Wildlife in the garden

Wildlife in the garden

ROY GENDERS

READERS UNION
Group of Book Clubs
Newton Abbot 1977

TO MAUREEN AND CLIVE WHO LOVE ALL WILDLIFE

❀ Preface ❀

Through the years, the wildlife attracted to our garden, whether through our efforts to encourage its visits to us, or through the part that nature herself has played, has provided us with as much pleasure as do the flowers it uses. By studying the requirements of birds for nesting sites, and providing the birds with winter shelter and berries for their food, we have enjoyed their company all the year round, whilst bees and butterflies have added to the interest in summertime. We have been fortunate in that the various gardens we have made through the years have always been situated near to the open countryside so that we have also had forms of wildlife not normally present in town gardens, though much can be done in built-up areas to attract wild visitors. I hope to be able to pass on the information I have collected for almost fifty years and that it will result in giving an additional dimension to my readers' gardening.

I am grateful to Mr. Malcolm Ness for allowing me to use the splendid photographs of birds taken in the garden and to the late Mr. Gordon Woods F.R.P.S. and his father, of Nelson, Lancashire, for other brilliant photographs of wildlife visitors to the garden. Also my thanks are due to Mrs. Molly Barraclough who brought these photographs to my attention.

My special thanks are due to Miss Sylvia Gatling for her attractive line drawings and to Miss Doris Gatling for the preparation of the MS with her usual thoroughness.

Last but not least, I am most grateful to the eminent entomologist, Mr. Arnold Darlington, for reading my manuscript and making a number of most interesting suggestions which I have gladly incorporated; and to my editor, Miss Eileen Brooksbank, for all the help she has given me with my book.

January 1976   ROY GENDERS

✿ Contents ✿

Preface		*page* 9
Illustrations		13
Introduction		15
Chapter 1	SHRUBS AND TREES TO ATTRACT BIRDS	25
	I. Wall-Plants	25
	II. Free-standing Shrubs and Trees	44
	III. Garden Hedges for Nesting Birds	56
Chapter 2	NEST-BOXES, BIRD-TABLES AND FEEDING UNITS	68
Chapter 3	NATIVE BRITISH BIRDS AND MIGRANTS	85
Chapter 4	BUTTERFLIES	130
	I. Native British Butterflies and Migrants	130
	II. The Butterfly Garden	159
	III. Breeding Butterflies	175
Chapter 5	MOTHS AND THE NIGHT-SCENTED FLOWERS	180
Chapter 6	BEES	192
Chapter 7	OTHER WILDLIFE IN THE GARDEN	208
Chapter 8	THE GARDEN POND	224
Appendix I	Birds and the law	251
Appendix II	Pesticides and fungicides	253

12 CONTENTS

Appendix III Some useful societies and their addresses 256

Bibliography 257

Index 259

❄ Illustrations ❄

PLATES

Between pages 96 and 97

1. Blue Tit
2. Great Tit
3. Marsh Tit
4. Redstart
5. Robin
6. Young swallows in nest
7. Painted Lady butterfly
8. Brimstone butterflies
9. Peacock butterfly
10. Humming-bird hawk-moth
11. Privet hawk-moth
12. Golden-ringed dragonfly
13. Hedgehog
14. Sow badger
15. Common lizard
16. Natterjack toad

LINE DRAWINGS

1. Plant support of galvanized wire	*page* 26
2. A hedge cut wedge-shaped	57
3. Battlement hedge formation	59
4. Nest-box fixed to trellis	70
5. Nest-box fixed to a tall tree	71
6. Nest-box for fixing to a wall	72
7. Nest-box fixed to a post	72
8. Wedge-shaped nest-box	75
9. Funnel-type nest-box	76
10. Nest-box for swifts	77
11. Combined feeding-table and nest-box	78
12. Scandinavian-type bird-house	80
13. Merry-Go-Round feeding unit	80
14. Free-standing bird-table	82
15. Queen of Spain Fritillary	138
16. Red Admiral butterfly	141
17. Small Tortoise-shell butterfly	142

18. Common Blue butterfly   146
19. Swallowtail butterfly   150
20. Plan for a butterfly garden   174
21. A small garden enclosure   190
22. Plan for a bee garden   206
23. A miniature garden pool   228
24. A small formal pool   229
25. A larger garden pool stocked with four types of
    plants   232

❦ Introduction ❦

One of the more pleasing aspects of this imperfect world is that
the modern generation is more interested in wildlife and its
preservation than previous generations. There is a ready aware-
ness that the balance of nature will be destroyed if wildlife is
further harmed and this is especially so with birds, many of
which feed upon those insects which are destructive to farm
and garden crops and which no amount of spraying can completely eliminate. I am thinking of the robin and of the garden-
warbler (though a summer migrant), which feed mostly on the
harmful insects of orchards. Contrary to general belief, the tit
is also an insect-eater (though it delights in suet and peanuts
in winter when other food is scarce) and so are the dunnock
or hedge-sparrow and the tree-creeper, numbers of which used
to keep my Somerset orchard free of harmful pests, thus
eliminating the need to use unpleasant sprays.

There are about 250 birds which breed in Britain each year
and every effort should be made to encourage them into our
gardens, not only for the valuable work they do in consuming
harmful insects, not least the cabbage white butterfly, but also
for the interest they provide. I have been fortunate in that the
homes I have had since childhood have been situated on the
outskirts of a town or village with woodlands and hedgerows
near by which gave hours of pleasure in the study of wildlife.
The gardens too were always filled with welcome visitors,
especially birds, but also summer butterflies, night hawk-moths
and bees, and we would do everything to encourage them to
visit us.

Bee plants are amongst the most delightful in gardens, many
being classed as herbs, and they have an informality all their own.
We planted them in small borders, in a window-box, and also a

bush or two of rosemary and lavender draped over the garden
path. The visitors would delight us throughout the year and the
garden would have as many of them from the wild as could be
found in the surrounding countryside. Our Somerset home was
surrounded by apple orchards which provided us not only with
many rare birds but with delicious fruit the whole year round.
Here, the tree-creeper, nuthatch and garden-warbler, usually
summer visitors but often remaining to winter in the warmth
of our orchard, would take food from the bird-tables we placed
there. Another regular winter visitor was the reed-bunting, for
we were close to Sedgemoor with its withy and reed-beds. The
cock is similar in its habits and appearance to the cock blackcap
and both measure about 6 in. (15 cm.) long, so it was a considerable time before we were able to distinguish one from another.

When we moved from the warmth of Somerset to the colder,
rugged coast of north-east Yorkshire, with its contrasting
scenery, our garden and its two acres of paddock and woodlands was also a paradise for birds, for on one side of the valley
were large conifer and hardwood plantations and on the opposite side was the North Sea with the moors in the distance,
situated between Forestry Commission woodlands and the sea,
and stretching away to Whitby. The views were superb at all
times of the year and there was a great deal of interesting wildlife although our house was close to a busy main road and the
number on the gate was 163, showing that we were included
with the town houses. Here we had entirely different birds as
visitors. Linnets would come in from the surrounding countryside where they built in gorse bushes and the yellow-hammer
would build in the Irish junipers in front of the house. Seagulls
would make their nests in any unused chimney pot and were
really pests, often attacking the fantail pigeons which we fed on
the lawn and for ever taking their food in winter. As we were
situated on the edge of open country, pheasants too would
make their nests in the safety and privacy of the garden and
paddock, for on one side of the house was a spinney of mature

birch and Scots pine, the grass beneath being left uncut, an ideal place for pheasants to build. Each evening they would strut across the lawn, the cock with his green head and white ringed neck, displaying his magnificent plumage to his female companion. Through the winter they never moved far away, as if sensing that if they did they would quickly fall to the guns which covered the moorland systematically, leaving only the minimum number of birds for breeding each year.

In winter, many birds different from those we knew in Somerset came into the garden. There were waxwings and redwings from Scandinavia, where they nest; they would arrive late in October and stay until March. Large flocks of bramblings and fieldfares would also come in winter and there would be the more familiar residents, the tits and the finches, the tree-sparrows and the blackcaps, the robins and wrens, most of which appreciated the protection of a nest-box to shelter in if the weather was severe, when driving winds from the sea would bring the taste of salt to one's lips and when breathing the cold air proved difficult to all but the strongest. At such times the birds appreciated the cover of an ivy-clad wall which faced away from the sea, and in the nest-boxes placed there blue tits and wrens would roost. Once, during a severe winter when foxes had been reported in the press as having been seen in that part of the town, people who did not know of its proximity to the open country, thought the press was guilty of gross exaggeration. On a number of occasions during prolonged snowy weather I have seen, by the light of the moon, foxes making their way from the woods and across the fields, through the garden and down the main road leading into the town, to scavenge from dustbins and leaving behind their tell-tale foot-marks.

We were fortunate in that our garden was mostly at the back of the house, away from the noise of traffic, and being so near the woodlands and moors, we had a never-ending stream of all kinds of wildlife and would do all we could to encourage it.

Again, we were fortunate in having a large number of mature
trees in the garden, and the paddock was surrounded with
thick hedges of bramble, thorn and wild rose. It was a bird-
lover's paradise and yet the most interesting visitors came because we had done something to encourage them, or so we
thought.

Against the back wall of the house there grew a Virginia
creeper, *Parthenocissus quinquefolia*. Its falling leaves in autumn
make extra work, as they form a wet mat if left to lie, but the
plant grows quickly, is self-clinging and the brilliant crimson of
its leaves before they fall in autumn is always an arresting sight.
What is more, its multitudes of pliant stems and dense foliage
make it an ideal place for birds to build their nests. It comes
into leaf early in May and retains its leaves until late September.
As soon as ours had grown about half-way up the wall, a pair
of spotted flycatchers made their new nest just above the sitting-
room window. They were virtually out of reach of cats, much
as these tried to get to them, and the nest was well hidden by
the large leaves which appeared early in May, the birds arriving
from the Mediterranean in this cold part of England later in
the month. Like the swallow, also a summer migrant, the
flycatcher will return again and again to the same nest, an
amazing natural instinct of these small birds, and this pair
which built so beautifully was no exception. Unlike many of
man's modern buildings, their nest was made to last, with an
outer 'shell' of tightly interwoven stems and coarse grasses, and
the inside thickly lined with feathers and moss. Soon after
arrival, the hen would lay four or five eggs of palest olive-green
speckled with reddish-brown, and for the next two months,
until the young left the nest, the cock would spend nearly every
moment of the day collecting food for his wife and family. This
activity gave hours of pleasure to all who watched. His job
was to feed his family and this is what he did, without a thought
for his own comforts. I had stuck a 5 ft. (1·5 m.) cane into the
lawn to be used to support dahlias but there it remained

throughout summer and each year afterwards, for I had noticed
that it was used by the cock as a lookout post from which to
make his forays to collect flying insects. A handsome little bird
with brown plumage and a white front, he would alight on his
perch, his quite long tail wagging perpetually, and there take
an upright position to enable him to survey the entire lawn.
Then, after a moment's hesitation, he would fly around and
around, always in an anti-clockwise direction, never more than
a few inches from the cane and about 12 in. (30 cm.) from the
top, taking the airborne insects in his beak. Then off he would
fly to the nest and in a moment transfer the food to the hen and
once again fly back to the cane with an occasional call of 'zip-
zip' to show how pleased he was with his family. After a few
moments' rest, he would begin flying around the cane once
more, always in the same direction, always the same distance
from the top, never varying. He would begin at daybreak and
continue until dusk and must have been exhausted by his
activities at the end of the day. We, and those visitors who came
to the house, would watch for hours, fascinated by his behaviour
and marvelling at his enthusiasm being sustained throughout
each day for several weeks. Then, as soon as the young left the
nest, the family would disappear until they returned again the
following May when the cane would once again be in its usual
position for their arrival.

The spotted flycatcher is possibly the last of all migrating
birds to arrive. During one summer, after an illness, I sat for
hours by the window watching the bird which was quite un-
mindful of those who passed along the path so close to the nest
and the cane. As he flew around the cane I would time him to
find how long he was taking going to and from the nest. I
thought then that where there were invalids in a house, some
determined effort should be made to encourage birds to
come into the garden and build as close to the house as
possible.

Now that we have moved to the northernmost tip of Cambridgeshire, we have different species of birds and butterflies as garden visitors. Although our home was built in 1330, the garden was completely bare of plants and trees and when we moved in the only birds to be seen were a few house-sparrows. It was most depressing after the sanctuary we had left. But large numbers of trees and flowering shrubs were planted, even before the rooms were furnished, and nearly a hundred wall-plants put in, especially rapid growers like the Russian vine and *Clematis montana*, also the honeysuckle, *Lonicera japonica halliana* which keeps its leaves in most winters. Within twelve months these shrubs had climbed to the top of 10 ft. (3 m.) high walls built of old stone, and in a very short time all manner of birds were attracted to the garden. Wrens, blue tits and pied wagtails now build in the walls, shielded from the passing eye by the climbing plants, and blackbirds and thrushes build in the flowering currants and other shrubs we have planted. They are attracted to the garden by the shade the shrubs provide, especially as the ground beneath remains moist during the hottest weather. Here these birds spend hours with their young, scratching about for worms, in the company of robins and chiff-chaffs that also build in the evergreens.

When we came to the house, I noticed a large hole in one of its walls, some 20 ft. (6 m.) above ground, and this, I hoped, would be a suitable place for swifts to inhabit, they being amongst the most amazing of all migratory birds. When the rest of the wall was pointed, I enlarged the opening so that I could just get my hand in and was able to pull out the rubble and mortar up to my elbow, working in a horizontal position to the right so that a passage was made behind the large facing stones. Within days, a pair of swifts arrived. This was towards the end of May and they made their nest there, bringing out a pair of youngsters (two eggs are always laid) which flew around with their parents for several weeks before leaving at the end of August for their long flight to Africa. I enlarged the wall opening the following spring, pulling out more rubble in the opposite direction, and have been rewarded with the arrival of two pairs of swifts, which build in the hole, evidently well satisfied with their dark and dry nesting quarters.

Swifts will build in colonies, making nests near to each other as they will do on the face of quarries and always well above the ground. They have exceedingly long claws which enable them to alight on rough stone and they are never seen on the ground. They will mate in mid-air.

It has been pointed out to me by an eminent ornithologist that swifts show a remarkable adaptability in feeding. They depend entirely upon small insects (Diptera), caught on the wing, to feed to their young, and whenever the weather is wet and cold and the insects are in short supply, the nestlings take on the appearance and lower body temperature of amphibians, like torpid toads. They may remain like this for several days, then when the weather improves and feeding can be resumed, the body temperature rises again and they become metabolically active. This accounts for the diversity of opinion about the length of time the birds spend in the nest, which depends entirely on the weather. The swift is unique amongst our birds in this respect.

From earliest times swifts have always held a strange fascination for countrymen because they were regarded as bats, which they resemble with their piercing shrieks, and because these birds will continue on the wing in their search for insects far into the night during times of scarcity.

Many a town or suburban garden can easily be made into a place which many forms of wildlife will love to visit, not only birds, butterflies, bees and moths, but hedgehogs and dormice which will hibernate where conditions are suitable, and other small mammals may also arrive. When it is realized that the ground adjoining one's home may have cost almost as much to purchase as the house cost to build, and when the ever-rising cost of motoring and other forms of travel make it more than ever desirable to spend a greater part of one's leisure time in the garden, we should make the most of it whatever the size and shape of the garden may be.

A small pond will provide interest and will be a pleasing feature of the garden if properly constructed and maintained. It will provide drinking water for birds and animals, and fish of all hues will be an added attraction.

A charming old lady of my acquaintance who lives alone in a small Georgian house in Bath had, in her tiny paved garden, constructed a pool 5 ft. (1·5 m.) long and 3 ft. (91 cm.) wide. It was surrounded by paving stones so that she could maintain it by herself with the minimum of effort, and at all times the surrounds were clean and dry. She would sit for hours almost hidden from view behind a french window, open whenever the weather was warm, enjoying the birds and other visitors to her pond and the butterflies and bees to the flowers. There were rarely five minutes in the day when there was not at least one interesting visitor to attract her attention. So interesting was this small garden that it could well be copied by those living in the centre of a town or city. Urban areas surrounded by pleasant countryside are particularly suitable for the encouragement of wildlife, and in this respect one thinks of cities like Bath and Edinburgh which are so much enhanced by their trees and where open parks and running water attract wildlife. The Headingley district of Leeds, Fulwood and Millhouses in Sheffield and parts of King's Heath and Edgbaston in Birmingham, are also places which come to mind.

Mention should be made here of the Conservation of Wild Creatures and Wild Plants Act, steered through Parliament by Mr. Peter Hardy, M.P. for Rother Valley, which makes it an offence to uproot a considerable number of wild flowers and to take many wild creatures such as the mouse-eared and horseshoe bat, the natterjack toad, dormouse, sand lizard and smooth snake. The Large Blue butterfly is also protected. The Act gives the Secretary of State for the Environment the power to add or remove plants and wild creatures from the Schedules and every five years the Council for Nature must advise him of any changes thought to be necessary. Amongst those who have worked hard to ensure the protection of our rarest forms of wildlife are the Council for Nature, the Royal Society for the Protection of Birds, the Botanical Society of the British Isles and the Society for the Promotion of Nature Reserves.

The purpose of these introductory comments is to encourage you to follow some of the suggestions and advice I shall give you on how to attract as many forms of wildlife as possible to your own gardens, in the hope and expectation that this will give you as much pleasure as it continues to give me.

❀ 1. Shrubs and trees to attract birds ❀

I. WALL-PLANTS

If climbing plants cover the bare walls of home, outhouse, garage and stable, and the walls surrounding a courtyard, not only will they take away the bleakness but they will provide cover for birds to roost and build their nests. Wall-plants also give colour where this is lacking, and interest where there was none before. They will be the means of bringing the birds close to one's home so that their behaviour may be more readily observed.

Preparing a wall

First the walls may be brightened by treating them with Snowcem, a cement whitening which is also obtainable in several soft colours. It is applied with a large brush and will retain its freshness for several years. Against the walls may then be erected neat wooden trellises (possibly obtained from a garden shop) made in panels approximately 6 ft. (1·8 m.) high from planed laths, nailed to a frame of stouter timber. Painted green, they look most attractive against the white walls. First 'plug' the wall, then fix the panels at their four corners, placing them so that the laths are on the side of the frame away from the wall. This will allow a space of about an inch between the wall and the laths and make it easy to tie in the shoots of the plants and give them room to develop, whilst also preventing the foliage from becoming scorched during hot weather.

Wood is expensive and, as an alternative, Nu-Frame lattice

panels are equally reliable for supporting wall-plants. They are constructed from rigid p.v.c. laths, secured at their pivot points with tubular plastic rivets. These give additional strength and provide location points for fixing. The rivet heads keep the laths from the wall, thus providing space for the plants to twine round. The material is strong and light to handle; it is rot-proof and will neither split nor warp. It can be bought in either the diamond or square pattern, in 6 ft. (1·8 m.) × 2 ft. (61 cm.) sections.

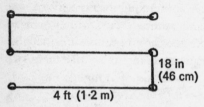

1. Plant support of galvanized wire

Another alternative is to use strong galvanized wire to support the plants. The wire is threaded through large nails containing an 'eye' which protrudes about 1 in. (2·5 cm.) from the wall, thus keeping the shoots away from the wall. The 'eyes' should be about 4 ft. (1·2 m.) apart, the wire being stretched across at intervals of about 18 in. (46 cm.) all the way up the wall to the required height.

By using the wire, the wall will not be disfigured and in time the plant will make sufficient growth to hide the supports. The wire may be pulled taut and kept so with the minimum of effort, whilst damage to the wall caused by its fixing will be at a minimum.

Auriol garden trellis, made of welded steel with a green or white plastic finish, gives lasting support for those plants which do not make too heavy top growth. A six-bar trellis will be 2½ ft. (76 cm.) wide, each 'window' being 10 in. (25 cm.) × 5 in. (13 cm.), and sections may be obtained of only half the width.

Remember that supports for wall-plants must take a considerable weight when the plants are established and are in full leaf and wet with rain, hence the need to 'plug' the wall before fixing any trellis. If the 'plugs' are allowed to protrude about 1 in. (2·5 cm.) from the wall, the shoots will have ample space in which to twine or be fastened.

Yet another method of supporting plants is to use wire netting, 3 ft. (91 cm.) in width and of any length, which is fixed to the wall on wooden 'plugs'. Wire netting is not so durable as wood or plastic, but one advantage is that against an old stone wall it cannot easily be seen from a short distance away, before the plant has covered it.

For all those plants with a drooping habit, such as the clematis, honeysuckle, vine and jasmines, some form of support is necessary. Wire netting or plastic wire frames may also be fastened around an old tree trunk and these plants grown against it.

Planting against a wall

There are a few rules to observe when planting against the wall and beneath the eaves of a house. Plant 8–9 in. (20–23 cm.) away from the wall so that the plant is not deprived of moisture, and to allow the shoots room to develop. There will also be room to erect a trellis to which the shoots are tied. Plants of a climbing habit should have a cane or stake inserted into the ground near the main stem, with the top of the stake against the lath frame up which the plant will continue to twine. A wall-plant will remain in place for many years and so should be given care in its planting.

First, remove the soil to a depth of 12 in. (30 cm.), and 12 in. (30 cm.) square. Line the base with rubble (lime rubble for those plants requiring an alkaline soil) and add an inch of peat; more peat for the acid lovers. To the removed soil add some decayed manure or hop manure and a little more peat or leafmould before replacing. Make it quite firm and it will then be ready for the plant. If possible purchase pot-grown plants, with the soil ball intact, so that the roots will be disturbed very little. In this way, planting may be done at almost any time, except when the ground is frozen. Bury the soil ball so that it is just covered, make quite firm and water in, giving the roots a good soaking. Climbing plants will usually be sent with a cane to support them.

During summer, never allow the roots to dry out and to avoid doing so, give a thick mulch early in June. All wall-plants will respond to a yearly mulch by putting out plenty of new shoots and in this way will quickly cover the largest of walls. They will also respond to an occasional watering with dilute liquid manure.

Self-clinging wall-plants

Perhaps the most important of wall-plants are those which are self-clinging, providing their own support by means of small suction cups on their stems. They are extremely hardy and so may be planted against a north wall. The fastest growing of these is *Parthenocissus quinquefolia*, a member of the vine family, which clings to a wall by means of discs which act in the same way as a suction dart. One with rather neater leaves is the Virginia creeper 'Beverley Brook', whilst *P. henryana* is perhaps the best of all, its silver and rose-coloured leaves being crimson on the underside. *Cissus striata* is more useful for birds to nest in, for it is evergreen, but may only be hardy in mild areas and should be grown on a south-facing wall.

Another beautiful self-clinging wall-plant is *Hydrangea petiolaris* which I have seen covering a Cheshire farmhouse the whole way round and to the eaves. It has glossy ivy-shaped leaves and in summer bears large flower heads more than 6 in. (15 cm.) across, like those of the Guelder Rose. The stems may need support by means of strong galvanized wires until it becomes established, for the plant has to carry a big weight when in leaf and bloom. I have seen the spotted flycatcher, whitethroat, chiff-chaff, willow-warbler and blackcap, all migratory birds, resting in it at the same time at about 6–7 ft. (1·8–2·1 m.) above ground. The plant will reach a height of 10 ft. (3 m.) in three years. Growth is so dense that it will completely hide nests built in it.

Those wall-plants which come into leaf late in spring will be suitable for those birds which build late, like the flycatchers and the garden-warbler, the greenfinch and redstart, all of them among the last of the summer arrivals. The early builders will require an evergreen wall-plant or shrub. All but the willow-warbler are residents and will begin to make their nests towards the end of March, before the deciduous plants begin to form their leaves. Amongst the earliest builders of the non-migratory birds are the chaffinch, chiff-chaff, tree-creeper, dunnock, blackbird, and the thrushes. They will build in a dense evergreen wall-plant which will also provide many resident birds with shelter during cold weather when they will be protected against cold winds by both the wall and the plants.

Amongst the best of evergreen wall-plants are the ivies which, contrary to popular belief, will not damage a sound wall. They should, however, be prevented from clinging to the wooden frames of windows for they will pull away the paint when the stems are removed and they will also grow into the cracks around the frame if it is not of the tightest fit. The shoots must also be kept away from gutters and the wooden eaves of a house. Ivies withstand clipping which is done at the end of summer, when the birds have left the nests, and the plants will then make new growth again before spring. As with parthenocissus and *Hydrangea petiolaris*, ivies should be planted early in spring so that they will get away to a good start; pot-grown plants should be used as all these plants resent root disturbance.

One of the best of the ivies is 'Silver Queen', its small grey-green leaves being edged with silver. Also interesting is

Hedera helix purpurea, the purple-leaf ivy, the foliage in winter taking on the glorious shades of the ampelopsis but having an advantage over it in that it is evergreen. Equally striking is 'Gold Heart' (syn. 'Jubilee') which has a neat small golden leaf, bordered with green, whilst *H. colchica* 'Dentata Variegata' has the colourings in reverse, on a somewhat larger and broader leaf.

Of the medium- to larger-leaved ivies, *H. helix angularis aurea* has bright green leaves splashed and edged with gold and *H. canariensis* 'Variegata' ('Gloire de Marengo'), slightly less hardy than the others, has large oval leaves of grey-green and silver. Of the 'green' ivies, *H. helix* 'Caenwoodiana' is most handsome, the dark green leaves having long narrow lobes.

Ivies appreciate an occasional syringeing during summer until fully established and old plants should be regularly cleaned of all debris such as old nests and dead leaves before being clipped and sprayed with a hose. In this way they will keep healthy and colourful for years.

In the wild, ivies are often found growing against trees but again, contrary to popular belief, they cause no harm in themselves although they may attract harmful insects. These will be found by birds which nest and roost in the ivy or in the trees. The woodland ivy bears yellow flowers in autumn and purple berries in spring, thus reversing the normal seasons of bearing flowers and fruit. Its fruit is much appreciated by birds in spring following a hard winter. Garden ivies rarely bear flowers and fruit unless unclipped, when they become untidy.

A handsome evergreen self-clinging plant for a sunny wall and a sheltered garden, or ideally a small walled courtyard, is *Campsis radicans*. It will attain a height of 25–30 ft. (7·6–9·1 m.) and is a plant in which many small late summer visitors will build. It is also known as *Tecoma* or the Trumpet Flower and it does like a warm, sunny wall and a sheltered garden. Against a whitewashed wall, the rich rust-coloured trumpet-shaped flowers and grey-green foliage provide a magnificent spectacle in July and August. *C. grandiflora* with its brilliant scarlet trumpets is equally arresting, though both may take several years to come into bloom. A hybrid, 'Mme. Galen', is hardier and more free flowering than either. The young plants should be provided with wire supports to start them off and they should not lack moisture. Plant them (and the ivies, too) in a soil containing some rotted manure, and mulch them in summer.

Another self-clinging evergreen is *Decumaria barbara*. It is a native of Florida and requires a warm sheltered wall in Britain. It will then make rapid growth, reaching a height of 20 ft. (6 m.) in three years. It has glossy leaves and from early summer bears clusters of small white flowers. Plant it in spring and use pot-grown plants. At planting time, pack peat or leaf-mould around the soil ball and plant firmly. It must not lack moisture in summer.

Wall-plants requiring support

There are a number of other plants, not self-clinging, to grow against a wall, the Russian vine, *Polygonum baldschuanicum*, being one of the most rapid in its growth. It requires support around which its shoots can twine and pull themselves up, and it will attain a height of 8 ft. (2·4 m.) in a single year. It will eventually reach a height of 30 ft. (9·1 m.) or more and will grow to a similar distance in width, its sprays of fluffy white flowers, borne in August and September, being most striking against the dark leaves. By then its growth will be really dense, but it will, like the more vigorous clematis species, have formed such a mass of wood that even when not in leaf it will still provide ample cover for birds to nest in. It is best grown against an old garden wall or about an old tree trunk surrounded with wire netting which it will quickly cover. If the wire mesh is quite large, it will not prevent small birds from making their nest in the tree trunk.

In addition to the Russian vine, there are various ornamental vines with twining stems, which are of similar rapid growth and which, though deciduous, soon form a mass of twiggy shoots. They could be used to cover an old wall or trellis, keeping the more exotic plants for the walls of a house. In a moist soil they will grow 10–12 ft. (3–3·7 m.) in two years and are chiefly planted for the rich autumnal colours of their leaves. Several will, however, produce a crop of small grapes in a warm summer and one of the best is *Vitis* 'Brant', its quite large blue-black grapes making delicious wine.

Amongst the truly ornamental species are, *V. coignetiae* which has very large, heart-shaped leaves which will turn rich crimson in autumn, and *V.* 'Purpurea', which has purple leaves. This is the wild vine which figures prominently in ancient sculptures such as those adorning the pillars of Southwell Minster. Equally fine is 'Miller's Burgundy'. I think it should more correctly be called 'Dusty Miller' for, like the old 'Dusty Miller's' auriculas, its leaves are covered with farina, as if they have been heavily dusted with flour. This vine bears clusters of small black grapes. Also attractive is the parsley-leaf vine, whose pale green leaves have the same indentations as the grape vines.

Another plant with twining stems and of similar vigorous habit is *Akebia quinata* which is fully evergreen in mild localities. Its leaves are composed of five oval leaflets and in May, before most other wall-plants are in bloom, it bears chocolate-purple scented flowers followed by interesting purple sausage-shaped fruits which grow to 3 in. (7·6 cm.) long. Like the Russian vine, it will grow on old trees or old walls.

Actinidia chinensis is a twining plant of interest, whose stems are covered with short red bristles. It will reach a height of 10–12 ft. (3–3·7 m.) and is known as the Chinese Gooseberry. It has large heart-shaped leaves 6 in. (15 cm.) long and in June and July bears clusters of fragrant creamy-white flowers which fade to pale yellow followed, in a good summer, by brown, edible fruit, 2 in. (5 cm.) long.

Celastrus scandens is also of twining habit and will quickly cover a pergola or rustic pole or, like the Russian vine, it may be allowed to cover a trellis which separates one part of the garden from another. It has pointed oval leaves which turn yellow in autumn, whilst its yellow flowers are followed by orange seed-pods which open to reveal brilliant red seeds which birds love to take.

Wistaria sinensis is a twining plant which will grow to huge proportions and entirely cover the large wall of a garden or house. It is deciduous but comes early into leaf, and an established plant will form such an abundance of woody stems close to the wall as to afford admirable nesting sites. Wistaria enjoys a rich, deeply worked soil which does not dry out in summer. Give it a mulch each year early in May when it comes into bloom. With its long mauve racemes it is one of the finest of all wall-plants when in bloom, whilst the pale green foliage is also pleasing. Plant from a pot, preferably in November, and each year in July after flowering pinch back the new shoots to the fourth or fifth leaf, and to the second or third in winter. This will encourage it to form flowering spurs; it is in the axils of the leaves that the flower buds are formed. If the shoots are allowed to grow unchecked, they will cover a wall more quickly but there will be few flowers.

Garrya elliptica is an interesting plant to grow against a north wall against which it will attain a height of 12 ft. (3·7 m.). A native of California, it grows better along the western side of Britain and south of the Thames. Its dark green oak-like foliage is evergreen and ideal for early nesting birds and in winter it is covered with long, drooping, silvery catkins which blue tits love to swing on and peck at.

Also from California, as are so many of the best wall-plants, is *Freemontodendron californicum*, for those British gardens which enjoy a favourable climate. There, on a sheltered wall, it will

attain a height of 20 ft. (6·1 m.) and will retain its leaves in all
but the severest of winters. It blooms from early June until the
end of summer, the cup-shaped flowers being of brightest gold
from which it derives the name of Californian Buttercup.

Solanum jasminoides, evergreen in a warm garden and a true
climber with its twisting stems, is useful for birds to build in.
Its leaves are like those of the jasmine in shape, and so are its
pale slate-blue flowers. Like freemontodendron, it has an
equally long-flowering season and it will quickly reach a
height of 15–20 ft. (4·6–6·1 m.). Perhaps more vigorous is *S.
crispum*, its dark blue flowers having a yellow cluster of stamens
at the centre; the best form is 'Glasnevin' which bears flowers
for a longer period, in large clusters 6 in. (15 cm.) across.

Also evergreen is *Berberidopsis corallina* which has heart-
shaped leaves 3–4 in. (7·6–10 cm.) long and, from July onwards,
blood-red flowers borne in large pendulous clusters. Like the
large-flowered clematis, it is happier when allowed to climb up
through another plant, or growing in shade, when it will reach
a height of 18 ft. (5·5 m.). Unlike clematis, however, it needs
acid soil.

A plant for a sunny wall is *Cytisus battandieri* with silvered
clover-like foliage and bearing, in June and July, lupin-like
panicles of pineapple-scented yellow flowers. It needs protection from cold winds.

When the summer jasmine, *Jasminum officinale*, is grown
against a trellis, many a bird will make its nest amidst the dense
foliage. It is semi-evergreen with twining stems which will
reach a height of 20 ft. (6·1 m.) if the shoots are tied in. It is
hardy and bears its clusters of pinkish-white flowers all summer,
but it is now rarely seen in gardens though it requires little
attention. Its long shoots with their small dark leaves fall in
cascading fashion and hide any nests from those who pass by.

J. nudiflorum, the winter jasmine, grows to only about half
the height but will spread out to clothe a low wall 8–10 ft.
(2·4–3 m.) high and the same in width. Plant it against a north

or west wall so that the early sun will not harm the frosted blooms which appear after Christmas and continue until early March, the bright yellow chalices lighting up the dullest day. The dunnock, chaffinch and goldfinch love to build their nests in its foliage. It is best grown against a trellis and the shoots tied in so that the young stems will cascade gracefully. The jasmines may be kept healthy and tidy by cutting out dead wood and removing nesting material where this is excessive.

Evergreen and of similar habit is *Trachelospermum jasminoides* which has dark green leathery leaves and, in July and August, bears clusters of fragrant pure white tubular flowers. Like the winter jasmine, it will grow 10–12 ft. (3–3·7 m.) high and only after several years will it need to have the dead wood cut out.

There is no finer plant for a wall 20 ft. (6·1 m.) high than the evergreen firethorns, the pyracanthas. They will make a dense hedge if supported by strong wires held on stout posts, or will cover a wall to a height of 20 ft. (6·1 m.). They have small glossy leaves and white hawthorn-like flowers which are produced in summer, followed by large trusses of orange or yellow berries which persist through winter. They will be happy on any wall except one facing due south, for the plants do not like heat. Indeed, they will withstand severe winds and hard frosts and all year their box-like foliage remains green and glossy; with their strong upright habit, they require the minimum of staking. Plant pot-grown plants and work some rotted manure into the soil.

The best species is perhaps *Pyracantha atalantioides*, its crimson berries hanging until the end of winter. There is also a yellow-berried form, 'Aurea'. The berries of *P. angustifolia* are also yellow, with orange tinting. This is the least hardy of the species, requiring shelter from cold winds. Of extreme hardiness is *P. rogersiana*, its graceful arching branchlets bearing orange-scarlet berries.

For covering old trees and garden walls or for growing

against a trellis or pagoda there are the honeysuckles and when these are fully grown, which will take about two years, many small birds will build in them. Those heavily scented at night are described in Chapter 5, for they are visited by humming-bird hawk-moths. *Lonicera tragophylla* bears scentless flowers, yet is one of the best of the climbing honeysuckles, reaching a height of 10 ft. (3 m.) and bearing its large deep-yellow flowers from early summer until autumn. The new season's shoots must be pinched back to encourage extra bloom. Also in bloom all summer is the hybrid 'Fireflame' which bears orange-scarlet flowers. *L. japonica* 'Aureoreticulata' is effective, for its leaves are mottled with gold and though it bears few flowers it makes dense growth and is semi-evergreen.

Truly evergreen is *Choisya ternata*, the Mexican Orange Blossom, which requires a warm wall to ripen its wood in the sun to better enable it to withstand a hard winter. It also re-quires a dry, sandy soil. It does not grow taller than 8 ft. (2·4 m.) but makes dense growth and bears its white orange-blossom-style flowers throughout summer. The honey-scented blossoms are enhanced by the golden stamens.

If one plants several species of ceanothus on the wall of a courtyard, they will give colour throughout the year. First to bloom is *C*. × *veitchianus* (*dentatus floribundus*) with its small round leaves and sky-blue flowers produced before the end of May and through summer. Then follows a hybrid, 'Cascade', which bears brilliant blue flowers just when *C*. × *veitchianus* is fading, and this is followed by *C*. 'Burkwoodii' and 'Autumnal Blue', in bloom from early August until October. 'Burkwoodii' is one of the most beautiful wall-plants. It is evergreen with small grey-green leaves and from mid-summer until well into autumn it bears masses of fluffy powder-blue flowers. It re-quires a sunny wall and is said to be not fully hardy in Britain, yet in my north-east coastal garden, lashed in winter by salt-laden winds which blow from the North Sea, it stayed ever-green all year, without so much as a browned leaf. It will grow to a height of 7–8 ft. (2·1–2·4 m.) and the same in width and all the pruning needed is to shorten long shoots and remove any dead wood.

All these are evergreen. The best of the deciduous kinds for a wall, and one which also blooms during late summer and autumn, is 'Gloire de Versailles' bearing broad panicles of sky-blue on upright stems, its flowers being sweetly but faintly scented. And, where it can be found, 'Charles Detriche' is worthy of planting, for its navy-blue flowers are delightfully different.

Of shrub-like habit, ceanothus requires the minimum of support, just a few lengths of strong wire to prevent it from being blown away from the wall. These shrubs are ideal for a small house, being in perfect proportion, and they are as at home in a suburban as in a country garden, being tolerant of soot deposits. Ordinary soil will suit them well but pack a little peat and rotted manure, or hop manure, about the roots at planting time. As with most wall-plants, plant them straight from pots, so that the soil ball is not disturbed.

The large-flowered clematis can be grown with a number of other wall-plants such as climbing roses and wistaria, and when established will provide sufficient twiggy growth and cover for birds to build in; by the front door of my home a blackbird makes her nest at the top of a clematis. But it is the species of clematis that make the most rapid growth and provide the densest cover, and they also come early into leaf. *Clematis armandii* is, in fact, evergreen and is a wonderful plant for a warm wall and one in which birds love to build. It has dark green leathery leaves which offset the sweetly scented pure white flowers. These appear in April from the axils of the leaves. There is also a pink form, 'Apple Blossom'. *C. cirrhosa balearica* (syn. *C. calycina*) is also evergreen but is only for a low wall, for it rarely exceeds a height of 8–9 ft. (2·4–2·7 m.). The foliage turns purple in winter, whilst the slightly cupped pale yellow flowers appear from late in November until early

March, at the same time as the winter jasmine. More rampant in
growth is *C. tangutica* which, when grown against a wall, is
best trained about a trellis. Extremely hardy, it has small pale
green leaves and is autumn flowering when it bears lantern-
shaped flowers of brightest yellow followed by white feathery
seed-heads which persist through winter.

More vigorous still, is *C. montana rubens* and the form 'Pink
Perfection'. For a garden wall or to cover an old tree quickly,
this, with its dense twiggy growth, is one of the best of wall-
plants and it also comes early into leaf. The bronze-tinted
leaves are enhanced by the masses of pale pink flowers which
appear in May. It may be grown against a trellis screen or over
a garden shed or garage. The new large-flowered form, 'Tetra-
rose', is also most effective. Of similar vigour is *C. chrysocoma
sericea* (syn. *C. spooneri*) which has dark green foliage and bears
large pure white flowers with yellow anthers. Plant in March
and cut back to within 18 in. (46 cm.) of ground-level so that
the plants will branch freely.

C. vitalba, Traveller's Joy, so called because it provides shade
for the weary traveller on foot, will give as much shade and
shelter for late nesting birds. It does well in chalk or limestone
soils where it is to be found in the wild, climbing about hedgerows or against old trees. It may be grown in a similar way in
the garden, or against an old wall or rustic screen, and will
grasp anything rough with its tendrils. Its white flowers in
May and June are replaced by fluffy white seed-heads in winter.

Another splendid species for birds to build in is *C. orientalis*
(or, more correctly, *C. o.* LSE 13372). It has finely divided
grey-green foliage and, in August and September, bears yellow
flowers which have thick curved petals like pieces of orange
peel, giving it the name of the Orange Peel Clematis. The
flowers are delicately scented. It is a plant of vigorous habit
and will quickly cover a wall.

Not only will clematis encourage birds to build in them,
completely hiding and protecting their nests from the winds,

but these rampant wall-plants will also offer the same shelter
and privacy to those birds building in an old garden wall. If a
small stone or brick is removed or even some mortar, a bird
will enter and scratch out more to make sufficient room to
build. Nesting-boxes, too, may be fixed near the top of a wall
and will then be covered by the rampant plants. Site and
situation are important.

The late-flowering clematis should be planted in full sun but
the montanas will flourish in a northerly position. They may be
grown against a trellis fixed so that it diverts the winds from a
wall or part of the garden which can then be expected to grow
the more tender plants. For example, if a ceanothus is being
grown against a sunny wall and a section of wooden trellis is
erected at an angle at the end of the wall to give protection
against the wind, it may be covered by *C. montana* or *C.
chrysocoma sericea* which will ensure greater warmth for the
ceanothus and other less hardy plants and more privacy for the
birds. Nest-boxes fixed to the wall will also receive protection
from strong winds which will be reduced in strength as they
filter through the plant-covered trellis. Make the trellis secure
so that it will not be blown down when heavy with the weight
of the plants.

Climbing and rambler roses are suitable for nesting if the
long shoots are tied in, and they will be effective where trained
against wooden laths. True, roses are deciduous but they come
into leaf early and, like all the deciduous wall-plants, will be
fully clothed by the time the later summer visitors arrive and
will also be available to those resident birds that build late.
They may be planted with clematis whose pliable stems provide extra nesting cover.

There are three climbing roses which may be recommended
to grow against a garden wall or to clothe a shed or garage, all
of which will make such heavy growth that they will be ideal
for nests of all types. Two of them, 'New Dawn', with its
trusses of blush-pink flowers, and 'Emily Gray', with its

coppery-yellow flowers, have large glossy leaves which they retain, if the winter is not severe, until early March when the leaves are shed, new ones appearing almost at once. These two roses are of great vigour and will quickly cover a large wall.

To make up the trio, there is the wonderful 'Zéphirine Drouhin', good as a hedge or against a wall, and though its foliage is a dull bronzy-green, it will also retain its leaves almost through winter. It is the first rose to bloom, its silvery-pink flowers, like small hybrid teas but borne in clusters, having an unsurpassable scent. It is also thornless and the shoots may be tied in without trouble.

Also suitable to grow against a tree or wall but only in a very large garden is *Rosa filipes*, 'Kiftsgate' which will cover a wall 30 ft. (9·1 m.) high and the same in length. It will send out its shoots to 15 ft. (4·6 m.) or more, from which will appear thousands of single white flowers with golden anthers, like orange blossom and with the same powerful scent. When open, the scent of the flowers will fill a large room. I have seen this rose covering one side of an old wall and cascading down the other side almost to the ground, to provide a home for spotted flycatchers and garden-warblers, chiff-chaffs and chaffinches which perch on the strong stems and sing for hours on end, a delightful sight and sound which could be enjoyed from a sitting-room window. To encourage the plants to send out shoots in all directions, cut back the main stems to 2 ft. (61 cm.) at the end of their first season, then tie in the new shoots as they grow.

In a sheltered garden and against a warm wall, *Passiflora caerulea*, the Passion Flower, will grow vigorously, clinging to supports by means of tendrils and bearing its interesting flowers from mid-June until September. The plant was brought into Europe by Spaniards from South America and was so named because the parts of its flower are thought representative of the Passion of Christ on the Cross. It may be cut down by hard frost but if the roots are covered with a thick mulch, the plant will survive and quickly grow again. The flowers are followed by edible orange egg-shaped fruits.

For a low wall, several of the cotoneasters will make dense growth and are evergreen, their flowers frequented by bees in summer and the fruits enjoyed by birds in winter. Hardy plants of easy culture, they are planted 5 ft. (1·5 m.) apart when they will grow into each other and hide the wall to a height of 5–6 ft. (1·5–1·8 m.). One of the best evergreen forms is *Cotoneaster henryanus*, its gracefully arching shoots clothed in small glossy leaves and hawthorn-like flowers which are followed by clusters of red berries in winter. *C. simonsii*, not perhaps fully evergreen, is also good; its bright glossy leaves turn red in autumn whilst it produces masses of orange berries. The deciduous *C. horizontalis*, called the Herringbone Cotoneaster on account of the arrangement of its stems which are like the centre and side bones of a herring, is also useful against a wall. Its leaves take on the brilliant colours of autumn before they fall, whilst the stems will retain the scarlet berries until removed by birds.

The camellia always does better against a west wall in a sheltered garden than elsewhere and will reach a height of 20 ft. (6·1 m.) or more, giving valuable cover for birds with its evergreen foliage and stiff shoots. It likes a lime-free soil, so pack plenty of peat about the roots at planting time. It must also be sheltered from cold winds which dry the leaves, causing them to turn brown and fall, and it must never lack moisture in summer. April is the best planting time and if the winter is severe cover the roots with a mulch and with sacking. Plants are more satisfactory if grown against a lath frame so that the shoots can be tied in and the wax-like blooms will not be bruised against the wall in windy weather.

Varieties and hybrids of *Camellia japonica* are the hardiest, of which 'Kumasaka', double pink with a centre filled with small petals, and 'Multipetala', of similar form, but rich crimson, are outstanding. The pure white 'Alba Simplex' with its conspicuous golden stamens, and the hybrid 'Mary Christian', single deep pink, are equally fine. All the pruning required is to cut out any dead wood as the plant ages. Outdoors, they mostly bloom in March when the first of the birds begin to make their nests in the matured plants. Plant them against a west wall so that the flowers are not damaged before the frost has left them by the early sun.

There is, then, a wide choice of plants to grow against a wall and the choice will mostly be governed by climate and soil conditions. Evergreens will encourage the early builders to make their nests but some plants will make such dense twiggy growth after a few years that even when not in leaf, birds will find them a suitable place for nesting.

A SELECTION OF WALL-PLANTS

Species or Variety	Height ft. (m.)		In Bloom	Colour
Actinidia chinensis (S)	12	(3·7)	June–July	Cream
Akebia quinata (S)	15	(4·6)	May–July	Purple-brown
Berberidopsis corallina (E)	18	(5·5)	July–Sept.	Coral-red
Camellia japonica 'Kumasaka'	8	(2·4)	Mar.–April	Pink
Campsis grandiflora	25	(7·6)	July–Aug.	Scarlet
Campsis radicans	30	(9·1)	July–Aug.	Scarlet
Ceanothus 'Burkwoodii' (E)	15	(4·6)	July–Nov.	Pale blue
Ceanothus 'Gloire de Versailles'	10	(3·0)	July–Oct.	Pale blue
Ceanothus × veitchianus (E)	12	(3·7)	May–Aug.	Pale blue
*Celastrus scandens	12	(3·7)	June–July	Yellow
Choisya ternata (S) (E)	6	(1·8)	May–Aug.	White
Clematis armandii (S) (E)	15	(4·6)	April–July	White
Clematis cirrhosa balearica (E)	9	(2·7)	Feb.–April	Yellow
Clematis montana rubens	20	(6·1)	May–June	Pink

Species or Variety	Height ft. (m.)	In Bloom	Colour
Clematis chrysocoma sericea	15 (4·6)	June–July	White
Clematis orientalis	15 (4·6)	Aug.–Sept.	Lemon
Clematis tangutica	12 (3·7)	June–Aug.	Yellow
Clematis vitalba	20 (6·1)	May–July	White
*Cotoneaster horizontalis	5 (1·5)	June–July	White
Cotoneaster simonsii	6 (1·8)	June–July	White
Cytisus battandieri (S)	10 (3·0)	June–July	Yellow
Decumaria barbara	20 (6·1)	May–Aug.	White
Fremontodendron californicum	20 (6·1)	June–Sept.	Yellow
Garrya elliptica (E)	12 (3·7)	Jan.–April	Silvery catkins
Hedera 'Gold Heart' (E)	12 (3·7)	—	Golden foliage
Hedera helix angularis aurea (E)	12 (3·7)	—	Golden foliage
Hedera 'Silver Queen' (E)	12 (3·7)	—	Silver foliage
Hydrangea petiolaris	20 (6·1)	June–Aug.	White
Jasminum nudiflorum (E)	8 (2·4)	Dec.–April	Yellow
Jasminum officinale (S) (E)	12 (3·7)	June–Sept.	White
Parthenocissus henryana	30 (9·1)	—	Coloured foliage
Parthenocissus quinque-folia	to 30 (9·1)	—	Coloured foliage
Passiflora caerulea	15 (4·6)	June–Sept.	Blue
Polygonum baldschuanicum	25 (7·6)	July–Sept.	White
*Pyracantha atalantioides (E)	10 (3·0)	June–July	White
*Pyracantha rogersiana (E)	10 (3·0)	June–July	White
Rosa filipes 'Kiftsgate'	30 (9·1)	July–Sept.	White
Solanum jasminoides	20 (6·0)	June–Aug.	Blue
Wistaria sinensis	30 (9·1)	May–July	Blue

* Plants forming brightly coloured berries or fruits.
  S=scented.
  E=evergreen.

II. FREE-STANDING SHRUBS AND TREES

Those shrubs noted for their dense growth as well as beauty will be those most visited by birds, especially the finches, but other small birds such as the goldcrest, yellow hammer and willow-warbler will be regular visitors too. When planning the garden, plant one part with shrubs. They are labour saving, requiring the minimum of pruning, and will last for many years, their vigour maintained by an occasional mulch of decayed manure.

The suburban garden, often long and narrow where the house is semi-detached, could have a shrub garden at one end, possibly 6–8 ft. (1·8–2·4 m.) wide, or shrubs may be used to divide the vegetables from the pleasure garden, perhaps planting shrubs to one side of a trellis over which climbing plants are grown. A triangular-shaped shrubbery can fit into a corner. Perhaps instead of a vegetable garden, a small apple orchard will be planted with those cultivars of compact habit such as 'Claygate Pearmain', 'Sunset', 'Egremont Russet' and 'Laxton's Fortune'. In warmer parts, 'Cox's Orange' with its pollinator, 'James Grieve', may also be planted. When established, the trees will accommodate those birds which love to build in the fork of a branch, well above the ground. The redstart and mistle thrush, chaffinch and lesser redpoll are amongst those with a liking for an orchard tree, for they are not shy when nesting. Plant the trees 8 ft. (2·4 m.) apart if in the bush form, but allow nearly twice the spacing if they are standards. Apples are hardy and will grow in most types of soil. Four or five years after planting, birds will begin to make their nests in them.

Daffodils and several of the blue-flowering bulbs so often

visited by bees in spring may be planted beneath the trees and will increase each year; or the ornamental crabs and cherries may be planted instead of apples. Their blossom will be as colourful and the fruit of the crab-apples will make excellent jelly. The trees are deciduous but come early into leaf and the tree-loving birds will build in them as soon as the branches are large enough for the nests. Whilst the trees are young, the finches will use them; later will come the lesser redpoll and redstart, then the blackbird and mistle thrush.

If the shrub border is planned in undulating curves, it will be more interesting, being wider in some places than in others. It may be separated from a lawn by a path of paving stone which will allow one to walk in the garden and admire the wildlife during wet weather. A low hedge of box kept clipped, or of dwarf lavender will provide a suitable edging to the border.

When planting a shrub border, arrange the plants so that the taller ones are at the back with the more compact to the front, and plan them so that there will be colour and nesting sites over a long period. Evergreens will provide the early nesters with cover, and a group of cupressus trees in their different greens, planted here and there, will be colourful in winter and available for those birds that build in March, the chaffinch, pied wagtail, chiff-chaff and dunnock.

Better than *Chamaecyparis* (formerly *Cupressus*) *allumii* with its widely spaced upright branches is *C.* 'Fletcheri', conical in outline and with dense feathery branchlets of a beautiful grey-green. *C.* 'Elwoodii' is similar but of blue-green, whilst 'Green Pillar' is mid-green. These conifers have a rounded base but taper to a point and are dense right down to the ground. After two or three years, small birds will begin to build in them for they are an ideal place for nests, providing complete cover and at the same time protection from wind and rain. Others of similar value are the Golden Cypress, *C.* 'Lanei', of neat pyramidal habit and with closely set branches, and 'Golden King', a graceful tree with slightly drooping branches. *C.* 'Stewartii' also has golden foliage with dense overlapping branches.

The junipers, too, are ideal for nests and in autumn birds will enjoy their uniquely flavoured blue berries, ejecting the stones after eating the flesh. *Juniperus virginiana* 'Canaertii' is the best, for it has a wide base and its upright branches taper to a point. The foliage is deep blue-green, its fruits turquoise-blue. The Irish Juniper, *J. communis* 'Hibernica', is an erect, almost columnar, form of greyish-green.

The true cupressus, *Cupressus glabra* 'Pyramidalis', with its brilliant blue foliage, will give dense cover and it is broadly conical from the base to the top. Of similar density is *Thuja occidentalis* 'Vervaeneana' which will reach a height of 6–7 ft. (1·8–2·1 m.) but will grow 5 ft. (1·5 m.) in width whilst it does so. Like all the thujas, it likes a heavy wet soil; given this, it will form an efficient windbreak or background tree with its feathery foliage of bronzy-green colouring. Several Scots pines, *Pinus sylvestris*, may be planted to the back of a border for there are a number of birds which delight to search for insects about the flaky chocolate-brown bark of mature trees.

A small garden within a garden may be made by siting a summer-house so that it faces south or west, to receive the evening sun, and planting at the back and to the sides some of the densely foliaged conifers in their various hues. Here one may sit for hours at all times of the year and until the hours of darkness, watching the birds either making their nests or singing from the high branches of a Scots pine. In spring, if the weather is cold, one may sit behind glass watching the courting antics of the birds and when the pines are about 10 ft. (3 m.) tall, nest-boxes may be fixed to the trunks and will be partially hidden by the slower-growing conifers beneath. With them may be planted a number of those conifers of dwarf, spreading habit. Amongst these, *Juniperus squamata* 'Meyeri' grows as wide as it grows tall, about 3 ft. (91 cm.) with radiating branches and rich blue foliage. Handsome, too, is *J.* × *media*

'Pfitzeriana Aurea' which makes a wide bush of golden-green, whilst 'Blue Cloud' has glaucous blue foliage. Birds delight in perching on them, and small birds will build in them when the trees are fully grown. Another fine dwarf conifer is *Thuja occidentalis* 'Rheingold' which makes a low-spreading tree turning more orange than gold in winter, when it provides a striking splash of colour in the sombre winter garden.

Group the dwarf conifers together or plant in small groups in the shrubbery, allowing 4–5 ft. (1·2–1·5 m.) between each to allow sunlight and air to reach all parts of them, otherwise the branches will die back. If planted too near together, the trees will grow into each other and their interesting outlines will be obliterated.

Plant in April with as much soil on the roots as possible, for they will be slow to re-establish themselves if the roots are bare. Pack some moist peat around the roots at planting time and make the soil firm. Water them in and, during the dry weather, spray the foliage. During their early years, protect the plants from cold winds by erecting a screen of canvas or hessian around them from early December until March.

The dawn cypress, *Metasequoia glyptostroboides*, long thought to be extinct but rediscovered in China in 1941, will make a tall dense tree planted as a specimen. It has slender upturned branches of deep green and a fine dark brown trunk. Though deciduous, it comes into leaf early in spring and it will retain its leaves almost to the year's end.

One of the best of small garden trees for birds to nest in is the double-flowering thorn, *Crataegus oxyacantha* 'Paul's Scarlet' ('Coccinea Plena'), with its trusses of double red flowers in June, whilst 'Rosea Flore-Pleno' is the pink form. If grown in the standard form they will quickly make a large dense head. Though deciduous, they come into leaf earlier than any other tree and birds will build in them when the trees are quite young.

The double-flowering thorns or Mays will not form haws,

the fruits so much loved by hawfinches and bullfinches, but several of the haw-bearing trees, those producing single flowers, will be equally valuable for birds to nest in, though they will not be as colourful in the garden.

Crataegus submollis makes a densely headed tree with broad leaves and bears clusters of bright orange-red berries in autumn, whilst *C.* × *lavallei* is a neat upright tree with silver-coloured, almost thornless, stems and glossy leaves which remain on the tree until December. The large round orange haws are remarkable in their size, being as large as the hips of many wild roses, and they will last through the winter.

The cockspur thorn, *C. crus-galli*, with its long thorns, makes a widely spreading tree and is particularly attractive in autumn when its foliage turns to shades of yellow, crimson and bronze. The crimson haws are borne in large clusters, and persist on the tree most of the winter. A hybrid, 'Autumn Glory', bears glossy leaves like *C.* × *lavallei* and scarlet fruits as large as cherries.

The hornbeam is also used by nesting birds, for it is a dense small-leaved tree which will, in a mild winter, retain its foliage until March. The tall-growing *Carpinus betulus* 'Fastigiatus' is the densest of fastigiate trees, whilst its beautiful pale green foliage turns brilliant gold in autumn and this is retained through winter. It, too, comes early into leaf again. It likes a heavy soil.

For its berries in winter and for the dense cover of its dark green spiny leaves, the holly is loved by birds. Owing to its slow growth, it is rarely planted in modern gardens but in many old gardens it was used for hedges as an alternative to yew, and birds of every description made use of it for building. Bees also make use of the flowers in summer. Amongst the best is *Ilex aquifolium* 'Pyramidalis', a tree of pyramidal growth, bearing plenty of red berries; it is self-fertile and a single tree will set fruit. Another is *I. a.* 'Argenteo-marginata'; the leaves have silver edges, and it berries well.

One of the best shrubs for nesting birds is *Berberis darwinii*, an evergreen with shiny holly-like leaves, bearing clusters of orange flowers in spring. It is happy in semi-shade and suitable for a wild garden. Pheasants build beneath its branches, for it grows 4 ft. (1·2 m.) wide and the same in height. The tree-pipit, willow-warbler and redbreast will also make their home beneath its protective branches, especially if coarse grass is growing beneath. *B. julianae* also makes a dense bush with large olive-green sharply pointed leaves which are evergreen, whilst its lemon-coloured flowers are much visited by bees. Both plants bear, in autumn, purple-black fruits which are much enjoyed by birds, especially the blackcap and hawfinch and winter visitors from Scandinavia such as the waxwing and fieldfare.

The closely related *Mahonia japonica* is equally good for providing cover for those birds which build close to the ground and, like the berberis, it will grow as well in shade as in full sun. At the ends of the leafy shoots the pale yellow flowers appear in February and have the scent of the lily of the valley. It prefers some peat in the soil. In bloom at the same time is *M. aquifolium* (known as the holly-leaved barberry and sometimes, wrongly, as the Oregon grape), also evergreen, its dark green leaves turning purple in autumn. It bears its yellow flowers in dense racemes and they are followed by large round, black grape-like fruits covered in 'bloom', which make excellent jam.

Stonechats, linnets, bramblings and several of the finches will make their nests in a gorse bush and the best is the double form, *Ulex europaeus* 'Plenus', which grows 5 ft. (1·5 cm.) tall and the same in depth. Though covered in sharp spines, the leafless stems will be ablaze with its golden, pineapple-scented flowers through late winter and spring.

The evergreen ceanothus hybrid 'Autumnal Blue', with its glossy leaves and dense growth, may be planted in the shrub border as well as against a wall. It bears its soft powder-blue

flowers from early July until early October, a time of year
when the border is not as colourful as in mid-summer. Plant
it in March, in a well-drained soil and in a position of full
sun.

I have seen many a chaffinch and the yellowhammer build in
a mature *Cornus mas*, which is the best of the dogwoods for a
small garden and which will attain a height of 6–7 ft. (1·8–
2·1 m.) in three years. It will then have grown as wide as it is
tall. The dogwoods will tolerate partial shade and even a
badly drained clay soil. *C. mas* is the cornelian cherry, its small
yellow flowers in February and March being followed by large
red cherry-like fruits which birds enjoy. *C. alba*, of similar
habit, bears small white fruits in autumn, whilst its red stems
are most colourful. *C. a.* 'Sibirica' has stems of sealing-wax
red and will be a striking addition to the winter garden. The
dogwoods are not evergreen but are dense when in leaf and
they produce their foliage early in spring.

One of the best evergreen shrubs for its density and colour is
Elaeagnus pungens 'Maculata' which makes a bush 6 ft. (1·8 m.)
tall and 5 ft. (1·5 m.) wide. It is hardy and will grow in any soil,
and against a north wall. The leaves which measure 3 in. (7·6
cm.) in length and are 1 in. (2·5 cm.) wide have a centre of
brilliant gold and a dark green margin. *E. p.* 'Variegata', which
is of similar habit, has dark green leaves with a cream margin.

The elaeagnus is tolerant of salt-laden sea-breezes, as is
Griselinia littoralis, also evergreen, which makes a dense bush
8 ft. (2·4 m.) tall. The leaves and stems are of bright golden-
green, so at all seasons it is colourful, whilst a fully grown
plant provides excellent cover for nesting birds.

Another plant resistant to salt-winds is *Olearia macrodonta*,
one of the daisy bushes, which grows 6 ft. (1·8 m.) tall and the
same across. A beautiful evergreen, it has holly-like leaves
covered in grey down and in July and August the plant is
covered in white flowers like Michaelmas daisies. *O.* × *haastii*
does not grow quite so large and has small oval leaves, green

above, grey below. It, too, is tolerant of sea-winds and in July and August covers itself in scented white daisies.

Where it can be grown close to the sea, to ensure its protection from frost, or in the more favourable climate of western Britain, *Laurus nobilis*, the poet's laurel, is a delightful evergreen with dark green leaves, terminating in a point and deliciously aromatic. Where it may need winter protection, it should be grown in a tub as a standard, possibly one on either side of an entrance to an inner garden bordered by stone walls, and it may then be lifted and placed under cover (an open shed is ideal, or a garden room) towards the end of November, before the frosts, and replaced in April. Or it will usually survive if the head is covered with sacking or plastic sheeting for the winter. In spring the dense heads are a favourite nesting place for chaffinch, blackcap and long-tailed tit.

The garden laurel, *Prunus lusitanica*, also known as the Portugal laurel, with its long pointed leaves of dark glossy green is an evergreen which the larger birds use for nest building. The plants make thick woody stems which branch out from the main stem, in the arms of which quite large nests can be built. This laurel should be planted at the back of a border for background or as a windbreak. Its scented white flowers, borne in 'tassels', are followed by large purple berries.

One of the best of the small-leaf evergreens is *Lonicera tatarica*, 'Hick's Red'. Though of the same family, it bears little resemblance to the climbing honeysuckles, being a dense upright shrub 6 ft. (1·8 m.) tall and 5 ft. (1·5 m.) across, with numerous twiggy stems and small dark green leaves. It is ideal for small birds to nest in and, early in summer, covers itself in small, tubular rosy-red flowers. It is hardy and grows well in all soils. The flowers are followed by red berries which birds enjoy. Also almost evergreen in a sheltered garden is *L.* × *purpusii* which grows 6 ft. (1·8 m.) tall with slender pointed leaves, and bears sweetly scented creamy-white flowers through winter. *L. frangrantissima* is similar in habit and in its flowering whilst its flowers are also deliciously scented. It, too, blooms in winter; if the weather is severe it will drop its leaves but new ones form early in spring.

Osmanthus heterophyllus is autumn and winter flowering, its small, white, honey-scented flowers appearing in October, partly hidden by the evergreen holly-like leaves which are sharply toothed. It is a taller plant than *O. delavayi* and of greater density so it is better for birds to build in and it is also hardier.

The photinia is an interesting tree-like shrub, of erect habit and reaching a height of 10 ft. (3 m.), but its short, twiggy branches are so close together that birds can easily make their nests in them. *P. serrulata*, known as the Chinese hawthorn, is partially evergreen and famed for the brilliant red colours of its young foliage formed on the new shoots. It later turns deep green. The older leaves turn red again before falling but the young leaves are retained through winter, so there is always coverage for birds. The small white flowers are borne in clusters in spring. *P. villosa* is deciduous, its leaves turning orange-red before they fall. Its white hawthorn-like flowers are followed by scarlet berries in early autumn.

Hebe 'Midsummer Beauty' is an evergreen which grows 5 ft. (1·5 m.) high and 4 ft. (1·2 m.) across, its small fleshy leaves tolerant of sea-breezes. It is the tallest variety with plenty of foliage and in August and September it bears long spikes of scented violet flowers which are frequented by butterflies.

Viburnum tinus, a wind-tolerant evergreen which does well in semi-shade, will also be visited by birds. It grows 5 ft. (1·5 m.) tall and is so dense that it may be used for a hedge. It blooms from November until March, the large flower-heads being sweetly scented and succeeded by dark blue berries late in summer.

Viburnum × burkwoodii is also evergreen with large oval leaves terminating in a point and bearing clusters of clove-scented white flowers, which first appear as pink buds, in spring. The evergreen *V. davidii* which makes a low-spreading bush, growing wider than it grows tall, may be planted not so much for nesting as for its turquoise berries in autumn, for which both male and female plants must be planted together.

The Wayfaring Tree, *V. lantana*, which is not evergreen, grows 10 ft. (3 m.) tall and 6 ft. (1·8 m.) wide. It bears white flowers in large clusters during early summer and these are followed by red berries which later turn black and are much enjoyed by birds. The best form of the Guelder Rose, *V. opulus*, is 'Notcutt's Variety' which makes a tree 10 ft. (3 m.) tall and 8 ft. (2·4 m.) across. It comes early into leaf, its flowers being followed by large scarlet berries. The cultivar 'Xantho-carpum' does not exceed 6 ft. (1·8 m.) in height but makes a broad bush, its white lace-like flowers followed in autumn by translucent golden berries which persist well into winter.

It may not be realized that *Cytisus* × *kewensis*, with its grace-ful arching stems clothed for weeks in early summer with creamy white flowers which give the plant an all-white appear-ance, is a much frequented nesting place for those birds which prefer to build close to the ground—the marsh-tit and willow-warbler, robin and yellow wagtail. Although it grows no more than 2–3 ft. (61–91 cm.) tall, it reaches 5–6 ft. (1·5–1·8 m.) across and when in bloom, it is impossible to see the ground beneath it. Similar is *Spiraea* × *arguta* which grows 4–5 ft. (1·2–1·5 m.) tall, its twiggy stems providing a cascade of brilliant white from top to bottom during April and May when the birds are nesting. Both these flowering shrubs provide shade and protection for small birds when they need it most and look most colourful if planted near dark evergreens.

Most popular of all berries as far as birds are concerned is mistletoe. It is to be found mostly in Worcestershire, Hereford and Shropshire, for in Britain the apple tree is the most suitable host-plant for this parasite, though most of our Christmas mistletoe comes from France where it grows on poplar trees. To grow it, fully ripened berries must be used and they will not be ready until about 1st March. The seeds need light to germinate and are pressed into cracks in the bark of apple trees. There they are left to germinate, which they will if birds do not take them. To guard against this, tie a few strips of tinfoil in the tree where they will jangle in the breeze and frighten off the birds until the seeds have sprouted.

By the end of summer the seed may have germinated and a small shoot will be seen. It will take five years to have made sufficient growth for a few stems to be cut at Christmas. Even then it may not bear berries, for the plant bears male or female flowers and the males set no fruit. To make sure of getting some berries, quite a number of ripe berries should be inserted into cracks in several trees: in any case, only a small number will germinate.

If trees are to be staked in a windswept garden, do not use pieces of felt or sacking, for in spring the birds will use it to line their nests and it will be necessary to replace it at regular intervals. Instead use rubber or plastic tree-ties of which there are several efficient makes. There will then be no fear of the stakes cutting into the bark of the trees. Also, use a strong stake which will not easily break in high winds, and drive it well into the ground to hold the tree firm.

A SELECTION OF FREE-STANDING SHRUBS AND TREES

Species or Varieties	Height ft. (m.)	In Bloom	Colour
*Berberis darwinii	3 (0·9)	Mar.–May	Orange
*Berberis julianae	2 (0·6)	Mar.–May	Lemon
Carpinus betulus 'Fastigiata'	20 (6·1)	Foliage	Pale green
Ceanothus 'Autumnal Blue'	5 (1·5)	July–Oct.	Blue
Chamaecyparis 'Ellwoodii'	to 20 (6·1)	Foliage	Blue-green

Species or Varieties	Height ft. (m.)		In Bloom	Colour
Chamaecyparis 'Fletcheri'	to 20	(6·1)	Foliage	Grey-green
Chamaecyparis 'Lanei'	to 12	(3·7)	Foliage	Golden
Chamaecyparis 'Stewartii'	to 20	(6·1)	Foliage	Golden
*Cornus mas	8	(2·4)	Mar.–April	Yellow
*Crataegus crus-galli	12	(3·7)	May–June	White
*Crataegus lavallei	10	(3·0)	May–June	White
Crataegus 'Paul's Scarlet'	12	(3·7)	May–June	Red
*Crataegus submollis	10	(3·0)	May–June	White
Cypressus glabra	to 18	(5·5)	Foliage	Blue-green
Elaeagnus pungens	6	(1·8)	Foliage	Green & gold
Griselinia littoralis	8	(2·4)	Foliage	Green & gold
Ilex 'Argenteo-marginata'	12	(3·7)	Foliage	Silver
Ilex 'Pyramidalis'	18	(5·5)	Foliage	Dark green
Juniperus 'Meyeri'	3	(0·9)	Foliage	Blue-green
*Juniperus virginiana	to 30	(9·1)	Foliage	Blue-green
Laurus nobilis	6	(1·8)	Foliage	Dark green
Lonicera fragrantissima	5	(1·5)	Nov.–Mar.	White
*Lonicera tatarica	6	(1·8)	June.–Aug.	Rose-red
*Mahonia aquifolium	3	(0·9)	Dec.–Mar.	Yellow
Mahonia japonica	3	(0·9)	Feb.–Mar.	Yellow
Metasequoia glyptostroboides	to 40	(12·2)	(deciduous)	
Olearia × *haastii*	4	(1·2)	July–Aug.	White
Olearia macrodonta	5	(1·5)	July–Aug.	White
Osmanthus heterophyllus	5	(1·5)	Jan.–Mar.	White
Photinia serrulata	12	(3·7)	Mar.–May	White
*Photinia villosa	12	(3·7)	Mar.–May	White
Thuja occidentalis	6–7	(1·8–2·1)	Foliage	Dark green
Thuja occidentalis 'Rheingold'	4	(1·2)	Foliage	Golden
Ulex europaeus	6	(1·8)	Jan.–May	Yellow
*Viburnum tinus	5	(1·5)	Nov.–Mar.	White

* Plants forming brightly coloured berries or fruits.

III. GARDEN HEDGES FOR NESTING BIRDS

A well-grown hedge providing privacy and shelter will be the best of all places in a garden for birds to build their nests. Hedges give privacy to a garden as well as to the birds, and they also act as a valuable windbreak, not only for other plants but for wildlife. They may also be planted to separate one part of the garden from another, maybe to surround a small bird sanctuary where there is a seat or perhaps a summer-house and suitable trees for birds to frequent. In front of the summer-house one may place a stone trough raised on a pedestal, for birds to drink from. The entrance to the sanctuary could be through an opening in the hedge, preferably on the side away from prevailing winds, whilst around the bird-trough could be set paving-stones with carpeting plants growing between them, around which there could be planted a circle of dwarf lavender. Amongst the conifers and evergreen shrubs, those plants which are visited by butterflies and moths can be grown. Such a garden would be sheltered from the winds and so be more attractive to butterflies, birds and bees. Shelter is a very important factor in the planning of a garden and before planting a hedge one must consider its site with special care.

Hedging plants will grow more quickly if the soil is prepared before their planting, incorporating decayed manure or used hops, together with peat or leafmould. Keep the plants moist at the roots and spray the foliage during dry weather. They will also appreciate a mulch of lawn mowings, peat, or decayed manure early in summer. Clip them in summer to keep the hedge at the required height and bushy low down. A well-clipped hedge should be wedge-shaped so that the sun and air can reach as much of it as possible and snow will not lodge on the top.

The best hedge for birds to nest in is holly which, with its great density and spiny leaves, is impenetrable to all but the birds and thus provides them with a safe haven. It is rarely planted for it is expensive and slow growing, but it requires little attention. The cultivar 'J. C. van Tol', which yields a large number of red berries and will grow 6 in. (15 cm.) in a year in a soil fortified with some decayed manure, is the best

2. A hedge cut wedge-shaped

form. It could be planted with whitethorn (hawthorn, quickthorn), using one or two every 5 ft. (1·5 m.) so as to reduce expense, but it will be better to plant the holly in pairs, to give a good patch of green in winter. Plant holly 18 in. (46 cm.) apart, and whitethorn at 12 in. (30 cm.). Both holly and whitethorn are frequented by bees.

Whitethorn, which does well on chalk, on its own is a cheap and satisfactory boundary hedge, growing 15 in. (38 cm.) each year and with hard wooded intertwining stems which are covered with thorns. It is one of the first of all plants to come into growth in spring so it will provide cover for the earliest builders which find the strong stems ideal for their nests. The attractive pale green leaves herald the summer and a hedge bare one day will be brilliant green almost by the next as the buds begin to unfold. To keep the hedge bushy low down, clip hard back in the first years, then trim early in July and again in September.

Hornbeam and hawthorn are tolerant of a clay soil, whilst yew, beech and box will grow well over chalk. The hornbeam, *Carpinus betulus*, is rather quicker growing than beech. As hedging plants, both will retain their dead leaves through winter, falling only when the new leaves appear in spring. Hornbeam withstands hard clipping, as does beech, but all that is necessary is to remove any long shoots to keep the height even. Plant in November 18 in. (46 cm.) apart and 2–3 ft. (61–91 cm.).

For an inner or outer hedge, beech is admirable, and being early in leaf is used by birds which also find it of value for roosting in winter, during which time its then reddish-brown leaves maintain their dense covering. When in new leaf, the pale green is admirable as a background for darker evergreens. Plant 15 in. (38 cm.) apart and allow the main shoot to grow to the required height of the hedge before 'stopping' it.

Lonicera nitida, Berberis × stenophylla, thuja and privet are evergreen and fast growing, whilst hornbeam and beech are deciduous, though they will retain their leaves through winter when used as a hedge, losing them only in spring when the new leaves appear. Hawthorn and sloe will lose their leaves in winter but make dense prickly growth when used as a hedge, whilst they are among the first of plants to come into leaf— usually before the earliest of nesting birds begin to build. These are the thrush and blackbird, pied wagtail and dunnock, chaffinch and willow-warbler. Privet is one of the best hedges for the early builders but it requires clipping through the summer. Beech and hornbeam are less demanding in this respect and whilst *Thuja plicata* is as fast growing as privet, it will need clipping only once a year, as will beech and hawthorn.

The small-leaved evergreen *Lonicera nitida* makes a dense inner or outer hedge but needs about three trims a year to maintain its neatness. It will grow quite quickly and soon reach 4–5 ft. (1·2–1·5 m.). Good cover will be given to nesting birds if a double, staggered row is planted, allowing 15 in. (38 cm.) between rows and the same distance between the plants. The variety 'Fertilis' is the best form, its small glossy leaves appearing from top to bottom of the upright branching stems. If not trimmed too hard it will bear scented flowers, attractive to bees, in spring and black berries, which birds enjoy, in autumn. There is also a fine golden form, 'Baggesen's Gold', which may be preferred.

The oval-leaf privet, *Ligustrum ovalifolium,* evergreen in all but the most exposed gardens, is valuable where a rapidly growing hedge is required but it will need constant attention to keep it in trim. Like *Lonicera nitida* it is best planted as a double hedge, with the plants similarly spaced. The golden form is more colourful, and when well-tended is difficult to better. It may be interplanted with the dark green form, two or three plants of the gold and two or three of the green, and the effect is striking.

To make a privet hedge more attractive, clip into battlement formation, but not until it has reached its required height. First make the top level (A) with shears, then, using secateurs, cut away a section of hedge, using a length of board of the required size as a guide. Cut down to a lower line (B) and along the hedge. For several weeks the sections which have been cut

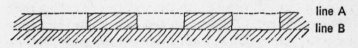

line A
line B

3. Battlement hedge formation

away will appear leafless and woody but these will quickly be covered by the formation of new leaf and both levels may then be kept neatly trimmed. Where planting the dark green and golden forms together, note that the latter is slow in growing and the green will need clipping more frequently to keep them at the same height.

Where the soil is heavy and wet and an evergreen hedge of density is required, *Thuja plicata* will be suitable. Birds love to build in it and it is one of the few conifers which, when cut hard back, will break into fresh growth even from the old woody stems. Constant clipping is necessary for it is a rapid grower. The time to plant is early May, 3 ft. (91 cm.) apart. Plant young trees 18–20 in. (46–51 cm.) tall; if older, they may be difficult to re-establish. Until the plants have reached their required height, pruning should consist of removing unwanted laterals. Regular spraying in summer will increase the beauty of the foliage. The cultivar 'Semperaurescens' could, with advantage, be planted with the dark green *T. plicata*, for it has contrasting golden-tipped foliage. *T. occidentalis* of North America is also valuable for hedge planting for it makes a large rounded plant 6–7 ft. (1·8–2·1 m.) high, clothed to the ground in feathery bronzy-green foliage. It is frequented by birds for making their nests.

In contrast to the thujas, the yew requires a dry chalky soil. As it is poisonous to animals, plant inside a garden where cattle and horses cannot reach it. The yew, *Taxus baccata*, makes a dense hedge and its almost black foliage is a most effective background for red roses and coloured foliage plants. If planted in well-manured soil, it will grow 6 in. (15 cm.) each year and need the minimum of clipping to maintain its shape. Plant 3 ft. (91 cm.) apart.

Lawson's Cypress, *Chamaecyparis lawsoniana*, makes a splendid hedge, growing into a dense upright tree with drooping branchlets. It withstands clipping and may be gently tapered at the top when at the required height. Jackman's 'Green Hedger' is another form, being deeper green than the type and faster growing. As with all conifers, plant in April when they are starting into new growth, and set them 2–3 ft. (61–91 cm.) apart. They require a well-drained soil.

A hybrid of *Cupressus macrocarpa* and *Chamaecyparis lawsoniana*, × *Cupressocyparis leylandii*, with the rapidity of growth of *macrocarpa* and the hardiness of the Lawson's Cypress, is rapidly becoming our most popular hedge. It will make a more valuable screen for inside the garden, rather than an outer hedge, and will grow at least 18–20 in. (46–51 cm.) in a year. It withstands wind and salt-laden sea-breezes and as long as the soil is well drained, it will be found to have few adverse qualities. For a thick hedge, plant in a double row 2 ft. (61 cm.) apart each way and allow the leader shoot to grow unchecked until at the required height. Pot-grown plants should always be used as × *Cupressocyparis leylandii* resents root disturbance.

The form 'Castlewellan', introduced by Pennells of Lincoln, has foliage of bright greenish-gold and all the good qualities of the parent with which it may be planted alternately.

Berberis stenophylla is one of the best of all hedges when in bloom and is evergreen, its gracefully arching stems being clothed with small dark green leaves, whilst in April the stems are covered in clusters of orange-coloured flowers. Plant 18 in. (46 cm.) apart, 2 ft. (61 cm.) apart if a double row is planted; November is a suitable time. Given the minimum of pruning, which should be done soon after flowering, the hedge will grow to 6 ft. (1·8 m.) in height and will be visited by most of the hedgerow birds.

Another berberis, *B. thunbergii atropurpurea*, will make a dense hedge 5 ft. (1·5 m.) tall, which is easily clipped into shape. It will retain its coppery-purple foliage all the year, so is always colourful. The variety *superba* is more vigorous and has deeper-coloured foliage than the type but both are excellent and, with their thorns, if planted as an outer hedge, will keep unwanted animals from the garden.

There is no plant of greater density than the box, *Buxus sempervirens*, an evergreen with small glossy leaves and pungent scent. In a chalky soil and in the west it makes a bush 6 ft. (1·8 m.) tall and almost as wide, clothed almost to the ground in its soft green foliage. It withstands hard clipping but grows slowly and will need trimming only once yearly. It may be left in the rounded natural state or clipped to form a square. Small birds love to build in it. Plant 2 ft. (61 cm.) apart in March.

It is only rarely that *Spiraea × arguta* is seen as a hedge. If used inside the garden it will prove an excellent haven for small birds which will visit the garden with more confidence where there is plenty of cover in which to take refuge when frightened, even though they may not build in this particular hedge. This plant will grow from 4 to 5 ft. (1·2 to 1·5 m.) and, though dense, it has a beautiful cascading habit. In April and May the shoots are covered in a multitude of white flowers, like snow in early summer. Plant 2 ft. (61 cm.) apart and trim if necessary after flowering.

The pyracantha, the firethorn, will make a wonderful evergreen hedge but the plants should be trained against strong galvanized wires held in place by stakes which may be left in as additional support. They will soon be covered by the plants which not only retain their small glossy bright green leaves through winter but will be a blaze of colour with pillar-box red berries. The hedge should be trimmed as little as possible so that the flowers (much frequented by bees) and the berries are not drastically reduced, though the plants will withstand hard clipping if necessary. The two forms for a hedge are *P. rogersiana* (this species is immune to greenfly attacks), its graceful arching branches covered in orange-red berries, and 'Orange Glow', a hardy and free-berrying form.

The common or prickly pear, *Pyrus communis*, will make a sturdy hedge or windbreak, to stand the severest of winds. It is seen at its best when planted alternately 5 ft. (1·5 m.) apart with the purple-leaf cherry plum, *Prunus* 'Pissardii'. Both flourish in a chalky soil and both withstand hard clipping, though being slow growing, all that is necessary is to prune gently in October. Plant 3 ft. (91 cm.) apart and when established remove the leader shoot to encourage the plants to grow bushy low down.

The same may be said of the blackthorn or sloe, *Prunus spinosa*, which also does well in a chalky soil. It is effective when planted alternately with the purple-leaf form, 'Purpurea'. Plant 2–3 ft. (61–91 cm.) apart and prune only rarely so as to enjoy its lovely white blossom, which appears early in spring and to which bees are greatly attracted. There is a double-flowering form 'Plena' and one, 'Rosea', which bears blossom of rosy-pink, but it is the wild single form that yields nectar. Another prunus of hedging value is *P.* 'Cistena' which grows to 6 ft. (1·8 m.) and if planted 15 in. (38 cm.) apart will make a thick hedge. It is most colourful in leaf; the foliage is crimson, the tips of the new shoots almost scarlet. Though it loses its foliage in winter, it is early into leaf and its whipping intertwining stems make it excellent for a hedge. But to keep it bushy low down, clip in autumn to about 15 in. (38 cm.) of the new growth each year.

Coastal hedges

For coastal planting there is the sea-buckthorn, *Hippophae rhamnoides*, a spiny shrub with handsome silvery foliage. It forms suckers to create a dense hedge and after flowering, in May, its stems will be covered in yellow berries all winter. Birds will rarely touch them but will build in an established hedge which can be grown to 6 ft. (1·8 m.) in height. Plant 3 ft. (91 cm.) apart, males and females together, and almost no pruning will be necessary. Both will make a hedge 10 ft. (3 m.) tall and 3 ft. (91 cm.) in width when fully grown and be clothed to the base in thorny shoots. Plant 2–3 ft. (61–91 cm.) apart.

The escallonia makes an excellent evergreen seaside hedge, for the plants thrive on the salt-laden breezes. The most vigorous kinds grow to 6–7 ft. (1·8–2·1 m.) and 3–4 ft. (91 cm.–1·2 m.) wide and they may be clipped into shape from an early age. The glossy dark green leaves have a sticky feel about them and are pleasantly resinous, whilst their tubular flowers are freely produced from mid-summer until late autumn. Plant in spring, 3 ft. (91 cm.) apart and in a light sandy soil and do any clipping to maintain the shape during April so that the flowers will not be lost. One of the best is 'Crimson Spire' which bears its red flowers from July until October and will grow to 6 ft. (1·8 m.) in three or four years. Vigorous, too, is 'Glasnevin Hybrid', also crimson flowering; plant with it, for contrast, 'Donard White'. *E*. 'Iveyi' is another good white variety.

Nor should the hardier fuchsias be omitted when considering a coastal hedge, though they will lose their leaves in all but the mildest climates. They grow well down the western side of Britain where they soon form large bushes and, as they require no pruning, may be left to produce their graceful stems which are clothed in flowers during the late summer months. *Fuchsia* 'Riccartonii' is the hardiest and will make a hedge 4–5 ft. (1·2–1·5 m.) tall and the same across. The dangling blooms have violet petals and crimson sepals. Though not quite so vigorous, 'Mme Cornelissen' has petals of white with contrasting scarlet sepals. It is hardy and free flowering. Plant in spring from pots, spacing them 2 ft. (61 cm.) apart. They like a deeply dug, well-manured soil.

The shiny-leaved euonymus makes a colourful low hedge and is as untroubled by sea-breezes as it is by the often polluted atmosphere of a town garden. It will grow to 5 ft. (1·5 m.) in height and if planted about 20 in. (51 cm.) apart will soon make a thick hedge for birds to nest in. The cultivar 'Ovatus Aureus' has pretty golden leaves whilst *Euonymus fortunei* 'Silver Pillar' has dark green leaves edged with silver. Both will make a thick low hedge about 4 ft. (1·2 m.) tall. Plant them in March, 20 in. (51 cm.) apart.

Rose hedges

Several species of rose will make an attractive hedge and, although they drop their leaves in winter, make a valuable nesting site for the later-building birds, whilst the plants give colour throughout summer and autumn. It is better to train the shoots along strong wires held in place by stout stakes at a height of about 4–5 ft. (1·2–1·5 m.) above ground with the wires 15 in. (38 cm.) apart. The early shoots may then be tied in and a sound framework built up. Or a wooden trellis of similar height may be used instead, the shoots being inter-twined about the trellis. In two to three years' time the hedge will have become so thick as to hide the trellis or wires com-

pletely and will be impenetrable to outsiders. The rose
flourishes in a heavy, wet soil where few other plants will do
well.

The most vigorous of the hybrid musk roses make a hedge
of great beauty, whilst requiring little or no pruning apart
from the removal of dead wood from older plants. 'Vanity' is
the most vigorous, bearing masses of deep pink flowers but
'Felicia', with its double flowers of shell-pink, is almost as
strong growing. They will make a hedge 5–6 ft. (1·5–1·8 m.)
high. 'Buff Beauty', with its apricot and cream flowers borne
in long elegant sprays, is a magnificent sight when in bloom
whilst 'Penelope', with grey-green foliage and creamy-pink
flowers, is also very fine. The single-flowering kinds are followed by bright red hips in autumn, so these hedges have an
added attraction.

A splendid rose for a hedge is 'Nevada' which in June and July
smothers itself in single creamy-pink flowers and has pale green
foliage. Equally vigorous is *Rosa moyesii* 'Eos' which makes a
tall, elegant bush, its semi-double blooms being followed by
enormous scarlet hips. The type bears clusters of single blood-
red flowers followed by red urn-shaped fruits, which make
this native of China one of the finest of all wild roses. A hybrid,
'Highdownensis', is equally fine, growing 7–8 ft. (2·1–2·4 m.)
tall and bearing single crimson flowers followed by enormous
sprays of slim crimson fruits. Several of these roses could be
planted together, 6 ft. (1·8 m.) apart, and in twelve months will
have closed up the gaps to form a dense hedge with their long
shoots.

'Zéphirine Drouhin' should not be neglected as a hedge. It is
useful to divide one part of the garden from another and will
make a thick screen or hedge if grown along wires or against a
trellis, whilst birds in their dozens will use it for nesting. A
Bourbon rose, it comes into bloom early in June and continues all through summer and autumn.

A thick hedge can be made with the white rose, *Rosa alba*

'Maiden's Blush', which will grow into a bush with handsome grey foliage and will flourish in the poorest of soils, eventually growing 6–7 ft. (1·8–2·1 m.) tall. Its flat double flowers are of a lovely shade of blush-pink. Another cultivar is 'Celestial', also with soft grey foliage and bearing double blooms of deeper pink.

R. rubiginosa, the sweet briar, so called because of the rich fruity scent of its foliage, is also admirable for a hedge, planted 4 ft. (1·2 m.) apart. Its single pink flowers in early summer are always a delight. The native dog rose, *R. canina*, with its single, sweetly scented flowers of pink or white, followed by long tapering hips of orange-scarlet, also makes a thick hedge but because of its considerable vigour it is more suited to field culture, where it will be a nesting paradise for large numbers of birds.

PLANTS OF DENSE GROWTH SUITABLE FOR A HEDGE

Species or Variety	Height ft.	(m.)	Planting Distance	
Beech (A)	8	(2·4)	15 in.	(38 cm.)
Berberis stenophylla (A)	6	(1·8)	18 in.	(46 cm.)
Berberis thunbergii (A)	4	(1·2)	10 in.	(25 cm.)
Buxus sempervirens (Sp)	5	(1·5)	2 ft.	(61 cm.)
Chamaecyparis lawsoniana (S)	12	(3·7)	2–3 ft.	(61–91 cm.)
Cupressocyparis leylandii (S)	12	(3·7)	3 ft.	(91 cm.)
Escallonia 'Crimson Spire' (Sp)	6	(1·8)	3 ft.	(91 cm.)
Escallonia 'Iveyi' (Sp)	6	(1·8)	3 ft.	(91 cm.)
Euonymus 'Ovatus Aureus' (S)	5	(1·5)	20 in.	(51 cm.)
Fuchsia 'Riccartonii' (A)	4–5	(1·2–1·5)	3 ft.	(91 cm.)
*Holly, 'J. C. van Tol' (Sp)	10	(3·0)	18 in	(46 cm.)
Hornbeam (A)	6	(1·8)	18 in.	(46 cm.)
Lonicera nitida (A)	5–6	(1·5–1·8)	15 in.	(38 cm.)
Musk Rose, 'Buff Beauty' (Sp)	6	(1·8)	4 ft.	(1·2 m.)
Musk Rose, 'Vanity' (Sp)	5	(1·5)	4ft.	(1·2 m.)

Species or Variety	Height ft. (m.)	Planting Distance
Privet (S)	6 (1·8)	15 in. (38 cm.)
Prunus 'Cistena' (A)	6 (1·8)	18 in. (46 cm.)
Prunus 'Pissardii' (A)	10 (3·0)	3 ft. (91 cm.)
Prunus spinosa (A)	8 (2·4)	3 ft. (91 cm.)
Pyracantha rogersiana (Sp)	10 (3·0)	2–3 ft. (61–91 cm.)
Pyrus communis (A)	10 (3·0)	3 ft. (91 cm.)
Rosa canina (Sp)	5 (1·5)	4 ft. (1·2 m.)
Rosa 'Highdownensis' (Sp)	7–8 (2·1–2·4)	5 ft. (1·5 m.)
Rosa moyesii 'Eos' (Sp)	6 (1·8)	4 ft. (1·2 m.)
Rosa rubiginosa (Sp)	6 (1·8)	4 ft. (1·2 m.)
Rosa 'Zéphirine Drouhin' (Sp)	6 (1·8)	4 ft. (1·2 m.)
*Sea Buckthorn (A)	6 (1·8)	3 ft. (91 cm.)
Spiraea × *arguta* (A)	4–5 (1·2–1·5)	2 ft. (61 cm.)
Taxus baccata (Sp)	10 (3·0)	3 ft. (91 cm.)
Thuja occidentalis (S)	7 (2·1)	3 ft. (91 cm.)
Thuja plicata (S)	12 (3·7)	3 ft. (91 cm.)
*Whitethorn (A)	6 (1·8)	12 in. (30 cm.)

* These plants form brightly coloured berries or fruits.

A = autumn trimming.

Sp = spring trimming.

S = summer trimming.

❀ 2. Nest-boxes, bird-tables and feeding units ❀

Nest-boxes

However well the garden itself has been planned to encourage the birds to come to it, more can be done by providing them with nest-boxes and, to win their confidence, by placing at their disposal objects from which they can feed and drink. This is important where making a new garden in which trees, shrubs and wall-covering plants will take several years to become established. The best time to make and prepare the boxes is during winter so that they may be in position for the birds to use in early spring. Often those birds which winter in Britain will have built and raised a family before the first arrivals from overseas have reached us and they will lay early, before many trees and shrubs have come into leaf, so nest-boxes are of real importance. Nest-boxes correctly placed will, whatever the state of the garden, be visited by birds of all types, not only for nesting but for roosting and winter protection. A little hay or straw placed in a box will encourage a bird to nest there. Wherever the nest-box is sited, let it face away from prevailing winds as most birds do not like wind. In Britain, the winds blow mostly from a south-west or north-east direction and the box should be positioned so that the opening faces either north-west, or preferably south-east. Some birds such as the tree-creeper do not take kindly to conventional nest-boxes, preferring a crack or hole in an old tree, but there are others which seem to prefer nesting in boxes rather than elsewhere in the garden, possibly because they are warmer and drier and afford greater privacy and protection from cats and also from magpies which will often attack young birds in open nests and take their eggs. Again, some birds prefer an open-fronted box and amongst these are the robin, water-wagtail and spotted fly-catcher, though all but the kestrel, which requires an open-front box, will build in a closed box if no other is available.

One is often asked how many nesting-boxes should be used in a small garden of, say, half an acre. Experience shows that perhaps four boxes may be used in a suburban garden, evenly spaced near the house and around the garden. Possibly two may be fixed to the house, as far apart as possible, with another half-way down the garden and a fourth near the end. Or if the garden is on both sides of a house, site one box on each side, as far from the house as practical. More birds will build in wall-plants and thickly foliaged trees and shrubs, especially ever-greens, which, like nest-boxes, will be available for the early nesters. The provision of different types of box, sited as far apart as possible, will encourage a wide variety of birds, whilst it will do much to prevent those birds which lay claim to a particular territory from becoming a nuisance to others. Should there be little suitable nesting vegetation for late arrivals, an additional box or two may be sited and the holes kept closed until early in May.

Be sure to secure the lid of any box with a hook-and-eye catch so that cats cannot open it. And where grey squirrels are prevalent, it is best to make the boxes of hardwood so that they cannot enlarge the entrance hole with their teeth.

Certain birds such as the robin and tree-pipit, which build low down, will often make their nests in an old boot, rusty bucket or old watering-can, even in a drain-pipe, and these objects should be sited about the garden but out of view. It is surprising how often they will be used.

A nest-box should be fixed where a tree, shrub or wall-plant will eventually hide it from view. This will give the birds greater privacy. The box may be fixed to a trellis on which a climbing plant is growing, or in the fork of an old apple tree, a young beech, or a white poplar, *Populus alba*. The box may

4. Nest-box fixed to trellis

be made both secure and inconspicuous by fixing it to a branch with an old leather belt of the same colour as the box and tree bark. It does not matter if the box is not fixed straight; a slight tilt to one side or with the hole in a downward direction will make little difference, for the birds will build their nest quite straight inside the box. Indeed, woodpeckers make the lower part of their entrance hole with a slope downwards from the front and most hole-nesting birds prefer an old woodpecker's nest to any other. But fix the box securely so that it does not rock in the wind or with the movements of the birds. If it does, they may not lay their eggs, even though they have built in it. This is why birds prefer to build in a wall-plant with its greater resistance to wind movement, rather than in a bush. If possible, cut away a small section of bark so as to give the box greater security; this can be done with a hammer and chisel or with a saw, taking care not to cut too deeply into the wood. Make sure that the box does not tilt backwards with the opening in an upward direction as this will make the birds too conspicuous, whilst admitting rain and snow. Nest-boxes should have a slightly green or black overhanging lid, covered with water-proof felt, to give greater protection from the weather. The lid will also give shade in summer and privacy, the young being reared in diffused light.

If one is fastening a box to a tall unbranched tree such as

Scots pine or ash, the box is first fixed to a piece of strong timber of ¾ in. (2 cm.) thickness which is cut about 2 in. (5 cm.) longer than the side of the box. This will allow 3 in. (7·6 cm.)

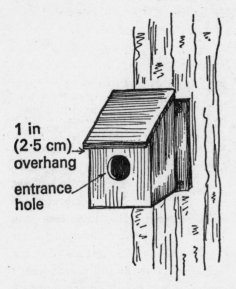

1 in
(2·5 cm.)
overhang

entrance
hole

5. Nest-box fixed to a
tall tree

nails to be driven in to fix the wood to the tree. In this case, make the lid so that when opened for cleaning the box, it will be clear of the fixing wood.

When fixing a nest-box to the wall of a house or outbuilding, screw the fixing timber to the back of the box horizontally and then fix it to the wall, after plugging the mortar between the bricks or stones to cause as little damage as possible. The timber fixed to the back will bring the box ¾ in. (2 cm.) away from the wall and so allow the lid to be opened for cleaning. In later summer after cleaning out the old nest, hold open the lid with a piece of wire fastened to a wall-nail to allow the box to be freshened by sunshine and air.

Nest-boxes may be fixed where the birds can be watched from the window of a sitting-room, though this may not always be possible if a number of boxes are being placed at strategic points about the garden. The first consideration is the birds; provide them with a suitable position and they will use the boxes freely and one may watch them when in the garden.

If a nest-box is fixed to a stout post so that it is about 6 ft.

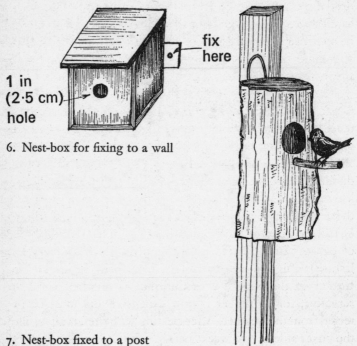

fix here

1 in (2·5 cm) hole

6. Nest-box for fixing to a wall

7. Nest-box fixed to a post

(1·8 m.) above ground, it will be protected from cats and other predators. It may be securely fixed to the post by means of a length of ¾ in. (2 cm.) timber fastened to the back of the box below the lid, cut 6 in. (15 cm.) longer than the back of the box. It can then be fixed to the box by two nails driven into the wood projecting below the box. Or a hollow log-type nest-box may be fixed to a post by brackets. The post may be close to a tall shrub, to provide camouflage for the box as well as shade and privacy. If the post and the box are painted green they will scarcely be noticed.

Boxes must be fixed at various heights as birds vary in their requirements. As the tree-pipit, robin and willow-warbler prefer to build low down, a box may be fixed to a short post driven securely into the ground near an evergreen shrub such as *Elaeagnus pungens* 'Dicksonii' or *Senecio greyi*, which will not be so dense in leaf as the cupressus and juniper in which birds will build naturally. Or boxes may be fixed near deciduous shrubs which provide camouflage as they come into leaf.

A box may be fixed in the corner where two walls meet and 6–8 ft. (1·8–2·4 m.) above ground, or to a post at the top of a fence. Barbed wire should then be fixed along the top of the fence to keep cats away. The back of a wooden shed is a suitable place for a nest-box and here a long box may be fixed, divided into six or more compartments, each with its opening, leaving some with the fronts partially cut away to encourage those requiring this type of box to build there. The boxes may be painted green or brown on the outside or left natural if made of oak or American red cedar, both of which are very long lasting though more expensive. Unpainted boxes are first treated on the outside with Cuprinol or another wood preservative, for all timber is now expensive and must be protected from the weather. After treating with preservative, allow the boxes at least two weeks before fixing, to enable any fumes to escape before the birds begin building. The most suitable timber for a nesting-box is 6 in. × ¾ in. (15 cm. × 2 cm.) deal or pine with a planed surface, for a box should be not less than 12 in. (30 cm.) deep at the back and 10 in. (25 cm.) at the front, with a gently sloping roof or lid with a 1 in. (2·5 cm.) overlap at the front. The lid is fitted with two hinges to allow it to be opened to clear out the nest in the autumn and thoroughly clean the box. First cut the timber to the required lengths with the end-pieces to fit inside the back and front pieces. If any attempt is made to dovetail the corners it must be remembered that the strength of a dovetail lies in the perfection of its construction, and a water-resistant glue is likely to prove more satisfactory. A good simple job is always better than a poor complicated one. When securing the side pieces, there is no advantage in using screws instead of nails, for screws will tend to split the wood whereas 2 in. (5 cm.) oval nails usually will not. For additional strength at the corners, an angle bracket should be screwed either on the inside or outside the box. The base should be drilled with several small holes for drainage, for some birds are not very particular as to their toilet habits. An entrance hole of only 1 in. (2·5 cm.) in diameter will allow almost all the small birds to enter, yet will keep out sparrows and starlings which may take over the boxes if given the chance. (The Royal Society for the Protection of Birds sells a small metal device which will reduce the size of an over-large hole.) If the hole is made 1¼ in. (3 cm.) in diameter, this will allow tree-sparrows and other birds to enter, but possibly house-sparrows, too. Make the hole with hammer and chisel after accurately drawing the correct diameter on the wood. The hole should be made 2 in. (5 cm.) from the top.

For those birds which require an open front, use only a piece of 6 in. (15 cm.) timber at the front, leaving 4 in. (10 cm.) at the top completely open. This will allow the nest to be built well down in the box. With the conventional box, additional air may be admitted by drilling two small holes of ½ in. (1·3 cm.) diameter on both sides or at the back, depending upon where and how it is to be fixed. If there are wrynecks in the area, they will often build in a nest-box if the entrance hole is made slightly oval.

For large birds such as the jackdaw and great spotted woodpecker, although the box dimensions will be the same, there should be a larger opening, 2 in. (5 cm.) square, made either at the front or the side. If there are boxes for both small and large birds, one will encourage a greater number of species into the garden.

Tree-creepers can be encouraged to build by providing a wedge-shaped box. Until the ornithologist, J. D. Mackenzie, suggested this, it was only rarely that the tree-creeper would use a nest-box. The box is made to the same dimensions as the conventional box but without the base, the front part being fixed to the bottom of the longer length which is cut about

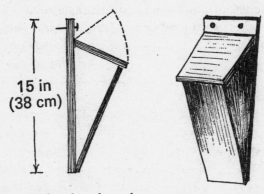

8. Wedge-shaped nest-box

16 in. (41 cm.) long. The roof or lid will therefore have a bigger slope. The entrance hole is made 1¼ in. (3 cm.) in diameter. Tits may also use this box. It should be sited in a near upright position on a tree trunk about 12 ft. (3·7 m.) above ground.

Owls and pigeons prefer a tray which has no roof or lid. The box should have sides 6 in. (15 cm.) deep and 10 in. (25 cm.) square (using two pieces of floor boarding for the base, glued together) for their nests will be composed of twigs and will be quite large. Such a box can be sited at the point where a chimney joins the roof, and may be held in position by two angle-iron brackets plugged into the chimney.

Owls will also use what is known as a funnel-type or drain-pipe box, if it is sited fairly high in a tall tree. It is made by nailing together four pieces of 8 in. × ¾ in. (20 cm. × 2 cm.) wood to form a square, and each piece should be about 30 in.

(76 cm.) long. It is provided with a base but no lid and is strapped to a part of the trunk where the box can be at an angle. Tawny owls, doves and jackdaws will use it even if it is fixed horizontally, but they like to get right down into it. To enable it to be cleaned, cut out a trap door some 12 in. (30 cm.) from the bottom and hinged. It is kept closed by means of a small hook and wire.

At my home, a small stone has been removed just beneath the eaves where each year several pairs of swifts bring up a family. As the old walls are 4 ft. (1·2 m.) thick they must make

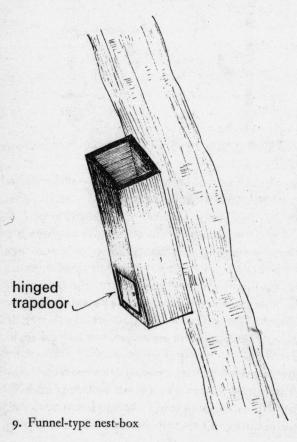

hinged trapdoor

9. Funnel-type nest-box

their 'nest' in a pocket left by falling rubble, for upon looking into the opening with a torch it is not possible to see or to feel any nest. Indeed the birds collect neither twigs nor grasses.

For the brick-built modern house, a special nest-box for swifts has been designed at the Edward Grey Institute at Oxford. This is a box made by fixing together two opposite lengths of 8 in. × ¾ in. (20 cm. × 2 cm.) timber and two of 6 in. × ¾ in. (15 cm. × 2 cm.) which are cut 2 ft. (61 cm.) long.

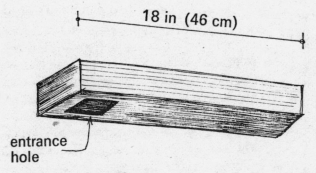

entrance
hole

10. Nest-box for swifts

The box has two ends and the 4 in. (10 cm.) square entry hole is made at one end. This will be on the lower side of the box when it is fixed against the overhanging eaves and close up to the wall. The birds will build at the opposite end to the entry hole and will be more inclined to do so if a circle of plaited straw, on which they can lay their eggs, is placed there.

Conventional nest-boxes will look more attractive if pieces of old bark are nailed to the outside, and they will present a more natural appearance to the birds.

For those who do not wish to make their own boxes, there are a number on the market which have been made by specialists to the exact requirements of the birds and which have stood the test of time. One of pleasing design, made of Burma teak, combines a feeding-table beneath the nest-box. It stands 6 ft.

(1·8 m.) high and the base timbers are drilled to take four wrought-iron pins which are driven into the ground to prevent the box from blowing over. It may be sited at a corner of the lawn, preferably close to a hedge or shrub border which the birds may use for privacy and shelter as they fly in and out of their house. If it is sited too close to passers-by or traffic, the birds will be too frightened to use the box.

11. Combined feeding-table and nest-box

The thatched bird-houses hand-made by Dornoms of Salcombe, Devon, are pleasing. About 18 in. (46 cm.) high, they are fitted with a hinged trap door at the rear for cleaning and there is a landing platform at the front, just below the entrance hole, which may also be used to feed the birds. This type of nest-box is best fixed against a wall, with a nail driven through a hook at the top into a plug in the wall so that the box will lie flat. These boxes are warm so are frequented by migrants from warmer parts.

The Nerine Nurseries, Walland, Worcester, make a selection of neat and well-designed nest-boxes. The log box, hollowed from a birch branch with the bark attached and with a hinged lid for cleaning, is ideal for smaller birds and for fixing to a tree or wall. They also make a larger box of rot-proof timber for flycatchers and redstarts.

The 'Wendy' tit-box is strongly constructed with a side blind for quick inspection of the occupants, whilst the entrance hole is adjustable from 1 in. (2·5 cm.) to 1½ in. (3·8 cm.) to accommodate all types of smaller bird. If a certain species is seen in the area, the entrance hole can be adjusted accordingly.

Bird-tables and feeding units

Scandinavian bird-houses are becoming popular for, as they are made from rigid weatherproof polythene, they are durable and inexpensive. If suspended from a branch they will be visited by members of the tit family who enjoy the movement more than other birds. They are fitted with perches and are perhaps more useful for putting in food rather than for nesting, as they do not provide the same privacy as those of more conventional design.

The 'mushroom' feeding-house, with its domed top and transparent cylinder for the food, is of neat design. There is room for the birds to alight and enjoy the food whilst an attachment underneath permits it to be fastened to a pole or broom handle driven into the ground.

Loved by the tits is the Merry-Go-Round feeding-unit (from The Mews, Gilston Park, Harlow) made of durable Burma teak and adjusted to fit on to a large cane or pole, the unit being suspended from a short bar. About 12 in. (30 cm.) long and 3 in. (7·6 cm.) wide, the teak block has four circular openings which go right through the wood and in which food is placed. The tits love to swing on the unit and climb in and out of the holes which are large enough for them but too small for larger birds, though finches will use them too. Each hole has a perch and the birds also use the top of the unit and the suspension bar. The unit should be fixed into the ground in a position from which the antics of the birds can be viewed from the house.

In a severe winter, thousands of birds will die from lack of food, especially in the country where household scraps are more difficult to find, but much loss of life may be prevented if scraps from one's plate are put out where the birds can find them. Pieces of bacon rind, crispy fried bread, bits of meat, the

12. Scandinavian-
type bird-house

13. Merry-Go-Round
feeding unit

skin from a cooked chicken, and bread crumbs (toast especially), are of the utmost value in keeping birds alive in winter. Each morning the scraps may be placed in a plastic-covered wire feeder, costing only a few pence, suspended from a wall 5 ft. (1·5 m.) above ground. If two are used, the scraps of the previous day are placed in one early in the morning and this is hung on a hook or nail when the other is removed. This will ensure that no food scraps, however small, are destroyed, nor do they become stale. A feeding basket made of plastic-coated wire mesh, with a lid, is equally efficient.

Many birds besides tits will enjoy peanuts in winter, possibly when the berries have all been taken from the shrubs. The nuts may be suspended from a tree or wall, about 6 ft. (1·8 m.)

above ground, in a plastic net on which the birds swing whilst they peck at the nuts.

Feeding equipment will require cleaning at least once a month. It should be dismantled as far as possible and scrubbed with soap and water, then washed down with clean water before reassembling. This regular care should be given to plastic-covered wire food-dispensers, for particles of sour food will collect between the wires.

Besides household scraps, birds in winter should be given seed whenever possible. Specially blended mixtures of proprietary makes are available from local pet shops or in larger quantities at wholesale prices from seed or corn merchants.

During autumn, birds will obtain all the seeds they require from flower-heads of the greater plantain, groundsel and shepherd's purse and these may be collected about the countryside and saved for winter feeding. A wonderful seed producer in the herbaceous border is *Achillea filipendulina*, a hardy plant which has handsome foliage and bears its large flat heads of a brilliant golden-yellow on 4 ft. (1·2 m.) stems. The seed-heads are removed in October when large quantities can be saved from a very few plants.

A most efficient bird-table is made by Jamie Wood Ltd. of Polegate, Sussex. Made of Canadian Douglas fir, the tray is about 18 in. × 10 in. (46 cm. × 25 cm.) and some 12 in. (30 cm.) above is a roof to protect the food in adverse weather. The roof is held up by a 5 ft. (1·5 m.) pole which goes through the centre of the feeding-tray, whilst two hooks beneath the tray enable plastic bags of nuts or wire food-containers to be suspended from them. The table is neat and solidly made by craftsmen and makes a pleasing gift.

A neat feeding-unit for small birds is that made by R. Dendy of Carshalton, Surrey. Hand-made of translucent fibreglass, it has a roof of 19 in. (48 cm.) diameter above the feeding-tray, which protects the food from rain or snow and prevents bigger birds such as gulls and crows from alighting on the tray. The six perches allow the birds ample scope for feeding from a circular trough 1½ in. (3·8 cm.) wide, whilst the droppings fall to the ground and do not foul the food. It is fitted to a wall or tree by means of a strong plastic-coated steel bracket.

The most inexpensive way of making a bird-table is to fix a board about 12 in. (30 cm.) square on to the top of a pole or post driven into the ground. To give additional stability, a short length of timber (a piece of builder's lath) should be fixed from underneath each corner of the tray to the post, some 8–9 in. (20–23 cm.) from the top. The feeding-tray should be about 4 ft. (1·2 m.) above ground; around the edge of the tray fix strips of wood 1 in. (2·5 cm.) wide so that they will come about ½ in. (1·3 cm.) above the tray, to contain the food.

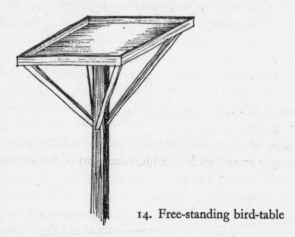

14. Free-standing bird-table

The Royal Society for the Protection of Birds has put on the market an efficient roofed table measuring 18 in. × 12 in. (46 cm. × 30 cm.), with hanging chains and a wall-bracket. Fitted beneath the roof is a seed-hopper to dispense seeds. It clips into a special fitment so is easily removed for filling. The equipment is made by the mentally handicapped in Cambridge and both the workmanship and materials are of the highest standard.

Birds must have water to drink and to wash in. In its correct setting, the stone pedestal bird-bath which may take the place of a sundial is admirable. It must be kept filled with water and cleaned out at least once a month. Butterflies will also use it.

More modest is the Rikden bird-bath, specially designed by a well-known ornithologist to place on the ground. It is of 20 in. (51 cm.) diameter with a gently sloping base so it is deep enough for a dove to use and shallow enough for a robin. What is more it has a sanded surface for good claw grip. Made of fibreglass, it will not crack in hard frost. It will hold a gallon of water and is easily cleaned and filled. Cleaning should be done frequently and one must keep special watch during warm weather to ensure that it is topped up often, for water in the open evaporates quickly and it is at this time that birds and other wildlife will be in most need of it.

Bird watching

The provision of nesting-boxes and bird tables will add greatly to the enjoyment of bird watching. Almost a necessity for the maximum enjoyment of birds is a pair of good binoculars. A lightweight model made to a high standard of workmanship is that made by the Heron Optical Co. of Brentwood, Essex. Field of view is 393 ft. at 1,000 yd. and magnifying 8 times with a front lens diameter of 40 mm. The Swift BWCF Mark II with a front lens of 44 mm., magnifying 8·5 times and focussing to 12 ft. is equally reliable.

Binoculars may be used from the home and about the garden, and they should be carried whenever going into the country so that the beauty and characteristics of all birds may be closely studied. The more one may learn about birds in the country-side the more will they be appreciated in the garden.

Buy as many books about birds and bird watching as you can afford and carry about a notebook to record all that you discover about them, especially in the garden. Note when any migratory species is first seen each year, when it leaves, and when and where a nest is made and the number of eggs laid, always approaching the nest with the minimum of noise and disturbance. Note which species visit which shrubs for their berries, and when they feed upon them. If they are seen in the countryside or in someone else's garden, you may then introduce the same plants to your own garden. Note also those trees and shrubs most often built in so that others may be planted if there is space. Also note which nest-boxes are most used and by which birds.

Become a member of the R.S.P.B. so as to receive their valuable bi-monthly magazine, *Birds*, for it contains news of the nature reserves and the birds to be seen there at any given time of the year and it is useful to note this information. But it is in the garden, where in the years ahead more of one's time may well be spent, that the birds may be studied to advantage. When digging, stop occasionally for a few minutes and look around to see where the birds are and how they are behaving. Have in the pocket some small pieces of suet or coconut, some chopped bacon rinds or bits of nut, and throw them a yard or two away, to win the birds' confidence. They will gradually come closer and closer and will have such faith in their friend that they will build in the garden with as much confidence as they would do in woodland and hedgerow.

Those who have a record player will be well rewarded by purchasing records of bird songs and those with tape recorders will enjoy making their own recordings. (Such recordings were first perfected by the late Ludwig Koch.) It is a pleasing way of getting to know the chatter and song of our birds so that they are instantly recognizable when heard in the garden and countryside.

Of all wildlife visitors to the garden, none are more welcome than the birds, both those which are indigenous to Britain and the summer visitors, and every effort should be made to encourage them to make their nests in our gardens, more especially in places where they may be observed from the house or garden room.

There are few gardens which cannot cater in some small way for birds. Plants may be grown against the wall of a tiny court-yard, either in tubs or planted directly into the ground by removing a small section of concrete or a stone slab, and their flowers and foliage will not only provide colour, but nesting space too. Here a tit box, hidden by the plants, will provide the household with hours of pleasure during the year. Even in a town garden, in the most densely built-up areas, many birds may be encouraged to make their home in an old tree or in a plant growing on a wall and several will return to the same nest year after year. It should not be thought that because one's house, and maybe quite small garden, are situated near to the centre of an industrial town, wildlife cannot be encouraged. There are parts of Leeds, on the north side where Roundhay Park covers a large area; of Sheffield, to the south, which is well served by the beautiful Ecclesall Woods; and the King's Heath district of Birmingham, where birdlife is almost as prevalent as in the open countryside. In Sheffield, the Botanical Gardens and Endcliffe Woods are within a mile of the city centre and here many quite rare birds are to be seen each year: they could be encouraged to visit gardens in a wide area around. The industrial towns of the North and Midlands are fortunate in having many large parks within their confines, Nottingham, for example, and Chesterfield with its lovely Queen's Park. The parks bring birdlife almost to our gates, and all that is necessary to enjoy the birds in one's garden in such areas is to give a little thought to its planning.

Writing in *Birds*, the highly readable journal of the Royal Society for the Protection of Birds, Mr. R. Glover of Hackney, a member of the Essex Bird Watching Society, reports that more and more birds of the countryside, at one time rarely seen in town gardens, are becoming more common in built-up places. He calls them 'refugees from an increasingly hostile countryside' where large areas of woodland are felled and hedges grubbed up in the interests of efficient farming. In addition to this, the use of herbicides is depriving many birds of important sources of food, especially goldfinches and linnets which feed on thistle seeds. The suburban gardener can do much to replace the now 'hostile countryside' by providing food and nesting places.

The Report of the Council for the Preservation of Rural England, published in July 1975, states that 3,000 miles of hedgerows are being grubbed up by farmers every year, this destruction no longer being confined to the arable lands of eastern England, for it has now spread on a similar scale to the Midlands and West Country where the fields, formerly thick with hedgerows, are now being made so bare that the traditional landscape is fast changing its appearance, and wildlife is now being driven to the outskirts of towns.

In a letter to *The Times* of 14 September 1974, Mr. K Doughty, Librarian and Curator to the Borough of Southwark, makes mention of much wildlife to be found in his borough, close to the city centre—a part where one would think little natural beauty could be found, for the area covers the Surrey Docks and Peckham Rye. But it also contains some rural areas: Mr. Doughty notes, for instance, that the little owl breeds in Dulwich Wood, this being its nearest point of breeding to central London, and also the long-tailed titmouse, the lesser redpoll and the three better-known woodpeckers; whilst in Peckham Rye Park, even closer to the city centre, he says that more than fifty different birds have been counted, including the heron and kingfisher. He adds that in these areas wood-mice and water voles, hedgehogs and grey squirrels can be found, and foxes have become a major pest.

It is often said that when fruit and vegetables are grown in the garden, birds should never be encouraged, for they will do more damage than good. True, blackbirds are dreadful thieves of ripe strawberries and redcurrants and these fruits should be covered with netting in their season. Blackbirds will also take elderberries and blackberries from the hedgerows, but without depriving one of too much free food, whilst bullfinches and house-sparrows may, in a dry spring, attack the blossom of apple and plum trees. Yet it has been observed at the East Malling Research Station in Kent that of a thousand Victoria plum trees attacked by house-sparrows, less than 10 per cent had their blossom so badly damaged as to prevent them setting fruit and in only 5 per cent were the styles damaged. Both the great tit and the bullfinch will take the fruit buds from apple and plum trees, as well as from blackcurrants in winter, but will rarely do so where there are berries for them to feed upon, whilst both birds will feed on caterpillars of the destructive winter moth and the larvae of other fruit pests, thus more than balancing the harm they do. The jay, too, will eat redcurrants but also devours the harmful larvae of the click-beetle. The hawfinch will remove ripe cherries to get at the stones and remove the hard outer shell with its powerful bill to reach the kernel, but it also eats caterpillars and beetles and does more good than it does harm. Bullfinches and house-sparrows need no encouragement, they make their home wherever man makes his. It is the other birds that need encouraging to come into the garden and almost all these are insect-eaters, taking them either from the ground or from trees and when upon the wing.

Another of the avid insect-eaters is the wren, which will

make its nest close to the house with the least encouragement. It likes nothing better than the dense growth of *Clematis montana* which may be trained against a trellis or supported by strong wires fixed to a wall. Each morning at sunrise, the cock will begin his song, perched on the top of the partly domed nest, before he disappears for hours in search of food for the hen whilst she sits patiently on her large clutch of eggs. When the chicks have hatched she will rarely go far, preferring to sit on the edge of the nest opening, gazing down on them with maternal contentment.

These British birds rely on insects for their main diet and are special friends of the gardener:

Blackbird	Pied flycatcher
Blackcap	Pied wagtail
Brambling	Redbreast (robin)
Chaffinch	Redstart
Chiff-chaff	Song thrush
Dunnock	Spotted flycatcher
Garden-warbler	Stonechat
Goldcrest	Swallow
Goldfinch	Swift
Great spotted woodpecker	Tree-creeper
Green woodpecker	Whitethroat
Jackdaw	Willow-warbler
Jay (larvae)	Wren
Lesser redpoll	Wryneck
Mistle thrush	Yellow wagtail

As few deciduous plants come into leaf before the arrival of our first summer visitors, evergreens should be available for their nesting and also for those resident birds which lay early. There should be climbing plants too, for even if they are not yet in leaf, an abundance of intertwining stems will provide nest cover and privacy for the birds. These plants may be grown against a trellis or garden wall, which is where birds prefer to build, there being little or no movement to the nests in strong wind.

Migrating birds

Much can be done to help our visiting birds, besides providing them with food and nesting, for it must be realized that at least twenty million are lost each year during migration. Nothing can be done to mitigate such vagaries of the weather as occurred in the autumn of 1974, when large numbers of swallows crossing western France on their journey to Africa were blown off course by the unusually early gales, and were found in Switzerland in an exhausted state. Many were saved in a massive rescue operation and flown to the African coast by those who cared. In France and Italy, however, thousands of trappers, mostly small farmers, lie in wait each year, in late spring, as the birds make their journey back to Britain and Northern Europe, and again in autumn as the birds journey south, and it is estimated that at least ten million are taken for food in each of these countries.

Migrating birds follow two main air-streams as they fly from Northern Europe to winter in the warmer parts. They are amongst our loveliest birds—the sedge- and garden-warblers, the chiff-chaff, the blackcap, the skylark and the linnet, and pied wagtail which are both resident and migratory. Millions of them whose melodious songs have delighted us all summer will never return.

The birds, after crossing the Channel, fly down the western seaboard of France where at Les Landes, just before reaching the Iberian Peninsula, multitudes are taken—and it is quite legal to do so—usually caught in nets, strung up between high poles and made of such fine wire that birds cannot see them. Those that escape fly on to Gibraltar where more trappers are waiting. Those birds that are lucky fly on to North Africa, wintering in comparative safety, but in spring they once more have to evade capture at these checkpoints before they once again reach the safety of our gardens. Those from central Europe pass over Italy and Malta, and in Italy nothing that flies is let go, more gun permits being granted per head of the population there than anywhere else on earth. In view of this, the Italian Bird Protection League can do little.

A third migratory route is through Poland, the U.S.S.R. and Bulgaria, across the Bosphorus and down the west coast of Turkey, where the birds are comparatively safe until they reach Cyprus. Here a big trade is done in picking small birds for the gourmet markets of the Mediterranean ports. In Cyprus the birds are trapped by covering branches with a lime and glue mixture which causes the feet of the birds to stick to the perches.

Now that Britain is a member of the European Community, all bird-lovers can make themselves heard by writing to the French and Italian Embassies, also to their M.P.s, asking them to raise the matter at all levels, both in Britain and at the E.E.C. headquarters in Brussels, and elsewhere in Europe, until the migrating birds are assured of a safe passage over these countries. If every visitor to France and Italy were to voice his disapproval to officials everywhere, something would be done. There must be some who care.

We can also do more to encourage those birds which are both resident and migratory to remain with us during winter by planting hedges (the use of *Cupressocyparis* × *leylandii* for town gardens is a step in the right direction), evergreen shrubs and wall-plants and by giving every assistance to those birds returning each year so that they can find a suitable place to build as soon as they arrive, and then bring up their families in safety.

Notes on some of the birds seen in our gardens

Barn owl

A resident, it is present throughout Europe and Asia. It is also known as the white owl for when in an upright position, its white breast feathers are most noticeable in the twilight, though its back and wing feathers are mid-brown and less conspicuous. It inhabits old buildings, churches and barns being its main haunts, where mice, its favourite food, abound. It will also eat rats, even swallowing them whole, later disgorging the skin. Barn owls will sit for hours in an old tree, hissing if disturbed and often letting out a loud shriek, but they do not 'hoot'. They roost in the daytime, in an upright position, surveying the world through slit eyes, their feet with sharp talons with which they catch their prey, wrapped around a suitable branch. Barn owls are large, 12–14 in. (30–35 cm.) in height and quite broad, with a wingspan of about 12 in. (30 cm.). They are attracted to those gardens where there are ivy-clad trees and old outhouses and as they are as good as cats at keeping a place free from vermin, their presence is much to be desired. Late in April, five or six round white eggs are laid directly on to the rafters of an old building, probably in a church tower or barn, and a second brood usually follows. The chicks, upon hatching, are covered in snow-white down.

Blackbird

It is both a resident and a visitor, for some winter in southern France, returning north in March when they begin their song, loud and clear but tailing off, unlike that of the song thrush. The male is an incessant fighter over its territorial rights and both hen and cock will attack a cat or dog if it is thought to be too near the nest.

Whilst the female is of a dull brownish-black, the male is

sleek and glossy and jet-black all over, with orange bill and
eye-rims which are in contrast to the rest of its colour. An
adult male measures about 10 in. (25 cm.) long. Though the
blackbird is a visitor to most gardens, it will build only where
its nest is concealed from man. The female blackbird builds in
a bush or hedgerow early in March when five or six pale green
eggs, blotched with brown, are laid.

Blackcap

A member of the warbler family, all of which have one thing
in common, a glorious song, clear and melodious, likened by
countrymen to that of the nightingale. It is both resident and
an early summer visitor, some leaving late to winter in France
and North Africa, some wintering in southern England, or
even in the north if the winter is not too cold. The jet-black
head of the male and the blue shading in its throat makes it a
familiar garden bird. It feeds on insects or berries during
autumn and winter, favouring especially the berries of the
cotoneasters. Its nest resembles that of the garden-warbler and
is built in ivy or evergreens, usually 3–4 ft. (91 cm.–1·2 m.)
above ground. Late in May four or five pale olive-coloured
eggs are laid, mottled with brown.

Blue titmouse

A resident and the most common of the tit family, it is a
regular visitor to the garden nest-box and bird-table. It is a
sociable bird and delights us with its acrobatics as it takes food
from a coconut cut into halves, or removes peanuts from a
container suspended from a wall. It will spend hours pulling
scraps of meat from a bone and as it feeds it continually utters
a crisp 'tee-tee' as if to call its friends to share in the feast. All
the year it sings its cheerful song from hedgerow or bush, often
close to the house where it will make its nest in a hole in an old
wall or in ivy. It will also use a hole in an old tree, but it is never

happier than when using a nest-box which seems to give it the protection necessary to bring up a large family.

The blue tit measures 4½ in. (11·4 cm.) long, of which its tail is 1¼ in. (3 cm.). It often hangs upside down to take its food, and the bright lemon-yellow of its breast is then most noticeable, whilst its pale blue head and back feathers and the white patch below the eyes give it a quaint appearance. Between ten and twelve eggs are laid in May but more have been recorded, and they are dull white, shaded with grey and with quite large markings of darker grey and brown, mostly at the broader end. The nest is made of moss, hair and lichen, lined with feathers and wool. One egg is laid each day and it will take a fortnight to lay the clutch; yet all will hatch within twenty-four hours of each other and the young leave the nest within four hours after the last has been hatched. To feed the hen and the chicks, the cock will make at least 500 sorties a day to bring grubs and caterpillars and thus, like the robin, the blue tit is a great benefactor of the gardener.

Brambling

The hardiest of the finches, it breeds in the pinewoods of northern Europe and reaches Britain in November where it stays until late spring. Here, it feeds mainly on beechnuts, so spends much of its time in beechwoods. The birds were frequently seen beneath the six mature beeches which stood sentinel on the northern side of my previous garden. They also feed on grubs and other insects of orchard trees and should be encouraged where fruit trees are grown. They appear in flocks, often with chaffinches, but may be distinguished by the jet-black heads of the males and the white flash on their back, though the chest feathers are of the same ruddy colouring. The female is without the striking black head. Its call is a crisp 'cheep-cheep' and often in the depths of winter its clear song can be heard from a distance.

Brown owl

Rather larger than the barn owl, the brown or tawny owl is almost as common, though it confines its habitat to woodlands and old trees, its presence unmistakable from its clear and regular hooting. At night, in search of food, it will visit built-up areas where there are tall trees to fly to, and it helps to keep the district free from vermin. It may also take roosting birds if other food is scarce. It builds a flat nest of a few twigs in the hollow of a tree where, in April or May, three or four round white eggs are laid. At first the chicks are covered with white down but soon become barred with buff. Fully grown birds are of a warm reddish-brown colour with buff breast feathers. They continue to feed their young for long after they have left the nest, defending them with ferocity and attacking humans and animals whom they consider a danger.

Bullfinch

It is one of the few birds of ill-repute, for its main diet is fruit buds, both soft and hard fruits falling prey to its destructive habits. Yet it will also consume the larvae of winter moths on fruit trees, and in this way balances the good with the bad. A resident, the bird is a little over 6 in. (15 cm.) long with a black head and tail, steely-blue back and huge bill, though this is possibly not so powerful as that of the hawfinch. The male is conspicuous with its chestnut-red throat and breast, whilst its presence may be detected by its clear 'chip-chip' call.

Its nest, built high off the ground in a tree or hedge, is made of twigs and here four to six pale blue eggs, speckled and marked with red at the broader end, are laid in April.

Chaffinch

This bird, which measures 6½ in. (16·5 cm.) long, is resident but in a severe winter will move to the milder western side of

Britain, returning north in spring. With its circle of pale blue around its head of pinky-red, its long tail and the white flash on its wing feathers, the male's presence in the garden is unmistakable; the female is light brown and inconspicuous. In North Yorkshire gardens it is more common than the sparrow, its staccato 'pink-pink' call being a familiar sound, whilst in spring it sings at the top of its voice for hours on end, finishing its notes with an abruptness unknown with most birds' songs. It is the gardener's friend, feeding on aphis and other harmful insects and is skilful in catching flies on the wing.

It builds in an orchard tree or in a hedge or dense evergreen. The nest, which is almost entirely made by the hen, is of moss, lined with wool and thistle-down. Five or six eggs are laid in April and are white but so heavily marked with red as to give the egg a reddish appearance. A second clutch is usually laid.

Chiff-chaff

A small migrant which measures about 4 in. (10 cm.). It does not go further south to winter than North Africa and Southern Europe and so does not need to leave us until mid-October, and continues with its song until then. Its food is similar to that of the willow-warbler (a bird it closely resembles and from which it is distinguished by its very dark-coloured legs) and it prefers to make its nest just above ground, either low down in a bush such as a hawthorn (which is early into leaf) or privet, or in an evergreen such as *Chamaecyparis* 'Fletcheri', the best of all the cupressus for nesting birds, which makes a broad conical tree, clothed almost to the ground in dense grey-green feathery foliage.

The chiff-chaff's domed nest resembles that of the willow-warbler but it lines it with feathers for extra comfort and enters by a small hole in the side. Six is the usual number of eggs, laid in April, and they are white with blotches of purple or red. The cock does not assist with the building of the nest but pays scrupulous attention to feeding the hen with a diet of flies and grubs. As it does so it utters its little throbbing cry of 'chiff-chaff-chiffchaff', from which it derives its name.

Coal-titmouse

The smallest of the titmouse family, measuring only 4¼ in. (11 cm.) long, it is so named from the coal-black head and throat. It is the least conspicuous of the tits, with olive-green back and tail feathers and paler green breast feathers. It has a white patch beneath both eyes and on the back of its head, which distinguishes it from the marsh-titmouse which is also slightly larger.

Whilst the coal-tit is an insect-eater, it also feeds on seeds of conifers, picking them from the cones, and it will visit gardens where there are mature larch and Scots pine trees and will be found near conifer plantations.

It builds in a nest-box or in a hole in an old tree trunk, usually low down, and may even build in a hole in a bank or in long grass, the nest being made of grass and leaves and lined with feathers and hair. There it will lay, in May, nine or ten dull white eggs spotted with red. As with all tits, a second clutch is rarely laid. Its call is a loud 'if-ee' which it maintains throughout the year.

Corn-bunting

Like the linnet, a bird of the open spaces which does not take kindly to the confines of a suburban garden though it is often seen in gardens near open country. A British resident, it will sing loud and clear throughout the year, its metallic song being likened to the jingling of a bunch of keys. It is 7 in. (17·7 cm.) long and the largest of the buntings, with a long tail. The male is a stout-looking bird with back and tail feathers of pale brown, streaked with darker brown, whilst the buff colouring of the throat extends around the back of the head. The throat and breast feathers have intermittent lines of dark brown. A characteristic of the bird is its short powerful bill.

1. Blue tit

2. Great tit

3. Marsh tit

4. Redstart

5. Robin

6. Young swallows in their nest

7. Painted Lady butterfly after alighting on thistle

8. Brimstone butterflies on red clover

9. Peacock butterfly

10. Humming-bird hawk-moth

11. Privet hawk-moth feeding on privet leaves

12. Golden-ringed dragonfly resting on leaves of yellow iris

13. Hedgehog

14. Sow badger

15. Common lizard

16. Natterjack toad

It builds on the ground, in long grass and weeds, and will do so in the garden spinney where grass is left uncut. The quite large nest is made of grass and straw and lined with hair. Five or six eggs are laid at the end of May, this bird being one of the last of the residents to lay. The pinkish-white eggs have large brown markings.

Dunnock

Also known as the hedge-sparrow and accentor, it is a resident and a familiar bird of hedgerows, its short, high-pitched song being constantly repeated. It resembles the house-sparrow but is without the black chest feathers, the throat and chest being of a soft shade of oyster-grey. It is also recognized by its jerky hop, putting one foot in front of the other as it searches amongst old leaves and rubbish for spiders and weevils. It also catches much of its food on the wing, so is a good friend of the gardener.

It makes its nest of twigs and grass in a hedge or dense evergreen, and lines it with hair and wool. Before the end of March it lays its four or five clear blue eggs. At least three broods are reared in the year.

Fieldfare

A winter visitor, nesting in Scandinavia, arriving early in October, and leaving at the end of March. It obtains its food from the soil, earthworms and grubs being its main diet, but in a severe winter it will eat the berries of rowan, berberis and hawthorn. It is a large bird, 10 in. (25 cm.) long, like a large mistle thrush, with a grey head, chestnut-brown back and black tail, the buff-coloured throat and breast feathers ticked with dark brown. In winter its bill is yellow. Its call is a sharp metallic 'sack-sack', quite distinct from the 'chit-chat' call of the mistle thrush and the 'chuck-chuck' of the song thrush.

It frequents mostly northern country gardens and will come whenever there is upturned soil. Like most of the winter visitors, the birds congregate in flocks at nightfall and perch on the branches of tall trees.

Firecrest

A winter visitor nesting in Northern Europe. During winter it is found in south-east England and is rarely seen as far north as Yorkshire. It is distinguished from the goldcrest by its green back and tail feathers, its buff-coloured throat and breast and by the prominent white streak over the eyes. Of the same size as the goldcrest, its diet is similar.

Garden-warbler

A summer resident throughout Britain, especially in East Anglia where its song is thought to compare favourably with that of the nightingale. Its back feathers in summer are more olive-brown than those of the sedge-warbler whilst the throat and breast are yellowish-green. Both sexes look similar in summertime. The largest of the warblers, being more than $5\frac{1}{2}$ in. (14 cm.) long, it is a bird of deciduous woodlands but will often venture into country gardens, selecting a dense evergreen shrub or wall-plant in which to build its nest which it constructs chiefly of grass and animal hairs. One of our later visitors, it will rarely make its nest before the end of May when four or five eggs, white, mottled with brown, are laid. Its food consists of insects on the wing and aphides from fruit trees, so where there is an orchard its presence is welcomed.

Goldcrest

Both a resident and a winter visitor, large numbers reaching the east coast from Northern Europe during October when their presence will be noticed by their high-pitched song which is kept up all winter and spring. It is a tiny bird, only $3\frac{1}{2}$ in. (8·8 cm.) long, and of a lovely shade of warm olive-brown with a crest of red and gold bordered with black and white markings on its wings. The tiny nest is made in a fir tree or in a hedge, the moss and lichens being wound round a twig or two to give support. It is lined with feathers and in April eight or nine tiny eggs are laid; they are white with red spots, as if made with a needle point, at the broader end. It feeds on tiny but destructive insects such as aphis and the larvae of fruit trees and usually hunts in flocks. Its presence in the garden is valuable.

Goldfinch

Like the greenfinch it is both resident and migratory and is one of the most attractive of birds, endearing itself to us by its captivating ways. At one time large numbers were sold as cage-birds, though in captivity, to which it takes kindly, it loses much of the charm it displays when feeding on the wing. In any case it is now fully protected. With its red face and contrasting bands of white and black around it, and its gold and black wing feathers which it uses to attract the female, its presence is unmistakable; it usually appears in spring in large flocks. The birds congregate in October in the north and fly to southern England, some to southern France and Italy, to winter. Its clear melodious song is most beautiful and, like the greenfinch, it twitters constantly as it flits about knapweeds and thistles and ripe teasel heads, the seeds of which are its favourite food. It also takes larvae of beetles and aphis from fruit trees and in orchard and garden it is a valuable friend. It will build in the forked branch of an apple tree or in a gorse bush or thick evergreen, lining its small round nest with thistledown. In late April or early May five or six eggs are laid; they are small and creamy-white with reddish-brown marks.

Great spotted woodpecker

Also known as the pied woodpecker, it is a resident of woodlands and parks, to be found wherever there is an old or diseased tree, being a frequent visitor to orchards and gardens, and its numbers are on the increase. Its 'call' is the well-known 'tapping' of the wood with its powerful beak, which is done

many times per second and repeatedly over several minutes. Its
food consists of wood-boring insects which it extracts from the
holes with its sticky tongue. It alights on the trunk and works
upwards in short hopping movements, assisted by its tail, and
removing small pieces of bark as it does so. It will also remove
aphides, so its presence in the garden is appreciated. Woodpeckers have two toes or claws at the back of the front ones, to
enable them to obtain a tighter grip on the bark. The male is a
handsome bird, about 9 in. (23 cm.) long with a black forehead
and a contrasting large white patch around the eyes. It has a
small red mark at the back of the head and patches of black and
white on its back, whilst the black wing feathers are barred
with white.

It makes its nest never less than 10 ft. (3 m.) above ground,
in an old tree, removing the dead wood and entering from a
small hole which it has bored into the tree. The nest is made
in a deep cavern, often 18–20 in. (46–51 cm.) below the entrance
and there, in the wood dust, six or seven ivory-white eggs are
laid late in May, this being one of the last birds to lay each year.

Great titmouse

Its plumage is the most beautiful of the tit family, the male
being 4½ in. (11 cm.) long and stouter than the other tits, with
the rich yellow of its breast continuing round the back of its
head. The head is black with a contrasting white patch below
the eyes, whilst the back, wing and tail feathers are of azure-
blue, shaded with yellow and with black and yellow markings
on the wings. Both sexes are of similar colouring, but the hen
is slightly smaller.

They will build in a hole in a wall or in a tree, lining it with
grass and leaves and any other soft material they can find. They
also take kindly to a nest-box. After the six or seven white,
red-spotted eggs are laid early in May, the hen will hiss loudly
if anyone approaches the nest. The young are several weeks old
before leaving the nest and the adults continue to feed them

for several weeks afterwards, mostly on caterpillars of the destructive winter moth, so the bird, contrary to general belief, does much good in the garden and orchard though it may take fruit buds to augment its diet in winter. It is also known to kill other birds if food is scarce, though I have yet to find evidence of this, but it will take bees whilst they are removing nectar from flowers and for this reason it is no friend of the beekeeper.

Greenfinch

Although resident in many parts of Britain, it also migrates during the early winter months when it is absent from northern gardens. At all times sociable, it is one of the most handsome and appealing of our birds, bringing joy to the countryside and garden with its constant twittering as it flies about the hedgerows, and is much missed when it departs. In summer the male has bright green plumage with a brilliant golden mark on the edges of wings and tail, which is noticeable when it is in flight. It is 6 in. (15 cm.) long. The female is duller, the yellow being less brilliant.

The nest is made of twigs and bracken, lined with moss and hairs, and may be built in a hedge or in ornamental conifers. This bird is fond of the dark seclusion of *Juniperus virginiana* where it may raise as many as three broods in a year. Five or six cream-coloured eggs, speckled with red or purple at the broader end, are laid. Its diet consists of weed seeds.

Green woodpecker

Though a native of most of the old world including Britain, Central Europe, Asia Minor and West Asia, here it is confined to the southern parts of England. In my Somerset orchard it was a regular inhabitant, its dark green back and scarlet head giving it a tropical appearance. It is a bird of some size, the males being more than 12 in. (30 cm.) long. It makes its way up a tree spirally as it searches for larvae which it takes with its very long tongue. Its call is a harsh laughing sound and it only

rarely uses the familiar 'tapping'. Besides larvae, ants form a
large part of its diet and it will come down from the tree and
travel long distances on the ground in search of its favourite
food.

Six or seven pure white eggs are laid at the end of April,
but though they are laid a month earlier than the spotted
woodpecker, there is only one clutch.

Hawfinch

Like the sparrow, it is found where there is human habitation
and though a shy bird, this resident makes its nest in suburban
gardens and in cherry orchards for, with its large blue bill, it
can easily open the stones to remove the kernel. It also feeds
on the berries of holly, yew and hawthorn and will discard the
pulpy outer covering to find the seeds, and will take peas from
the pods. But it also eats caterpillars and beetles and so balances
its harmful activities in orchards by doing at least some good
in the garden, though peas when reaching maturity should be
covered with muslin.

The male is 7 in. (17·7 cm.) long with a short tail and a grey-
blue bill of tremendous strength. In winter its back is reddish-
brown with the wings and tail feathers black and contrasting
with a white patch on the shoulders; the female has less red
colouring in her back feathers. It will build in the branches of
orchard trees or in a wall-plant well above ground, the nest consisting of twigs and roots lined with hairs, where, in April, four
or five eggs are laid, blotched and marked with grey and brown
on a cream-coloured ground. Its eggs are amongst the largest
of the smaller British birds.

House-martin

The small tail feathers and the white rump distinguish it from
the swift and swallow when in flight, and it is also without the
rust-red throat of the swallow. Wintering in Central Africa,
the house-martins come later than the swallows but before the

swifts; they nest in colonies, on cliffs or in caves, building their shallow cup-like nests with damp mud and hair and, like the swallows, twittering as they do so. They will nest beneath the eaves of a house or farm building, often a dozen or more pairs close together, which also distinguishes them from the swallows. They are one of the last to lay early in June; four or five white eggs make up the clutch and a second will usually follow.

Because of its lateness in raising a family the house-martin is one of the last of the migrants to leave, the birds gathering in large flocks in mid-October when they will group themselves in a tall spreading tree before taking off. It is a smaller bird than the swallow or swift, measuring rather more than 5 in. (13 cm.) long, but its habits are similar. It will return to its old nesting site year after year. Its food consists of insects caught on the wing.

House-sparrow

It is present in built-up areas, for it has made its home with man, building in holes in walls, beneath the eaves of a house, or in an ivy-clad wall. The male is distinguished from the tree-sparrow (which is not destructive to flowers) by its grey-black head, the throat and upper breast feathers being of similar colouring. It is not nearly so colourful as the tree-sparrow, nor so likeable. Its perpetual 'chirping' is well known and this continues all the year, yet it is not a bird that one encourages into the garden, for although it takes insects, it can, and invariably does, do a great amount of damage to spring flowers in its search for nectar. Yellow crocuses and primroses are the worst to suffer but it will remove the petals from flowers of all colours and is capable of doing much damage in a very short time. Black thread wound around small sticks and suspended above the blooms will prove a deterrent and small pieces of tin held on sticks above the plants will, as they jingle in the breeze, deter the birds from their attacks. The deterrents should be in place as soon as the flower buds are seen, for in a dry spring when moisture is scarce, the sparrows will begin to attack them as soon as they start showing colour.

The nest is of twigs and straw, lined with moss and feathers, and in March five or six pale blue eggs spotted with black or dark brown are laid. At least three and even four clutches are laid in a season, until the end of September.

Jackdaw

It belongs to the rook family of which it is the most endearing member. Unlike the rook, it will pair and build away from the flock, usually in a hole in a wall, the nest being composed of sticks, lined with hair which it collects from cattle and horses, or with wool pulled from sheep whilst it looks for 'ticks', its favourite food. It also feeds on wireworms and larvae in the soil and is the gardener's friend. But where jackdaws are present care must be taken to hide rings and other small brilliantly coloured objects which attract their attention, for they will steal them from a dressing-table near an open window.

The male is about 14 in. (35·5 cm.) long and has a blue-black head and is charcoal-grey elsewhere. The bill and legs are also dark grey, so it has a most sombre appearance.

Four or five eggs are laid early in May: of the palest blue, splashed with grey, brown and slate-blue, they are amongst the most beautiful of all birds' eggs.

Jay

It is a beautiful but timid bird, rarely straying far from woodlands, though it will frequent nearby gardens if there are large leafy trees for it to hide in. A member of the crow family, it is a thickset bird about 14 in. (35·5 cm.) long, the back of its head and breast being of richest buff, its wing feathers and tail black touched with white, with a black 'moustache' mark between beak and eyes. It has a white crest streaked with black and a striking patch of pale blue, barred with brown, beneath the wings. These blue feathers were at one time prized by men to wear in their hatbands.

Though its chief food is acorns and beechnuts in winter, it is also an egg thief, taking those of small birds, and even of pheasants, and is despised by the gamekeeper. It also takes peas and redcurrants from gardens and is not a bird to be encouraged where fruit and vegetables grow. On the credit side, it will devour click-beetles (the larvae of wireworms) by the hundred.

It makes its nest of grass and moss in an evergreen or in a hedge, where six or seven eggs are laid early in May. They are buff coloured, speckled and lined with grey and brown at the broader end.

Kingfisher

One of our most colourful and interesting birds. In my father's garden in the suburbs of Sheffield, kingfishers built in a low bank of soil by the side of a large natural pond, and they may come into any garden where there is water, but are rarely seen further north than this. It has blue-green back plumage and tail feathers, a white flash on each side of the head and red in the neck and belly. With its long pointed beak it takes small fish from pond and stream with amazing precision. The nest is made in a burrow some 3 ft. (91 cm.) into the bank and in June six or seven white eggs are laid, the young being fed on small fish, water-beetles and dragonflies.

One may watch the male darting down over the water from an overhanging branch, snatching a minnow and returning to its perch where, holding the minnow's tail in its beak, it will bang the fish's head against the branch until it is dead and then swallow it, always head first.

Lesser redpoll

A common resident in the north, it has many of the lark's characteristics, singing from on high and swooping down and around in erratic flight. Whilst feeding on grass and weed seeds, which they do in flocks, the birds twitter endlessly and all the time dart here and there to peck out the seeds from a dandelion or thistle head. They also feed on aphis and other injurious insects of orchard and garden and are welcome visitors.

The male is about 4 in. (10 cm.) long with a handsome dark brown back and pink throat and breast feathers, resembling the linnet but distinguished from it by a red mark on the forehead.

It will often make its nest in a small tree or bush, usually 5–6 ft. (1·5–1·8 m.) above ground, the deep untidy nest being built of sticks and lined with coarse hair and feathers. There, late in May, four or five eggs are laid. They are of deep bluish-green, speckled with reddish-brown.

Lesser spotted woodpecker

Distinguished from the great spotted in that it is only about half its size, measuring some 5 in. (13 cm.) long. It has a beautifully barred back, hence its other name of barred wood-pecker, whilst the black forehead of the larger bird is replaced by one of brilliant red in the smaller.

It is a retiring bird, spending most of its time in tall wood-land trees and is thus less well known than the great spotted, but is often present in orchards. Its habits are similar, feeding as it does on the larvae of wood-boring insects and of moths and making the same rattling noise. It enters its nest through a hole of little more than 1 in. (2·5 cm.) diameter. Here, 12–15 in. (30–38 cm.) below, six to eight pure white eggs are laid late in May and both birds take turns at sitting. The Forestry Commission use woodpecker holes as indicating the diseased condition of a tree.

Linnet

Like many of the finches, the linnet is both resident and migratory, those from Northern Europe reaching Britain in late autumn, whilst those already here move further south, to southern England and France. It relies for its food on weed seeds and indiscriminate use of weedkillers has greatly reduced its numbers; in parts of Britain the bird is now rare though in my North Yorkshire coastal garden, surrounded by much uncultivated land, it was a regular visitor, building in gorse bushes and hedges but spending much of its time in the open countryside. The nest is small and made of twigs and grass, lined with feathers and thistledown. The male is 6 in. (15 cm.) long with chestnut-coloured back feathers, its throat and breast being crimson, whilst it also has a crimson mark on the forehead. In April, four or five eggs are laid. They are palest blue with slight grey or brown markings at the broader end.

Long-tailed titmouse

It is 5½ in. (14 cm.) long and half this is the tail, it being one of the longest of all the smaller resident birds. It is an even greater acrobat than the blue tit for its long tail enables it to balance. A bird of the hedgerows, it will rarely use a nest-box, whilst in winter it feeds mostly in flocks, taking insects and larvae from upturned soil and from orchard trees. I have seen birds congregate in hundreds on rose bushes, removing every insect they could find.

Its presence is noted by the delicate 'see-see' of its call as it flits about the hedgerows. The female has a nearly snow-white head and throat, and is almost owl-like, with her tiny black eyes, whilst the back and tail feathers are black with slight russet shading beneath the wings. This is also present on the male which has a black streak over the eyes and more of the russet in the throat. The long tail is black above and of contrasting black and white on the underside.

Its deep oval nest is intricately made, both male and female taking 2–3 weeks to construct it in a hedge or dense bush. There the birds will continue uninterrupted for hours, weaving together tiny pieces of moss, wool, hair and even cobwebs, until the thick walls and dome are made to their satisfaction. Not until then does the building stop. The tiny entrance hole is near the top. In mid-April ten to twelve minute eggs are laid; they are white, with tiny marks of red. Though only the hen incubates the eggs by day, she is always joined at night by the cock, and perhaps the reason for the high dome is to enable the birds to hold their long tails above their heads as they sit huddled together for warmth, for the long-tailed tits are the least hardy of our resident birds. Many will be killed by the cold of a hard winter unless they can find adequate shelter.

Magpie

A resident, it is a member of the crow family and is increasing as a garden bird. Though one of the most beautiful of our birds, it is one of the least endearing, for it has many unpleasant habits. About 18 in. (46 cm.) long, it is familiar to all with its black and white plumage. It is present in gardens and parks and about the open countryside and, like the jackdaw, it has a liking for bright objects. It will eat anything, including insects, grain, small birds and their eggs. Often it is to be seen raiding another bird's nest and coming under attack from those it has plundered.

Like the rest of the family, it will build in a fairly tall tree, the nest being made of large twigs banded together with moist clay. It will also build in a thick hedge.

Between six and eight eggs are laid in early April; they are greenish-blue, speckled with red or brown. Only one brood is reared, the young resembling their parents when fledged but without their handsome gloss.

Marsh titmouse

A resident bird which, as its name implies, will spend much of its time in marshland, but it is a frequent visitor to the garden where there are hedgerows or evergreens. The absence of the white mark at the back of the head distinguishes it from the coal-tit, the sexes being similar. The call is a sharp 'zip-zip'. Its main diet is insects and larvae but it will take thistle seeds and is a friend of the gardener.

Like the coal-tit, it builds low down in an evergreen or even in a hole in the ground, a grassy bank suiting it, or in a hole in an old tree. It will first line the hole with pieces of decayed wood, then add an inner lining of moss and wool where, early in May, it lays eight or nine white eggs speckled with red at the broader end. The hen does the incubating and will hiss and even peck at those who place a hand in the nest to see if it is in use.

Mistle thrush

A bird of Northern Europe, it is resident in Britain, though some will migrate to southern France when the winter is severe, returning in March. Yet it is a hardy bird and will continue its beautiful song through the severest winter. Only in July and August, when moulting, does it not sing. Though not quite so melodious as the song thrush, it still remains one of the most tuneful of our song birds.

It takes its name from its liking for mistletoe berries and is common in parts where mistletoe abounds, as in Hereford and Shropshire, but it will also feed on the berries of yew and holly, hawthorn and juniper. In summer snails and insects are its chief food, and it may be seen breaking the shells of snails on a large stone.

A larger bird than the song thrush, measuring 12 in. (30 cm.) long and of stouter build, the back, wings and tail feathers are chocolate-brown, whilst the buff-coloured face and breast are spotted all over with darker brown. Both male and female are similar but the male is rather more brightly coloured.

The nest is often made in open country between large boulders or in the fork of an orchard tree, in full view of all who pass by, and after she has laid the female will attack dogs, and even man, when she thinks he is too near her nest. I once had a bird build in a low-branched apple tree close to my garage and each time I passed to take out the car, she would fly into my face, flapping her wings and letting out a fearful screech. She gave a sheepdog I owned the same treatment, until the poor animal became too afraid to go near the nest. He would whine with fear at the sight of her, his tail between his legs.

The open nest is made of coarse grass and bracken and is then lined with mud before the inner lining of moss and feathers is added. The nest is of tremendous strength, capable of withstanding the gale-force winds to which it is invariably exposed. In my east-coast garden during a hurricane I have known the female sit motionless on her eggs when all around her was devastation. She did not budge an inch during twenty-four hours of the most appalling conditions, her courage being remarkable.

Towards the end of March three or four eggs are laid; they are greenish-white speckled with purple and grey. A second clutch is laid.

Nuthatch

A resident which is rarely found north of the Yorkshire Dales. It is one of the most handsome birds, about 5 in. (13 cm.) long and resembling a kingfisher in its appearance, its beak being straight but long and pointed. The head and back are steely-grey, in marked contrast to the pinkish throat and breast feathers. The tail is short and strong but is not used to assist in climbing; this is achieved by placing one foot higher up the tree than the other, the bird clinging with its sharp claws. It climbs up the tree in this way and then climbs down in a similar fashion, always head first, whereas the tree-creeper climbs a tree and then flies down to the base of another.

Its song consists of a single trilling whistle. Though mainly insect-eating, the birds are able to open acorns and other nuts with their powerful beaks, which they do on a stone, hence their name, derived from 'nut-hack'. They are territorial and will stoutly defend their territory against all comers.

They mostly build in the hollows of dead trees or in crevices large enough to accommodate their small nests. They love an old woodpecker's nest and will also build in a concealed nest-box or in a wall crevice, when they will almost block up the entrance hole with clay until it is less than 1 in. (2·5 cm.) diameter, so few other birds can enter.

Between six and eight eggs are laid early in May; they are white, lightly spotted with red. The young are ready to leave the nest after twenty-four days, when they will begin to climb at once and be quite independent of their parents in searching for food.

Pheasant

Those whose garden is near the open country will often be visited by this handsome bird and where there is long grass in a spinney or orchard, it will make its nest. In my east-coast garden adjoining open country and moorlands at least one pair made their nest in long grass each year.

The largest and most handsome of game birds, this Asiatic species (*Phasianus colchicus*) has for long been naturalized in Britain. A terrestrial bird which feeds and nests on the ground, though roosting in trees, its curved wings are suitable for a quick take-off, but the birds are unable to sustain their flight for more than a short time. Their diet consists of worms and grubs, augmented by berries.

Though the female is dull brown with black markings on the wing and tail feathers, the cock is most decorative, being of shades of brown, metallic blue and green, with red markings and a white collar around the neck. They are large birds, the tails measuring 10 in. (25 cm.) or more in length. They have a harsh grating call and when frightened rise from the ground with a loud 'squawk'.

The large round nest is made of grass and straw and lined with feathers and in May as many as ten to twelve eggs are laid; they are olive-green, faintly spotted with red. The female incubates on her own and the chicks are hatched covered in down and with their wing feathers developed. They are soon able to leave the nest with their mother and will roost with her at night. Though of great value as game birds, the pheasant is so magnificent in appearance and so majestic in its movements that it is difficult to eat its delicious meat after having had these birds nesting in the garden. A few plants of the evergreen *Berberis darwinii* about the spinney will encourage them to nest.

Pied flycatcher

A rare summer visitor, this attractive bird is found mostly in the dales of North Yorkshire and in the Lake District, for it never builds far from water. It may be encouraged to nest in gardens and a small pond will attract it to do so. It is a small bird 4½ in. (11 cm.) long, the male having a jet-black head and back which contrasts with the snow-white throat and breast feathers. Its long tail is also black and there is a large white patch on the wings. It is smaller than the spotted flycatcher and depends for its diet on caterpillars and larvae, rather than on winged insects. These it takes from orchard and other trees so it is greatly to be encouraged to come into the garden. It resembles the pied wagtail in that its tail for ever moves up and down, and it has a similar sharp metallic call. It will build in a hole in a tree and in a nest-box suitably concealed in a wall-plant. Grass, moss and hair are the materials used and early in June it lays six to eight sky-blue eggs, it being one of the last birds to lay. It is also one of the first to leave, shortly after the swifts, and has gone by the first days of September. Like the swallow, it will return again and again to its nest, the male always coming first to set up home and guard his territory whilst awaiting the arrival of his partner.

Pied wagtail

It is also called the water-wagtail and is both native and

migratory, returning in February. It is 7½ in. (19 cm.) long and delights in paddling about the edge of a pond, often leaping into the air to take a midge or some other fly which makes up its main diet. Its long graceful tail, which is held horizontally, is continually 'wagging' up and down and if a partially sub-merged stone be placed in the pond with the surface just un-covered by the water, the wagtail will alight on it and from there seek out its prey, in the same way as will the spotted fly-catcher from the top of a pole.

Though usually building near water, in a hole in a wall or in a dense bush, it will venture far in search of flies and will follow the plough for hours, or seek out larvae from a farm-yard manure heap during winter and early spring when flies are less numerous.

The male is a handsome bird with a black back and throat feathers and an almost white head and breast. Its tail is black on the upper part, white on the underside. The black wing feathers are also marked with white.

Between four and six eggs, white, speckled with grey, are laid in April, followed by a second clutch.

Red-backed shrike

Known as the Butcher Bird, for it slays anything it can catch, it is one of the most interesting and rare garden birds, reaching Britain early in May and rarely nesting north of a line drawn from Southport to Hull, though it appears to be on the de-crease everywhere. The handsome male with his reddish back and grey-blue head is usually 7 in. (17.7 cm.) long and is possessed with tremendous strength, making quick work of killing anything that takes his fancy. He has a particularly pleasant song during courtship. The rather untidy nest, made of grass and moss, is lined with wool and hairs and is made in a thick hedge away from the passing crowd. Not until early June are the eggs laid; four or five make up the clutch and they are pinkish-white with grey blotches at the broader end, surrounded with a circle of reddish marks. The male is most attentive in feeding his family and will swoop down from a tall post to pick up with his hooked bill almost anything which moves, even including mice and small lizards, and then remove his prey to a hawthorn hedge where he impales it on the sharp thorns. Wasps and beetles are also included in the diet.

Redbreast

We know it as the robin, one of the most delightful of British birds and the tamest. It is the male robin only that has the red breast. He is 5¾ in. (14·6 cm.) long and has a red face, throat and breast, bordered by a wide margin of palest blue which runs from the forehead to the belly. The back and wing and tail feathers are light brown. Wherever man turns over the soil, the robin is there to pick up the grubs, never more than a few feet away, showing the utmost trust in its friend. Its presence is noted before it is seen by the 'click-click' of its call, whilst its clear melodious song, so powerful for such a small bird, is to be heard in summer and winter. It will make its nest in an old kettle or plant pot thrown into the hedge bottom, or even piled up at the back of the potting shed. It will also make use of a nest-box but prefers to build low down, often on the ground at the foot of a tree. The nest is made of old leaves and grass and lined with soft hair and moss and there, towards the end of March, five or six eggs are laid. They are of muddy-white, speckled with red, and two or even three broods are reared.

Redstart

A summer visitor, wintering in North Africa and arriving early in April. By the end of that month it will have become distributed throughout Britain. It is a bird of parks and sub-urban gardens, has the same inquisitive look as the robin and is of similar colouring. The male is 5¾ in. (14·6 cm.) long, with grey back and wing feathers which contrast with the orange-red breast and tail feathers. It is the only bird able to move its tail in every direction, which it does when alighting on nest or perch. Its food consists entirely of winged insects. The call is a staccato 'ee-tic-tic' and its song is heard mostly at dusk.

It will build in a hole in a tree or in an old wall, the nest being of hair and moss and lined with down and feathers. Between six and nine dull pale blue eggs are laid early in May and it is usual for the birds to return to the same nest for many years.

Redwing

Breeding in Northern Europe and Asia, it winters in Britain where it arrives early in October, leaving again in April. It is a bird of the open fields, feeding on worms and grubs as they are turned up by the plough, though in a severe winter it will be found in gardens on the outskirts of towns and villages where it comes for the berries of juniper and yew. Its call of 'zee-yip' denotes its presence. It is found in flocks which move during the hours of darkness and roost on the branches of pine and larch.

It is a large bird, about 8 in. (20 cm.) long, in appearance like a small thrush, its throat and breast of buff being spotted with brown and with slight reddish shading near the wings. The back and tail feathers are olive-brown in winter.

Reed-bunting

It will often appear in a garden where there is water and, unlike the dipper, it is as happy by still water as running water. In the Norfolk Broads it builds in the reeds, but if rushes are planted in quantity by a pond, it will build low down, making its nest of reeds and coarse grasses and lining it with hair and feathers. Between four and six eggs are laid early in April and they are of the colour of reeds, marked with darker brown. Both birds incubate the eggs and a second clutch usually follows. The call is a loud 'eep' and it will sing its metallic song for hours, from early March until September.

The female resembles the corn bunting but the male is more striking, with its jet-black head and throat and white collar circling its head from one side of the beak to the other. The white breast feathers are free from markings. It feeds on pond insects and the larvae of moths and will fly down to catch them and then return to its look-out post which is usually a reed on which it hangs with one foot above the other.

Sedge-warbler

One of the largest of the warblers, about 5 in. (13 cm.) long, it has little of the yellowish colouring of the others, its back being reddish-brown and pale buff in the throat. It is recognized by a pronounced inch-long thin white streak running from its bill to just above the eyes. The sexes are alike. (The reed-warbler, closely related, is rare in gardens for it prefers running water.) If there is a pond in the garden, suitably planted with aquatics and with a degree of privacy, afforded by a dense hedge or shrubbery close by, this member of the warbler family is sure to make its presence known by its sweet, melodious song. It is a great imitator and will follow, note for note, the song of a willow-warbler, so it is often difficult to realize there are two different birds singing. It will perch on a willow branch above a pond for hours, singing at the top of its voice and often well into the night, and will continue its song until it leaves our shores late in August.

It arrives late, not reaching us until early May so is here for only four months. It will build in willows or where there is any coverage near water, but no more than 3 ft. (91 cm.) above ground, its nest being similar to those of the other warblers. Five or six olive-green eggs, speckled with brown and marked with curious scribbles, are laid towards the end of May.

Song thrush

Slimmer and sleeker than the mistle thrush, about 9 in. (23 cm.) long, it is found throughout Northern Europe and Asia and in

Britain it is both migratory and a resident, frequenting wood-lands and hedgerows. A common garden bird, it will build in a wall-plant or evergreen, being more secretive than the mistle thrush and not so vicious. Also known as the throstle, its melodious song rivals that of the nightingale; indeed it is called the northern nightingale, for in the north it reigns supreme and, like the nightingale, it sings at dusk and into the night.

The male is of a rich olive-brown with a buff-coloured throat entirely without spots (unlike the mistle thrush) and well-spotted breast feathers. But on the underpart, the spotting is not so heavy as on the mistle thrush. It has the endearing characteristic of holding its head on one side, as if listening, as it picks up a worm or grub to take to the female; after giving it to her, it will depart with a happy twitter. Worms, snails and grubs make up its diet.

The nest is made of grass and leaves and, like that of the mistle thrush, it is first lined with mud before it is given an inner lining of moss and feathers. The female does the building, usually taking no more than two days to do so, and two days later four eggs are laid. They are of sea-blue colouring, spotted with black, the first clutch being laid early in March, followed by a second.

Spotted flycatcher

One of the last of our summer visitors, rarely arriving before May, coming from as far south as the Cape. Like all migrating birds, it feeds on insects taken on the wing and none is better at doing so, whilst its feeding of its family in the nest is one of the wonders of nature. Both male and female are about 5 in. (13 cm.) long and are greyish-brown, not in any way spotted. It is known as the post bird, for the male takes up its position on top of a post or cane from where it can make its forays, swooping on any insect that passes in sight. It therefore likes an open situation, though it will nest in a wall of a house or barn or in a dense creeper. The nest is of grass lined with hair and feathers. Four or five eggs are laid early in June; they are white, covered all over with tiny red spots from which the bird takes its name. The call is a soft 'zit-zit'. Early in September the birds depart, having raised only one brood.

Starling

One of our commonest residents, yet it has few friends apart from the gardener and farmer; it feeds on wireworms and the larvae of destructive beetles wherever the soil is upturned.

Its constant chattering and the fact that it is so gregarious, large flocks darkening the sky as they rise up to roost at dusk, have contributed to its unpopularity, and it is said to attack pears and plums as they ripen in autumn, though this I have never seen. Its harsh notes and its habit of screaming when frightened, also go against it. Yet in addition to its valuable feeding habits, it has a number of endearing qualities as it struts about the land, its long pointed beak darting here and there to pick up grubs. In its winter plumage of metallic blues and greens, flecked all over with white, it is a handsome bird, almost 9 in. (23 cm.) long. It will nest anywhere, in an old wall, in a barn or nesting-box and there, in April, lays six or seven clear blue eggs, followed by a second clutch.

The birds will take food from a bird-table but they tend to be greedy, taking more than their share and often, by sheer weight of numbers, preventing other birds from feeding.

Stonechat

It is both resident and migrant, many moving south from northern England to winter, and moving back again early in spring. It is to be found about the open moorland, amidst gorse bushes and outcrops, usually near the coast. It has a scraping-like chatter, like small stones being rubbed together, and when on its perch its tail has the same movement as the wagtail. Its song resembles that of the robin, being clear and melodious, whilst it is similar in size, with brown back and tail feathers and a russet-buff breast. A black patch covers face and throat, and around it is a crescent of white (absent in the female) making it conspicuous everywhere.

Its diet consists of insects and their larvae and, like the robin, it will eat small worms. Spiders also figure in its diet. Those whose garden is close to moorland can attract the birds by planting the double-flowering gorse and evergreens for, again like the robin, it likes to build low down. It is rarely seen in a town garden. It makes its nest of moss and grass and lines it with wool and feathers and there, early in April, five or six pale blue eggs, speckled with red, are laid. A second clutch follows.

Swallow

The most familiar of summer visitors for, although it winters in South Africa and India, it is an early arrival, reaching our shores in late April or early May, to the sound of bat and ball heralding another English summer, though in the north it may be the last days of May before it is seen. It leaves in late September when large numbers gather together, soaring and swooping before the whole flock perches on nearby telephone wires as if to organize themselves before taking wing in a southerly direction, feeding as they go on flies and, if the day is calm, often flying at a height of 10,000 ft.

Both male and female are alike. They are $7\frac{1}{2}$ in. (19 cm.) long and are distinguished by their rich steely-blue colouring, the throat and forehead being of rust-red with a steel-blue band beneath, and white breast feathers. The forked tail feathers, longer than those of the martin and swift, have a white mark. The rust throat also distinguishes it from the martin and swift.

It builds its nest of mud, hair and straw beneath the eaves of a house or shed or inside a barn or garage, twittering as it does so, and both birds help. This is done in wet weather so that the moist materials will bind together better and then set hard. Four or five white eggs, speckled with red, are laid late in May and a second clutch will invariably follow. The young have to be taught to fly over several days and at this time cats must be kept away from them, for the young spend much of the time on the ground. They will return to the same nest year after year, patching the nest before the eggs are laid and thus saving time in rebuilding.

Swift

One of our latest summer arrivals, for not until May is well advanced (even into June) do we hear the piercing screech which tells us that the birds have completed their 3,000 mile journey from South Africa, Kenya and the Congo. More than is the case with any other bird, it is built for speed and for flying long distances, for it is about 7 in. (17·7 cm.) long and sleekly built, with a short but powerful neck and long curved wings, though the tail feathers are short compared to those of the swallow. The plumage of both male and female is charcoal-black, as are the beak and legs. Soaring to a great height, it glides for long distances with its outstretched wings but descends only slowly so that it need expend little energy in maintaining its height over thousands of miles.

Two white eggs are always laid early in June and as soon as the young are ready to fly, the parents begin their training by taking them first on short 'sorties', then for longer distances and higher and higher, all the time continuing their piercing shriek like dive-bombers, as they soar and descend like lightning. They also show the same frightening characteristics if one approaches anywhere near their young whilst they are in the nest.

Sadly, they are the first to leave. By early August the young are strong enough to make the long journey and will depart fully a month before the swallows. They are with us for only about ten weeks at the end of which one realizes that another summer is almost over.

Swifts live entirely on insects caught on the wing and as

insects are most active in thundery wet weather, so too is the
swift, and because of this countrymen believe that when swifts
are plentiful, the summer will be poor. This was certainly so in
1974. (See also pp. 20, 77.)

Tree-creeper

This interesting small bird, with its chocolate-brown plumage
and white underfeathers, is a resident and, though nowhere
plentiful, is fairly well distributed throughout Britain. I have
watched them for hours in a Somerset orchard and in our
north-east coastal garden, as they climb a tree in short, jerky
but rapid movements. They are assisted in their climbing,
which is upwards never sideways, by their short but wide, stiff
tail feathers which are pressed against the bark as they cling
with sharp, curved claws. Woodpeckers make use of their tails
in a similar way. Unable to fly very far, tree-creepers have short
wings and in all measure rather less than 5 in. (13 cm.) long.
As they climb they search for insects in the bark, which they
remove from the tiniest cracks with their curved beaks.

The nest is made in old ivy or in other climbing plants and
consists of twigs and bark, lined with moss and feathers. Six or
seven eggs are usually laid, but up to nine have been recorded.
They are white, marked with tiny spots of reddish-brown. The
birds will also build in nest-boxes placed against an ivy-covered
wall.

Tree-pipit

A common summer visitor, it frequents parks and gardens
when it arrives in early May. Both the meadow and tree-
pipits resemble the lark in flight, soaring to a great height before
plummeting earthwards when the tree-pipit will alight on a tall
tree and begin its plaintive song. Its diet is composed of insects
which it takes on the wing.

A handsome bird 6 in. (15 cm.) long, the male is light brown
and speckled in the chest, so it resembles a small thrush. The

female is similar though not so bright. In spite of its name, it builds low down, on the ground in fact, in long grass or amongst bracken or beneath a hedge, the nest consisting of interwoven grasses. Four or five eggs are laid and are so heavily spotted with rust as to give the eggs a brown appearance. The cuckoo will lay its eggs, which have similar markings, in a pipit's nest.

Tree sparrow

It differs from the house-sparrow in that it is shorter and plumper, whilst the black throat markings are more clearly defined, and unlike the house-sparrow's black head, that of the tree-sparrow is coppery-red. A resident, it is shy and retiring. It makes its untidy nest in an old tree, often an apple, where it will build in a hollow between trunk and a branch. The birds usually build in colonies. The domed nest is made of sticks, moss and lichens and lined with hair or wool. Four or five eggs are laid. They are small and white, heavily marked with russet and brown, mostly at the broader end.

Waxwing

Nesting in Northern Europe and Asia, it is a winter visitor to Britain, arriving in October, often in large flocks. It is a delightful bird, trusting man as does the robin, its food consisting of winter berries provided by cotoneaster and pyracantha. The birds are about 7 in. (17·7 cm.) long and have a conspicuous erect crest of pale brown and a black streak from the bill and over the eye. The wings and tail feathers are black with markings of yellow and white and the bird takes its name from the red wax-like ends of the secondary flight feathers.

Whitethroat

Those gardens where there is a thick hedge of hawthorn or bramble are sure to attract this elegant-looking bird with its happy melodious song. The male is 5½ in. (14 cm.) long, slim (which enables it to traverse dense hedgerows) and elegant, with reddish-brown feathers, a white throat, which distinguishes it from the warblers, and a pinkish breast. The female is browner and without any red colouring. It arrives early, though wintering in South Africa, and it is one of the last to leave, remaining until late October. Its summer diet consists mainly of flies but in autumn it lives on elderberries and blackberries, though it may attack redcurrant bushes which should be covered with muslin.

It builds low down, the nest consisting of grasses, lichens and moss lined with hair and early in June, five or six eggs are laid. They are palest green, speckled with grey and red.

Willow-warbler

Also known as the willow-wren, it is one of the most common of our summer visitors, found in all parts of Britain. It arrives in the south before the end of March and by mid-April will have reached the far north, coming in continuous 'waves'. Its melodious warble extends the full length of the scale and ends in a gentle murmur: for strength its song rivals that of the song thrush, whilst the call of the young is equally loud.

The bird is one of the gardener's best friends, for it feeds on aphides and weevils taken from fruit trees, whilst doing the minimum of damage to the fruit buds. Like the flycatcher, it augments its diet by taking small insects on the wing.

It measures about $4\frac{1}{2}$ in. (11 cm.) long, both sexes being alike, the upper parts being a lovely greenish-yellow, the underparts paler with a brown bill and legs. Though of similar colouring, it is distinguished from the chiff-chaff by the lighter colouring of its legs.

Though the willow-warbler will often build in grass, it will also select a wall-plant where it builds close to the ground. Towards the end of April it will begin to build its dome-shaped nest which is made of grass, fresh moss and dried bracken and ferns. Early in May six to eight eggs are laid; they are white, blotched with pale brownish-red. By the first days of September the family will be ready to leave, for this bird winters in Africa, often at the Cape.

Wren

One of the best-loved of our birds, it is the smallest, measuring about 3 in. (7·6 cm.) long, and is as active as the robin in its search for insects. It loves to flit about a plant-covered wall where it will find insects, but it is a shy bird, and unlike the robin will keep away from people. Known as Jenny Wren and Stumpy, it has a beautiful and powerful song, amazing for so small a bird. Both male and female are of similar colouring, being chestnut-brown on the back, barred with darker brown, also on the breast and tail feathers. It will build in the strangest places, almost anywhere it can find to make its domed abode. I have seen its nest in the corner of a garage, occupying 2 in. (5 cm.) of space between an upright timber and the wall. It will build in a crevice of a wall, in a nest-box, or in the hole of a tree, often in sight of all who pass by, though the bird itself is rarely to be seen.

The domed nest is made of moss and dead leaves, lined with wool or hair, and six to eight eggs are laid in April. They are amongst the tiniest of eggs and are white with a few pin-head spots of red.

Wryneck

A summer visitor, it rarely ventures north of the Thames for it likes warmth and winters in North Africa, the Near East and India. It was an occasional visitor to my Somerset orchard but I have seen it nowhere else. The male, which arrives first, has almost the same mottling as the nightjar, its wide throat and neck being beautifully barred, whilst its blue-grey tail has three bars of brown. Though 6½ in. (16·5 cm.) long, its thick neck gives it a short, stumpy appearance. Though not quite so brightly coloured, the female has similar markings. It is not a shy bird and is to be found in woodlands, parks and gardens, and like the woodpeckers (it is of the same family), it makes its nest in a decaying tree. It is a climber and has the unusual ability of moving its head and neck almost completely round, independent of the rest of its body. It does not obtain its food from the bark but uses its long sticky tongue to pick up insects as they alight on nearby leaves and twigs, so is of much value in orchard and garden. Another peculiarity is that when the nest is approached the birds make a loud hissing noise which has been known to frighten away many a lad climbing in search of eggs. As many as ten pure white eggs are laid early in May; this number means that at least some should survive the long journey to and from their winter quarters, and thus ensure the survival of the species.

The birds will return to the same tree year after year, even if not to the same nest, and they will also take kindly to a nest-box placed among the branches of a tree, possibly an old apple tree.

Yellow hammer

A hedgerow bird, rarely frequenting woodlands, it is also known as the 'scribbling lark', for its white eggs are marked with scribble-like ink-marks, as if made with a mapping pen. It is also called the yellow bunting, for it is closely related to the bunting family. The male is 6½ in. (16·5 cm.) long and is handsome with its summer plumage of brightest yellow and dark brown rump. Its call is an oft-repeated 'chit-chit' to which it adds notes which children believe to sound like 'a little bit of bread and no cheese' when said quickly. It begins its song early in March and continues all summer. The nest is made in the matted grass, left uncut until late summer, of a spinney or a bank on which bulbs may be grown, or it may be built at the bottom of a thick hedge. The nest is made of grass and bracken and lined with moss. Two to five eggs are laid at the end of April and two clutches in a season, the male assisting in the incubation. The eggs are whitish, covered with dark blotches and streaks.

Yellow wagtail

Wintering in West Africa and southern Spain, it is one of our most charming birds, with a greater liking for water than the so-called pied or water-wagtail. A smaller bird, about 6 in. (15 cm.) long, the male has deep brownish-green back and tail feathers, whilst the throat and breast feathers are of brilliant yellow, enhanced by the jet-black beak and legs. Its habits are similar to those of the water-wagtail; it will search newly up-turned soil for grubs, as do the thrush and robin, occasionally letting out a soft twittering noise (though usually it is a silent bird) and all the time its tail will be wagging up and down.

It makes its nest in the ground, in an open field or orchard, and for this reason is less numerous in the garden than the water-wagtail. The nest is made of grass and lined with wool and feathers and in April five or six white eggs, speckled and lined with grey, are laid. They are usually followed by another clutch. By late September, the flocks will be ready to leave and gather in open fields before making their departure early in October.

BIRDS RESIDENT IN THE BRITISH ISLES

Blackbird	Jay
Blackcap	Lesser redpoll
Blue tit	Linnet
Bullfinch	Mistle thrush
Chaffinch	Nuthatch
Corn-bunting	Pheasant
Dunnock	Redbreast (robin)
Goldcrest	Reed-bunting
Great spotted woodpecker	Song thrush
Great tit	Starling
Green woodpecker	Tree-creeper
Hawfinch	Tree-sparrow
House-sparrow	Wren
Jackdaw	Yellow hammer

MIGRATORY GARDEN BIRDS

Chiff-chaff†

Garden-warbler‡

Goldfinch†

House-martin‡

Pied flycatcher‡

Red-backed shrike‡

Redstart‡

Sedge-warbler‡

Spotted flycatcher‡

Swallow‡

Swift‡

Tree-pipit‡

Whitethroat†

Willow-warbler*

Wryneck‡

Yellow wagtail†

* Returning in March
† Returning in April
‡ Returning in May

BIRDS THAT BUILD EARLY (MARCH) AND MAKE NESTS IN EVERGREENS

Blackbird

Chaffinch

Chiff-chaff

Dunnock

Goldcrest

Mistle thrush

Song thrush

Stonechat

Tree-creeper (old ivy)

Water-wagtail

Willow-warbler

The evergreen should be of a suitable density, such as ivy, privet, pyracantha or cupressus.

BIRDS THAT BUILD LATE (MAY) AND MAKE NESTS IN DECIDUOUS HEDGES

Blue titmouse

Garden-warbler

Goldfinch

Greenfinch

Lesser redpoll

Spotted flycatcher

These hedges, such as hawthorn or beech, will be in leaf when the birds nest.

BIRDS THAT BUILD IN OLD WALLS AND BUILDINGS

Blue tit
Great tit
House-martin
House-sparrow
Jackdaw
Nuthatch (occasionally)

Owls
Pied wagtail
Redbreast (robin)
Swallow
Swift
Wren

BIRDS THAT BUILD BY POND OR POOL

Marsh-titmouse
Pied flycatcher
Pied (water-) wagtail

Reed-bunting
Sedge-warbler
Yellow wagtail

BIRDS THAT BUILD IN TREES

Coal-tit
Great spotted woodpecker*
Green woodpecker*
Lesser spotted woodpecker*
Mistle thrush

Nuthatch
Redstart
Tree-creeper
Tree-sparrow
Wryneck*

* These build in holes in trunks of decaying trees. The rest
build in the forks of branches.

BIRDS THAT BUILD IN HEDGEROW, BUSH OR CLIMBING
PLANT

Blackbird
Blackcap
Brambling
Bullfinch
Chaffinch
Chiff-chaff
Dunnock
Garden-warbler
Goldcrest
Goldfinch
Greenfinch

Hawfinch
Lesser redpoll
Linnet
Long-tailed tit
Red-backed shrike
Song thrush
Spotted flycatcher
Stonechat
Tree-pipit
Whitethroat
Willow-warbler

BIRDS THAT ARE WINTER VISITORS TO GARDENS
BUT DO NOT NEST IN BRITAIN

Fieldfare   Redwing
Firecrest   Waxwing

BIRDS THAT FEED ON BERRIES IN WINTER

Blackcap   Mistle thrush
Fieldfare*   Redwing*
Hawfinch   Waxwing*

* Winter visitors.

4. Butterflies

I. NATIVE BRITISH BUTTERFLIES AND MIGRANTS

Butterflies must be included with birds as being amongst the most welcome of garden visitors, for they have similar characteristics and they are equally beautiful. Their name is, in fact, a corruption of 'beauty-fly'. With moths, which are mostly nocturnal and for this reason less well known to us, butterflies are of the order *Lepidoptera*, one of the largest of insect orders, and they are present in most parts of the world. In Britain there are about seventy breeding species, represented by eight families and sixteen tribes or sub-families. Several are extremely rare and may already have become extinct. Others are becoming less noticeable every year, due to the indiscriminate use of pesticides and weedkillers about the roadsides and hedgerows and the continual 'grubbing up' of hedges, now that it is so expensive for farmer and local authority to hire labour to keep them in trim. Again, many of the most important and once inaccessible breeding grounds have become so frequented by car owners that several species are in danger of becoming extinct, due chiefly to their being driven from their natural breeding grounds by petrol fumes or being taken by collectors. The Adonis Blue and Large Blue (first discovered in England in 1945), once familiar visitors to the gardens of southern England and to be seen often on downlands and hillsides of limestone formation, have become sadly depleted in recent years, whilst the Swallow-tail, once common in Wicken Fen, and so often seen in gardens of Cambridgeshire and Norfolk, has vanished completely from the scene and now breeds only on Horsey Mere and on the Broads at Hickling in Norfolk. The Large Tortoise-shell, once a common visitor to those gardens situated close to woodlands of eastern Essex and Kent, now appears to be on the point of extinction, for its natural habitat, the deciduous woodland, has in those parts been felled to make way for new towns and aerodromes, linked together by an enormous expanse of motorways. The rapid spread of the urban population and the pollution of the atmosphere by industry have also made it impossible for butterflies to survive in many parts of Britain, so we must give them all the help possible by providing them with the plants they need to feed and breed upon.

It is estimated that almost half of Britain's breeding butterflies, which are now confined to well-known but small areas, are in constant danger from collectors. They remain protected only in nature reserves, but elsewhere the collector or dealer can take dozens of those species which have now become rare. The Swallow-tail, Lulworth Skipper and Large Blue, come within this category, for they are now confined in their breeding to only a few local colonies.

The trade in butterflies, supplying them for ornamentation and to display in frames, as pictures, is much to be condemned and the time has come when all our butterflies should receive the same protection by law as birds and their eggs now enjoy. Butterflies are, to some extent, covered by the Conservation of Wild Creatures and Wild Plants Act, and it is hoped that the number protected will increase.

Butterflies have clubbed antennae, those of moths being tapered and feathered. The body is composed of three segments or sections which give flexibility—the head, the thorax to which the four wings and six legs are attached, and the abdomen. The wings are covered in what appears to be dust but which, in fact, is made up of tiny scales of coloured pigment which cover the wings like tiles on a roof. It is from this that the name of the order is taken, from the Greek *lepis*, a scale and *pteron*, a wing. Handling will cause the scales to be loosened and eventually to fall, thus reducing the butterflies' ability to fly and to protect themselves in wet weather, so they should never be touched. A butterfly has neither veins nor arteries, but a rudimentary heart provides the necessary circulation. Nor has it lungs, oxygen being absorbed through the body tissues by means of tubes, and this greatly restricts altitudes and flying distances.

All lepidoptera are scented and the butterfly is known as the 'flower of the air' not so much because of its beauty but because of its fragrance. It was the German naturalist Dr. Hermann Müller who first drew attention to this characteristic of the butterfly and he found that though scent varies in the different species, some smelling like jasmine, others like bean flowers, mostly they carry the scent of honey, which is close to the scent given off by the flowers of the buddleia and *Sedum spectabile*, the Ice Plant, both of which will be visited by butterflies more than any other garden flowers. The scent of butterflies is present only on the male and is due to an oil secreted at the base of a tuft of hairs folded along the inner edge of their wings. When mating, the oil is secreted along the hairs which the male brushes against the female, so covering her with perfume.

The function of the scent of butterflies was confirmed by Dr. Carpenter in 1914 when he reported on the observations of the courting and mating of several African species. He witnessed the male hovering above the female and protruding his scented hairs on to her. This went on for some time before mating took place.

The butterfly passes through a life-cycle of four distinct stages: (1) the egg or ovum; (2) larva (caterpillar); (3) chrysalis or pupa; and (4) the adult or imago state which may take several weeks to achieve, or even months. Females of most species lay about 200 eggs singly or in clusters. The adult's life may be over within a matter of 14–20 days or it may live for almost a year, the Peacock and Small Tortoise-shell often surviving the winter which is spent hibernating in an old building such as a stable or barn or even an attic. But shortly after the period of hibernation is ended they flutter around for several days and then die.

While most of those butterflies which breed in Britain complete their life-cycle here, there are migrant species, as with birds. The Camberwell Beauty with its mourning cloak of funereal black and wide border of pale yellow, is believed to come with timber boats from Northern Europe, which unload their cargoes at Hull, Scarborough and Harwich, an easy way for the butterflies to make the long flight across the North Sea. But the Queen of Spain Fritillary arrives in May from Southern France and the Iberian Peninsula, and the Painted Lady, being the most distant of our migrant butterflies, from North Africa and the Mediterranean regions. The Pale Clouded Yellow and the Red Admiral also come from Southern Europe, mostly from France and Italy. These species are the most powerful in flight of all our butterflies.

Butterflies, unlike bees, are drawn to a plant by scent rather than by sight. The female, searching for a suitable place to lay her eggs, will beat the leaf with her front feet so as to release the scent or smell and there, if the leaf is right for her, an egg will be deposited on its surface or underside. The eggs will be laid over a period of several days and are deposited as widely apart as possible, for the caterpillars of many species will often eat each other during a food shortage if they are too close together. It may happen that a female will refuse to mate if she cannot find the right leaves on which to lay or, if she has the already fertile eggs in her, she may not lay them, so it is important to provide the correct plants for butterfly breeding, whether it be in the garden or countryside. There will be no butterflies if the food plants are destroyed. It may well be that the interesting Comma, which in recent years has spread to the industrial Midlands from its original and unique breeding area of the Wye Valley, will become less prevalent in future, due to the necessary felling because of disease of the elm tree, still the most common hedgerow tree of the Midlands countryside.

Before any attempt is made to persuade butterflies to visit one's garden, something should be known of the terrain where they may be seen and of the plants on which they lay their eggs, also of those flowers which provide them with nectar at the time of year when they emerge from the chrysalis state.

The butterflies mentioned here are to be found in the British Isles, those that are now believed to be extinct or almost so are omitted. Not all can be persuaded to visit the garden, the Skippers group being especially difficult to entice, whilst the Purple Emperor rarely leaves the sanctuary of oak woodlands. Others are to be seen in only a few parts of southern England, rarely venturing north of the Thames. Butterflies are as diverse as birds in their characteristics, some hibernating (there are also hibernating caterpillars) and some which are woodland species, whilst others frequent dry sandy heaths and downlands.

Notes on butterflies seen in our gardens

FAMILY SATYRIDAE (the 'Browns')

Speckled Wood

With its colouring of Van Dyck brown and beautiful wing-markings of pale yellow, it is common in the south of England and south Midlands, also in Ireland, frequenting woodlands and tree-lined hedgerows. It is unusual in that the caterpillars from late broods hibernate in tufts of grass and do not change into chrysalids until spring, the butterflies, with a wing-span of about 1½ in. (4 cm.), appearing early in May and on the wing during May and June. Bramble blossoms are their source of nectar in late summer.

Wall Brown

Slightly smaller than the Speckled Wood, its wings are copper-coloured with dark brown markings and with conspicuous eye-spots. It is distinguished by its zigzag flight movements, whilst it will spend hours on a sunny wall or wooden fence. The first brood appears late in May, followed by a second towards the end of July. It is present, in all parts of Britain, except the north of Scotland, and on the wing from May to August.

Mountain Ringlet

With a wing-span of about 1⅜ in. (3·5 cm.), it is found only at the top of Langdale Pikes in the Lake District and in several parts of the Scottish Highlands, usually above 1,500 ft. It is believed to be one of the first butterflies to reach Britain after the Ice Age. It is dark brown all over with dull coppery markings towards the edge of the wings. It flies only during July. The caterpillars hibernate under rough grass and emerge to pupate there when the snow has melted.

Scotch Argus

It is found in Scotland and the Border regions and as far south as North Yorkshire. With a wing-span of 1¾ in. (4·5 cm.), it is a handsome species, of darkest brown with broad coppery markings towards the wing-edges. The wings have conspicuous eye-markings. It is found on grassy hillsides and is slow in flight. Its breeding characteristics are similar to those of the Mountain Ringlet, and it is on the wing during July.

Marbled White

One of the 'Browns' in spite of its name, it is fairly common, though becoming less so each year, in southern England and the south Midlands, as far north as Northampton and Hunting-don, and is on the wing from mid-July until late in August. Frequenting rough hillsides and deciduous woodlands, it is to be found mostly on the South Downs near the sea. It has a wing-span of 2 in. (5 cm.) and the female merely drops her eggs in the grass tufts, whilst pupation is on the ground. The caterpillars feed on grasses, especially sheep's fescue.

Grayling

It has a wing-span of 2 in. (5 cm.) and has the colour of very dark tortoise-shell with two black eye-marks on each side of the fore wings. It is found on moorlands and dry hillsides and is on the wing during July and August. It is almost invisible on the ground for it conceals its fore wings beneath the other two. The caterpillars hibernate in grass tufts to pupate in spring, after remaining in the chrysalis form for at least a month.

Hedge Brown

With a wing-span of about $1\frac{5}{8}$ in. (4 cm.), it is found throughout the south of England and the Home Counties but is rare elsewhere. The fore wings are copper-coloured, edged with brown and with two conspicuous 'eyes', the hind wings being dark brown with a coppery patch at the centre of each and a less conspicuous eye. It frequents brambles, taking nectar from the flowers, but like all the 'Browns' lays on grass. On the wing during August and September.

Meadow Brown

Distributed throughout the British Isles, its dark brown wings are relieved only by a bright copper-coloured eye-spot on the fore wings. Found in meadows and on commons, it has a wing-span of $1\frac{3}{4}$ in. (4·5 cm.) and is slow in flight. On the wing from June until early October.

Small Heath

One of our smallest butterflies with a wing-span of 1 in. (2·5 cm.), it is found in all parts of Britain, on hillside and heath,

and is on the wing from May until early October. The colour
is orange and yellow with a contrasting wire-edge of darkest
brown and a small brown spot on each of the fore wings. Slow
in flight, it rarely moves far above the grass on which it lays
and pupates.

Large Heath

With a wing-span of $1\frac{3}{8}$ in. (3·5 cm.), it is larger than the Small
Heath from which it is distinguished by its pale olive-brown
colouring and conspicuous brown veining of the fore wings,
whilst it has a double pale spot on the hind wings. Present in
northern England, North Wales and Ireland, usually on heathlands, and on the wing during July. The caterpillars hibernate
until late in spring.

Ringlet

Common everywhere, being darkest brown with double spots
on fore and hind wings, though these are hardly visible. It frequents shady woodlands, feeding on bramble blossom, and is
slow in flight and difficult to find. It is on the wing in July and
August. The females drop their eggs on to cocksfoot grass and
pupate on the ground.

FAMILY NYMPHALIDAE

Small Pearl-bordered Fritillary

It is difficult to distinguish it from the Pearl-bordered for it has
a wing-span of $1\frac{3}{8}$ in. (3·5 cm.) compared to the $1\frac{5}{8}$ in. (4 cm.)
span of the (Large) Pearl-bordered. The familiar dark brown
markings on paler brown are similar in the two species though,
if anything, the (Large) Pearl-bordered is of brighter hue,
being golden-brown with the wing-spots larger. The Small
Pearl-bordered is widely distributed about the British Isles,
especially throughout the Midlands and Wales, but does not

appear in Ireland. Found in woodlands where its markings are
a perfect camouflage in the dappled light and on the wing
early, during May and June.

Pearl-bordered Fritillary

This species confines its activities to the south, south Midlands
and South Wales. Like all fritillaries, it enjoys the dappled
light and shade of deciduous woodlands where it is difficult to
find. On the wing during June, the caterpillars hibernate and
pupate in spring.

Queen of Spain Fritillary

Larger than the Small Pearl-bordered and Pearl-bordered,
with a wing-span of 2 in. (5 cm.), and golden-brown with
clearly defined black marks evenly distributed. It comes from
southern France and the Iberian Peninsula, at any time between June and September, but remains along the south coast,
rarely venturing north. It very rarely breeds in Britain but is
common all over Southern and Central Europe where the
caterpillars hibernate in winter.

15. Queen of Spain Fritillary

Dark Green Fritillary

One of the largest in this group, with a wing-span of $2\frac{1}{2}$ in. (6 cm.), and one of the most beautiful, being of rich coppery-brown with black markings and with the hind wings green on the undersides. Found mostly in the north and Midlands, rare in the south and East Anglia, it is on the wing during August. It frequents moorlands and heaths and is strong in flight, being able to combat the stiff breezes. The caterpillars hibernate, pupation being in July.

High Brown Fritillary

Distributed through most of England but is rare north of Lancashire and Yorkshire. It is olive-brown with clearly defined black markings and with a wing-span of $2\frac{1}{8}$ in. (5·5 cm.). Present in deciduous woodlands, it feeds on the nectar of bramble blossom and is on the wing in July and August. It spends hours in the sun with little movement. The eggs are laid on the leaves of the dog violet in August but the larvae remain inside the shell until March.

Silver-washed Fritillary

The largest fritillary, on the wing in July and with a wing-span of more than $3\frac{1}{8}$ in. (8 cm.), the hind wings being large. Distributed in hedgerows and deciduous woodlands of southern England, the Midlands and Ireland, it lays its eggs in cracks in oak bark where the caterpillars winter, crawling down in spring to find the dog violet and to feed upon its leaves. On the wing from early July until early October. Pale olive-brown in colour with clearly defined markings and green shading at the edge of the wings, it takes its name from the silvered chrysalis which shines brightly in the sun. The courtship of these butterflies is unique. After the male has selected his partner, both fly off together with the male flying round and round the female; this continues for several hundred yards until they alight, usually on bramble flowers.

Marsh Fritillary

A rare butterfly of exquisite beauty, the wings divided into bands of yellow, orange, brown and black, the black dividing bands being broad and well defined. Found in only a few localities in England where it frequents damp meadows, marshes and woodlands. Small in comparison to its 2 in. (5 cm.) wing-span and weak in flight. Like the Red Admiral, it lays in large clusters, the caterpillars hibernating. On the wing during June.

Heath Fritillary

With a wing-span of $1\frac{3}{8}$ in. (3.5 cm.), it is one of the smaller fritillaries, found only in Epping Forest and in one or two coppiced woodlands in Kent and Sussex away from busy roads. As coppice management of woodlands is now rarely practised, this butterfly is in danger of extinction. Contrary to its name, it is never seen on heathland. The wings are divided into areas of yellow and coppery-orange, with wide bands of black separating the colours. Weak in flight, it is on the wing in July, when mating occurs. The caterpillars hibernate.

Red Admiral

One of the largest and most handsome of our butterflies, those pupating early migrate to the Mediterranean regions late in summer, returning here in spring. It has a wing-span of $2\frac{3}{4}$ in. (7 cm.) and measures 2 in. (5 cm.) from the tip of the fore wing to the extremity of the hind wing, so it is large in all respects. A large area of the wings is dark brown, with a wide belt of scarlet separating this colour from the black fore wing extremities which have white markings. There is also a wide scarlet edge to the hind wings, with pale blue 'eyes' or rings. It is distinctive and cannot be confused with other species.

16. Red Admiral

Strong in flight, it lays its eggs singly. The chrysalis is covered with 'bloom', like that on its wings. Migrations occur throughout summer and it continues to breed until October, being present in all parts of Britain. Its food is the juice of decaying plums and other fruits.

Painted Lady

The furthest migrant, coming by stages from North Africa and arriving early in June, aided by its strong wing-beats. Through spring it is to be seen resting with outspread wings in the sun on walls in France. It has a wing-span of 2¾ in. (7 cm.) and is of orange colouring, with broad black bands and a large black area at the fore wing tips with white markings. It is found in all parts of England and Wales, though mainly in the south, and is on the wing from early summer until late September.

Small Tortoise-shell

One of the most beautifully coloured butterflies, being orange with markings of black and yellow and with seven bright blue

17. Small Tortoise-shell

spots around the fore and hind wings, set in a broad black
band. It has a wing-span of 2 in. (5 cm.) and is extremely
active when on the wing from May to October. Common
throughout Britain, it frequents gardens and hibernates in old
houses and barns, venturing out with the first warm days of
April. The eggs are laid in large clutches in May, pupating early
July, with a second brood towards the end of August.

Large Tortoise-shell

A now uncommon species, to be found only on the borders of
Suffolk and Essex, and occasionally in Kent, spending its
entire life in remote shady woodlands and rarely venturing
into gardens. It has a wing-span of 2⅝ in. (6·5 cm.), its wings
having the irregularity of the Comma at the edges, with the
tips of the fore wings clipped. They are coppery-red with slight
markings of yellow and black and with a yellow and black
margin around the edges. Strong on the wing from April until
the end of August, it hibernates in old trees and is in flight
again in spring.

Peacock

When seen it cannot be mistaken for any other species, for on
the upper corners of both the fore and hind wings is a large
round 'eye', resembling the 'eyes' on a peacock's tail. The rest

is a reddish-brown colour with a pale yellowish-brown band around the wing edges. It has a wing-span of $2\frac{1}{2}$ in. (6 cm.). Present throughout Britain, it hibernates, frequenting old buildings. The eggs are laid in large numbers in May. The caterpillars weave a web between leaf and stem of the nettle beneath which they feed. On the wing from May to October.

Camberwell Beauty

A European species which reaches the east coast of England during early summer and is believed to come with timber boats. In those gardens near to the ports of Hull, Scarborough and Harwich, where timber is unloaded, the species is a regular visitor. It is the largest of our butterflies, with a wing-span of $2\frac{3}{4}$ in. (7 cm.) and is $3\frac{1}{8}$ in. (8 cm.) from the extremities of the fore and hind wings. It is known as the Mourning Cloak on account of the dark brown colouring of the wings which have a broad edge of pale yellow. Inside the edge is a row of pale blue marks running the whole length of the wings. It is a strong and high flyer and feeds on the sap of birch and conifers, also on decaying fruit. It is attracted to the garden where these foods are available and where willows are growing, for it is on the leaves that the eggs are laid in large clutches. On the wing from May to July.

Comma

With a wing-span of about 2 in. (5 cm.), it is not a large butter-fly but is one that, with its jagged wings, is familiar. It is rich coppery-red with black markings and takes its name from the white comma mark on the hind wings. On the wing from April to October, at one time it was confined to woodlands of the Wye Valley, but has spread to London and the Home Counties and across the south Midlands. A hibernating species, it lays on nettles, hops and elm leaves and feeds on cherry blossom when awakening from its winter sleep.

Purple Emperor

It has a wing-span of 3 in. (7·5 cm.) and is blackish-brown with
a broad, white band down the centre of the hind wings and
orange 'eyes'. Found in remote wooded areas of Norfolk and
Suffolk, Huntingdon and Northamptonshire, and in those
counties south of the Thames. It feeds on the decaying car-
casses of birds or rabbits, descending from tall trees to attack
them. The eggs are laid on willows and the presence of these
trees will be a clue as to where the species can be found. The
eggs, caterpillar, and chrysalis are brilliant green, a perfect
camouflage for the willows. On the wing mid-July until the
end of August, it can fly to a great height.

White Admiral

Like all the family, it frequents woodlands but will come into
any garden where there are bramble blossom and honeysuckle
(on which it deposits its eggs), to feed upon the nectar. It is
present in woodlands south of a line drawn from the Wash to
the Dee, especially in the New Forest, and is a handsome
species with a wing-span of 2 in. (5 cm.). It is dark brown with
an almost central band running from top to bottom of the
wings. There are almost inconspicuous orange-red 'eyes' on
the hind wings. It flies quickly, with graceful gliding movements but will remain for hours on the flowers it visits for
nectar. A hibernating species, spending the winter in old trees.
On the wing July and August.

FAMILY RIODINIDAE

Duke of Burgundy

The only species of the genus to be found in Britain, and
though widespread in southern England, it is seen nowhere
else. Although having a wing-span of only ¾ in. (2 cm.), its
flight is rapid. It is dark brown with paler brown markings, so

resembling the fritillaries. It frequents open woodlands where
there are cowslips and primroses on which it lays its eggs in
June, and is attracted to gardens south of the Thames where
primroses or cowslips are growing in a spinney or shrubbery.
It remains in the chrysalis state for ten months, emerging in
May when, shortly after, mating begins. On the wing mid-May
to the end of June.

FAMILY LYCAENIDAE (the 'Blues')

Short-tailed Blue

A migrating species, found along the south coast of England
and the South Downs, it does not breed here but is usually
found on gorse. It has a wing-span of 1 in. (2·5 cm.) and is
dark blue, shading to purple at the wing-edges with two small
tail-like appendages to the hind wings. On the wing July to
September.

Long-tailed Blue

A migrating species from Southern Europe, it does not breed
here but may be seen in gardens of those counties south of the
Thames. It is on the wing from July until September, when the
tree lupin is in bloom, for this is its favourite food. With a
wing-span of 1¼ in. (3 cm.), the male is brilliant blue with a
thin black edge to its wings. The hind wings each have two
tiny black spots and quite long 'tails'.

Small Blue

Like all the 'Blues', with the exception of the Common Blue, it
prefers the warmth of the south, rarely venturing north of the
Thames, though it is present in Southern Ireland. It has a wing-
span of only 1 in. (2·5 cm.) and is dark blue on the upper surface, pale blue on the underside of the wings. The caterpillars
hibernate and pupate early in May, remaining on the wing

until early August. Preferring the chalk country, they are seen
in chalk quarries and gravel pits but will visit gardens if the
kidney-vetch can be provided, for this is their main source of
food and they lay their eggs on it.

Silver-studded Blue

With a wing-span of 1 in. (2·5 cm.), the sexes look entirely
different, the males mid-blue with prominent black veins, the
females brown with reddish spots near the edge of the wings.
They always congregate together, whether on the wing or
whilst resting and feeding. Found on heathlands in the Home
Counties, Hampshire, Devon and Cornwall, they are on the
wing in July and August when the eggs are laid, but these do
not hatch until spring.

Brown Argus

Despite its name and brown colour, it is one of the 'Blues',
common as far north as Derbyshire, and is present in the Low-
lands of Scotland but not in Ireland. Two clutches of eggs are
laid, usually on the common rock rose, but the caterpillars
pupate on the ground. With a wing-span of 1⅛ in. (2·8 cm.),
both sexes have a band of coppery-red close to the wing-edges.
They frequent sandy heaths and are on the wing from May to
September.

Common Blue

Widely dispersed over the British Isles on sandy heaths and
downlands and on the wing from May until September, the
sexes are of different colouring but both have a wing-span of

18. Common Blue

1¼ in. (3 cm.). The males are bright violet-blue, the females dark brown with reddish markings near the edge of the wings. They fly by rapid wing movements and feed on leguminous plants. When resting, the wings are closed. Eggs are laid in spring and a second clutch in August, the caterpillars hibernating, to begin feeding in spring.

Chalk-hill Blue

The second most widely distributed 'Blue', found on the South Downs and across the south of England to Devon and also in Bedfordshire, feeding only on horseshoe vetch. The green caterpillars remain below ground by day and feed only after dark. The males are of brilliant sky-blue with black edging to their wings, the females being mid-brown. On the wing from mid-July until October.

Adonis Blue

Present across southern England from Kent to Devon and feeding on horseshoe vetch. The male, which has a wing-span of 1 in. (2·5 cm.), has wings of vivid blue with black veins and a wire-edge of black, the female brown with a narrow band of orange towards the wing-edges. Two clutches are laid, the last in October, the larvae hibernating to pupate in spring. On the wing from early June until late October.

Holly Blue

More violet than blue, the female only having a wide edge of black on the wings. Common through England and Wales, feeding on and laying amongst the flowers of ivy and holly. The wing-span is 1⅛ in. (2·8 cm.). Often seen in gardens and parks close to industrial towns and on the wing from early May until late in August. Caterpillars that hatch in September remain in the chrysalis state over winter.

Large Blue

Found only on the northern coast of Devon and Cornwall, and now protected by Act of Parliament. It has an amazing affinity with ants which suck the honey from the caterpillars and then take them underground to pupate; the emerging butterflies make their way along the passages formed by the ants to the sunlight and then fly away. This takes place early in July when they mate, and the amazing procedure begins again. Male and female are of brilliant blue with five black markings on the fore wings and an edging of black around the wings. On the wing in July.

Small Copper

Common throughout Britain and on the wing from early May until late October, it lays on sorrel and dock leaves and feeds on fleabane in autumn. The male is of coppery-orange, the fore wings marked and edged with brown, with large brown areas on the hind wings. The female has the same markings as the male but where he is copper, she is pale yellow. The wing-span is $1\frac{1}{4}$ in. (3 cm.). Common on heaths and about waste ground, a few plants of sorrel will usually attract it to the garden. Several broods of eggs are laid, those laid in autumn wintering at the base of the plants to pupate in spring.

Green Hairstreak

So called because when its wings are closed they are of brilliant green which is camouflaged by the pale green of the broom and gorse on which it feeds and lays its eggs. Common about heaths and downland, the upper surface of its wings is a milk-chocolate colour. It is on the wing only during June when it lays, the caterpillar spending longer in the chrysalis state than any of the species, often for ten months or more. It has a wing-span of $1\frac{1}{8}$ in. (2·8 cm.).

Brown Hairstreak

Though one of the 'Blues', it is dark brown with two broad markings of orange on the fore wings, whilst the hind wings have the irregular edge of the Comma. When the wings are closed, they are palest orange-yellow with white streaks. On the wing in August, and with a wing-span of 1⅜ in. (3·5 cm.), it is found in woodlands south of a line from the Dee to the Wash, and though it will visit wooded gardens, it is not conspicuous, for it hides beneath the foliage of the blackthorn to which it is attracted for its egg laying, whilst it feeds upon the blossom. The eggs are laid in August on the stems of blackthorn and do not hatch until spring.

Purple Hairstreak

Only the female has the purple 'bloom' over its dull brown wings but both sexes have a short 'tail'. Common in Britain and Southern Ireland, it is present in woodlands and well-treed gardens and is on the wing in August when it lays on oak leaves, the eggs hatching in spring. The caterpillars climb down the trunk to pupate on the ground, which takes about a month. It has a wing-span of 1¼ in. (3 cm.) and usually stays high above ground.

Black Hairstreak

With a wing-span of 1¼ in. (3 cm.), it is of darkest brown with a broad orange band down the edges of the wings and both sexes have a short 'tail'. On the wing in July when the eggs are laid on the blackthorn. The caterpillars are cannibalistic if too close together; they do not hatch before spring and it is three months before they pupate. Frequenting woodlands, the Black Hairstreak is found only in a few haunts in Huntingdonshire and Northamptonshire and will visit gardens in those parts only where there is blackthorn.

White-letter Hairstreak

So called because of the peculiar white 'W' mark seen when the wings are closed. It has a wing-span of 1¼ in. (3 cm.) and is darkest brown, the colour of the female being relieved by yellowish shading. It lays on elms in the south of England and the Midlands. It will be attracted to the garden by privet flowers for it feeds on the nectar. On the wing early in August when it lays, the eggs remaining dormant during winter.

FAMILY PAPILIONIDAE

Swallow-tail

The largest and most beautiful of our butterflies with a wing-span of 3⅛ in. (8 cm.) and measuring 3¾ in. (9 cm.) from the tip of the fore wing to the 'tail'. Found only on Hickling Broads and Horsey Mere in Norfolk, and on the wing from early July to late August, it will visit nearby gardens and those situated close to the rivers Yare and Bure, especially if fennel or milk parsley, on which it lays its eggs, are available. The first eggs hatch early in May. The chrysalis will attach itself to the plant

19. Swallowtail

by means of a girdle of silk and is conspicuous with its markings of black and yellow and with its two long 'tails' on the hind wings on which there are two large 'eyes' of red and blue. It can be recognized in the air by the flapping of its large wings and by its laboured flight. It is the only member of this family in Britain.

FAMILY PIERIDAE

Large White

Together with the Small White, the only 'pest' amongst butterflies. It is known to all, especially vegetable growers, for its caterpillars feed on brassica crops and if not controlled will destroy acres of plants in a few days. It is on the wing from early May to October and is to be found throughout the British Isles. With a wing-span of $3\frac{1}{8}$ in. (8 cm.), it is white with black tips to the fore wings. On the female only are also two black spots and a bar. The eggs are laid in large clutches on any plant of the *Cruciferae* family and in batches throughout summer at regular intervals. Those caterpillars born late winter in the chrysalis stage.

Small White

Distinguished from the Large White by its much smaller wing-span of only $1\frac{7}{8}$ in. (4·8 cm.), and by the smaller amount of black on the fore wing tips. The female has two spots on the fore wings and one on the hind wings whilst the male has only one spot on each wing. Present throughout Britain, and on the wing from May to October, it is also a pest of brassica crops, if not to the same extent as the Large White which it resembles in its breeding habits.

Green-veined White

Distinguished from the Small White in that the female has

three spots of black instead of two on the fore wings, whilst the pronounced black veining in both sexes, when seen against the pale yellow ground-colour, gives the veins a greenish tint. The smallest of the three indigenous 'Whites', with a wing-span of $1\frac{5}{8}$ in. (4 cm.), like the others, it spends the winter as a chrysalis. It lays mostly on hedgerow *Cruciferae* and spends much of its time there. On the wing May to September.

Bath White

It has a wing-span of $1\frac{5}{8}$ in. (4 cm.) and attractive black mark-ings about the tips of the fore wings, whilst the female is also marked on the hind wings. A migrant, it arrives from the Continent in late May and can be recognized by its flight close to the ground. It is on the wing until the end of August and remains mainly south of the Thames. It lays on hedge-mustard and its life-cycle is completed within thirty days.

Orange Tip

Present throughout Britain, it has a wing-span of $1\frac{5}{8}$ in. (4 cm.) and both sexes have black tips to the fore wings, but only the male has the brilliant orange which comprises almost half the fore wings. It bears only one brood, depositing the eggs singly and usually on the flowers of Lady's Smock or Dame's Violet, which will attract it to the garden and upon which it feeds. It passes the winter as a chrysalis of unusual shape, looking rather like an aeroplane with swept-back wings. It is the earliest of our butterflies on the wing and is active only in May.

Pale Clouded Yellow

Now a rare migrant though once common, arriving from the Mediterranean regions early in June and on the wing until September, it is seen only in those counties south of and immediately north of the Thames. It has a wing-span of $1\frac{5}{8}$ in. (4 cm.) with large areas of black at the tips of the fore wings and with a black spot at the centre, and an orange spot on the hind wings. Both sexes are pale yellow when the wings close but only the male shows yellow on the upper surface, the female being ivory-white. The eggs are laid on lucerne and it is important that early frosts do not damage the plants before pupation.

Clouded Yellow

One of the most beautiful of our butterflies with a wing-span of 2 in. (5 cm.), both sexes being of brilliant orange with a wide margin of black on both fore and hind wings, whilst each has two black spots to the centre of the fore wings and orange spots on the hind wings. They arrive from Southern Europe early in June and continue to come until early September, during which time they lay their eggs and feed upon white and pink clover and bird's-foot trefoil. They remain south of the Trent and are most common in the west country. They may be encouraged into the garden by sowing clover patches in a sunny corner or in an orchard.

Brimstone

The male is of deep brimstone-yellow, the female pale lemon coloured, but each sex has a small single orange spot to the centre of each wing. Free from any other markings, the wings terminate to a point and when folded resemble the leaves of the buckthorn on which it lays. Present throughout England and Wales but not in Scotland and only in Southern Ireland, it hibernates in ivy and other evergreen wall-plants and will fly around from spring and through summer, being the longest living of our butterflies.

Wood White

The smallest of the 'Whites' with a wing-span of $1\frac{5}{8}$ in. (4 cm.), it spends most of its life in dense woodlands south of the Thames and on each side of the Severn Valley and is on the wing from May to August. Slow of flight, it is almost moth-like, with its narrow wings and long body. It lays and feeds on tufted vetch and other leguminous plants, and caterpillars from a late batch will over-winter in the chrysalis form. This butterfly does not damage brassica crops with its caterpillars, nor does it lay its eggs on them.

Dingy Skipper

A small species with a wing-span of only 1 in. (2·5 cm.), it is common in southern England and the south Midlands but is rare in the north. Dark brown with tiny yellow spots around the wings, it is moth-like in its habits, fluttering low over heaths and downs and, when nesting, folding its wings over its body. It is about very early in spring, and will lay on bird's-foot trefoil during June, the caterpillars hibernating until early the following April, pupating in May.

Grizzled Skipper

Smaller even than the Dingy, with a wing-span of ¾ in. (2 cm.), its brown wings being mottled all over with yellow. It is found over much the same territory as the Dingy and lays on the leaves of wild strawberry or raspberry. The caterpillars spin a silk web over the leaf and there hibernate for almost ten months, during most of this time as chrysalids, pupating in May.

Chequered Skipper

The male is brown, spotted all over with orange, the female with yellow. It frequents woodlands and is found only in the east Midlands, possibly within a twenty-five mile radius of Stamford. Its life-cycle follows the same pattern as all the skippers, hibernating in the caterpillar stage through winter and remaining six weeks as a chrysalis during April and until

mid-May, the butterfly then living only until the end of June.
It has a wing-span of 1 in. (2·5 cm.) and lays on ground ivy
or slender false-broom grass, the caterpillars weaving a shelter
on the leaves so that they become like slender green tubes.

Small Skipper

Found in the same parts as the Chequered, it remains for eight
months encased in a cocoon before changing into a chrysalis
and emerging early in summer. With a wing-span of 1 in.
(2·5 cm.), it is pale coppery-orange with prominent brown
veins and a wire-edge of brown around the wings. To be seen
in woodlands flying about the trees, making a humming sound
as it does so.

Large Skipper

Common throughout England and Wales and in Scotland as
far north as Perth, it has a wing-span of 1¼ in. (3 cm.) and is
copper coloured with patches of black. It is stronger in flight
than the Small Skipper and larger in all respects. On the wing
from June until late August, laying on Yorkshire fog grass or
couch grass on which the caterpillars hibernate for ten months.
Before pupating it builds a cocoon and will be a month inside
it before emerging as a butterfly.

Essex Skipper

Found only near the Thames Estuary, on the Essex and Kent
coasts and in Cambridgeshire, and with a wing-span of ⅞ in.
(2·3 cm.), it is one of our smallest butterflies and is coppery-
brown with black veins and a wide margin of black. On the
wing in August when it mates and lays on Yorkshire fog or
couch grass, the eggs remaining in a dormant state for nearly
nine months, it is only two months as a caterpillar and chrysalis.

Silver-spotted Skipper

Present on chalk and limestone downlands on each side of the

Thames as far west as Wiltshire and also in Hertfordshire and
Cambridgeshire. It has a wing-span of 1¼ in. (3 cm.) and is
coppery-brown, heavily marked with black but when the
wings are closed, they are green and yellow, dotted with pale
blue, making them difficult to see when resting. Its eggs are
laid in August on sheep's fescue and are dormant through
winter. In April the larvae climb down into the clumps of grass
and within two months will have pupated.

Apart from the Large Skipper, all skippers are fairly local
and seem to keep to the downlands rather than gardens.

SUMMARY OF WHEN BUTTERFLIES ARE ON THE WING AND WHERE THEY CAN BE SEEN

Species	Where seen	On wing
Satyridae		
Speckled Wood	S. England & S. Midlands	May & June
Wall Brown	All Britain	May–Aug.
Mountain Ringlet	Langdale Pikes	July
Scotch Argus	Scotland & N. England	July
Marbled White	S. England & S. Midlands	August
Grayling	All Britain	July–Aug.
Hedge Brown	S. England & Home Counties	Aug.– Sept.
Meadow Brown	All Britain	June–Sept.
Small Heath	All Britain	May–early Oct.
Large Heath	N. England, Wales, Scotland, Ireland	July
Ringlet	All Britain	July–Aug.
Nymphalidae		
Small Pearl-bordered Fritillary	All Britain	June–July
(Large) Pearl-bordered Fritillary	S. England, Midlands, Wales	June

Species	Where seen	On wing
Nymphalidae—cont.		
*Queen of Spain Fritillary	S. England	June– Sept.
Dark Green Fritillary	N. England & Midlands	August
High Brown Fritillary	S. England & Midlands	July–Aug.
Silver-washed Fritillary	S. England, Midlands, S. Ireland	July
Marsh Fritillary	Few localities in England	June
Heath Fritillary	Few localities in S.E. England	July
*Red Admiral	All Britain	May–Oct.
*Painted Lady	England & Wales	May–Sept.
Small Tortoise-shell	All Britain	May–Oct.
Large Tortoise-shell	S.E. England	April–Aug.
Peacock	All Britain	April–Oct.
*Camberwell Beauty	East Coast	May–July
Comma	W. Midlands & Home Counties	April–Oct.
Purple Emperor	East Anglia, S. Midlands	July–Aug.
White Admiral	S. England, S. Midlands	July
Riodinidae		
Duke of Burgundy	S. England	Mid-May– June
Lycaenidae		
*Short-tailed Blue	S. England	June–Sept.
*Long-tailed Blue	S. England	July–Sept.
Small Blue	S. England, S. Ireland	May–Aug.
Silver-studded Blue	S.W. England, Home Counties	July–Aug.
Brown Argus	England, S. Scotland	May–Sept.
Common Blue	All Britain	May–Sept.
Chalk-hill blue	S. England, Home Counties	July–Oct.
Adonis Blue	S. England	June–Oct.
Holly Blue	England, Wales	June–Oct.
Large Blue	N. Devon & Cornwall	July

* Does not breed in Britain.

Species	Where seen	On wing
Lycaenidae—cont.		
Small Copper	All Britain	
Green Hairstreak	All Britain	June
Brown Hairstreak	S. England, S. Midlands	August
Purple Hairstreak	All Britain, S. Ireland	August
Black Hairstreak	Huntingdon & Northants	July
White-letter Hairstreak	S. England, Midlands	July–Aug.
Papilionidae		
Swallow-tail	Norfolk Broads	July–Aug.
Pieridae		
Large White	All Britain	Early May–Oct.
Small White	All Britain	May–Oct.
Green-veined White	All Britain	May–Sept.
*Bath White	S. England	June–Aug.
Orange Tip	All Britain	May
*Pale Clouded Yellow	S. England, Home Counties	June–Sept.
*Clouded Yellow	S. England, S. Midlands	June–Sept.
Brimstone	England, Wales, S. Ireland	May–Sept.
Wood White	S. England, W. Midlands	May–Aug.
Hesperiidae		
Dingy Skipper	S. England, S. Midlands	May–June
Grizzled Skipper	S. England, Midlands	May
Chequered Skipper	E. Midlands	June
Small Skipper	S. England, Midlands	June–Aug.
Large Skipper	England, Wales & S. Scotland	June–Aug.
Essex Skipper	S.E. England	August
Silver-spotted Skipper	S. England, Home Counties	August

HIBERNATING BUTTERFLIES

Brimstone
Comma
Large Tortoise-shell

Peacock
Small Tortoise-shell

* Does not breed in Britain.

HIBERNATING CATERPILLARS WHICH PUPATE IN SPRING

Adonis Blue   Marsh Fritillary
Chequered Skipper   Mountain Ringlet
Dark Green Fritillary   *Queen of Spain Fritillary
Dingy Skipper   Scotch Argus
Grayling   Small Blue
Green Hairstreak   Small Copper
Heath Fritillary   Speckled Wood
Large Heath

* Does not breed in Britain.

Butterflies possibly now extinct (or almost so) in the British
Isles:

Black-veined White   Milkweed

These butterflies are extremely rare in the British Isles appearing
in only one or two local colonies where they are easily taken by
collectors, and all should be protected:

Bath White   Large Tortoise-shell
Berger's Clouded   Long-tailed Blue
Black Hairstreak   Lulworth Skipper
Chequered Skipper   Mountain Ringlet
Glanville Fritillary   Purple Emperor
Large Blue   Swallow-tail
Large Copper

II. THE BUTTERFLY GARDEN

By providing as many plants as possible on which butterflies
will lay their eggs and caterpillars subsequently feed, you will
attract many species to the garden. If there is room for a small

spinney at one end of the garden, this will be ideal as a breeding ground for many butterflies. The Speckled Wood, for instance, lays on cocksfoot, *Dactylis glomerata*, and couch grass, *Agropyron repens,* which will be included in most of the cheaper grass seed mixtures (obtained from an agricultural seedsman) for spring sowing in a spinney. The rough sward will attract both birds and butterflies. The Marbled White of southern England mostly lays on or near sheep's fescue, *Festuca ovina*, though often the eggs are laid on the ground nearby. The Grayling, widely distributed about the British Isles, will also lay on sheep's fescue and on the handsome tufted hair-grass, *Deschampsia cespitosa*.

Berried trees and shrubs may be planted in the spinney, together with a few dense evergreens, and the area enclosed by a hedge of hawthorn or blackthorn, *Prunus spinosa*. The total area need not be more than about 20 ft. (6 m.) square or it may be triangular, occupying a corner of the garden away from the house and divided from the rest of the garden by a trellis, against which ornamental vines and other rapid-growing climbers can be grown (as suggested for a shrub garden, in Chapter 1). The area will give privacy and shelter to birds and other garden visitors and if in a sunny part, will afford conditions which butterflies enjoy—sun and shelter from cold winds. It would be an excellent breeding ground for butterflies, and many species may be artificially introduced.

In parts of England south of the Wash, and confined to East Anglia and Huntingdon and nearby counties, the Brown and the Black Hairstreak will mate on a blackthorn hedge and the female will deposit her eggs on the leaves. If hops are used to cover a trellis in the Midlands and Home Counties, the Comma will most likely be found, for the female likes to lay her eggs on hop plants, as well as elm trees. In Huntingdon and Cambridgeshire, the White Admiral will be present and will lay her eggs on the leaves of the honeysuckle *Lonicera periclymenum*, which may also be used to cover a trellis. When established, many small birds (and the blackbird too) will build in its twiggy stems, the nest being hidden from view by the honeysuckle's trailing shoots.

Around the sides of a spinney, beneath the hedge, plant a few stinging nettles, *Urtica dioica*, and allow them to spread, for the leaves are the favourite food of the caterpillars of the Red Admiral, Peacock and Small Tortoise-shell. The caterpillars spin a protective web over the leaves which they devour before moving on to another stem.

Of other familiar species, the Brimstone, which is common throughout England and Wales, lays on the leaves of the buck-thorn, *Frangula alnus* (syn. *Rhamnus frangula*), and the Purple Emperor on leaves of the pussy willow, *Salix caprea*, which grows in the water meadows of Northamptonshire and Hun-tingdon and south to Oxford and into Hampshire where the species is most likely to be found. This is a splendid willow to plant by a pond or in damp ground.

The leguminous plants, the tree lupin, gorse, perennial pea and Spanish broom are the favourites of several species, in-cluding the Long-tailed Blue of southern England, the Silver-studded Blue which is confined to Hampshire, Dorset and Berkshire, and the Green Hairstreak which is common throughout Britain and which also frequents the dogwood. They deposit their eggs at the base of the flowers, the cater-pillars feeding on the petals.

The pretty Orange Tip, common throughout most of Britain, lays on the flowers of several of our loveliest cruci-ferous plants, especially the Lady's Smock, *Cardamine pratensis*, Dame's Violet, *Hesperis matronalis* and honesty, *Lunaria annua*, all plants of the cottage garden of earlier times, the Dame's Violet being delightfully scented at night to attract hawk-moths for its pollination. The planting of gladioli, dahlias and geraniums in place of the old-fashioned flowers has done much to deprive our gardens of butterflies.

The fritillaries deposit their eggs on the leaves of violet and

Heart's-ease, members of the family *Violaceae*, the first to arrive being the Small Pearl-bordered Fritillary. The High Brown and Dark Green deposit their eggs on violet leaves late in July and the caterpillars at once go into hibernation and do not begin eating the leaves until the following spring. The Painted Lady lays its eggs singly on the leaves of thistles, the caterpillars spinning a web around the leaves on which they hatch and which they devour. The Scottish thistle which grows 3 ft. (91 cm.) tall is one they seek out. It may readily be grown from seed and should be in every herbaceous border, if only for the brilliant red of its flower-heads and grey-green leaves.

As survival of plant and insect is interrelated, those flowers in which the nectar is secreted at the end of a long tube will be those to which the lepidoptera, with their long tongues, are attracted. The long tapering spike of the buddleia flower is made up of multitudes of tiny flowers with long tubes, at the bottom of which is secreted the nectar. This is accessible only to the long tongues of the butterflies and, to a lesser extent, to honey-bees. When the butterfly is flying or resting, its tongue (or proboscis) is curled up under its body, like a coiled wire spring, and with it the butterfly can reach the nectar in a tube more than $\frac{5}{8}$ in. (1·5 cm.) long. The insect collects the nectar by means of a sucking action, and this is its only food. It takes up water or moisture, such as the juice oozing from decaying fruit (plums especially) or birch tree sap, in the same way.

The flower of *Sedum spectabile*, the ice plant, is flat but similar to the buddleia in that it is composed of numerous small tubes. Both are pink, deepening with age, as does the red clover which is also visited by butterflies and bees and which opens pale pink, becoming reddish-pink after fertilization and as it ages. The red clover has the same honey-like scent with musky undertones as the buddleia and *Sedum spectabile*. It would appear that butterflies mostly visit flowers of pink (or pale mauve) colouring in their search for nectar. I have on many occasions observed that they will always alight on a pink dianthus in preference to a dianthus of another colour, if the blooms are in a similar state of freshness; they will visit red or white dianthus if the pink ones have been removed or have faded. In the same way I have noticed that butterflies will prefer the flower spikes of pink lavender rather than the blue, though they will spend considerable time on the blue if the spikes of the pink variety have faded or have been removed. As with the buddleia, the dianthus flower-spikes consist of a number of narrow tubes, the bottom of which the proboscis of the butterfly can easily reach. It should be noted that the blooms of the common honeysuckle, *Lonicera periclymenum* of the hedgerows, which are scented by day and by night, are tinted with pink when viewed from above, whereas *L. caprifolium* of Southern Europe, which is scented only at night to attract night-flying lepidoptera, is coloured white and yellow. It has a tube almost $1\frac{1}{4}$ in. (3 cm.) in length so its honey is available only to those moths with a proboscis of similar length, which abound in Southern Europe. In comparison, *L. periclymenum* has a tube of only $\frac{3}{4}$ in. (2 cm.) in length, so is adapted for pollination by butterflies as well as by moths, and the flowers open by day to accommodate them.

Not all the species will visit honey-scented flowers, for the Speckled Wood frequents bramble blossom for its main source of nectar, and in spring and early summer the Small Copper may be seen on forget-me-nots, the Small Tortoise-shell on coltsfoot flowers.

CATERPILLAR FOOD PLANTS ON WHICH BUTTERFLIES LAY THEIR EGGS

Species	Plant
Satyridae	
Speckled Wood	Cocksfoot; Couch grass
Wall Brown	Annual meadow grass
Mountain Ringlet	Mat grass
Scotch Argus	Blue moor grass

Species	*Plant*
Satyridae—cont.	
Marbled White	Cat's-tail; Sheep's fescue
Grayling	Tufted hair grass; Rat's-tail
Hedge Brown	All grasses
Meadow Brown	Meadow grass
Small Heath	Annual meadow grass
Large Heath	White beak-sedge
Ringlet	Cocksfoot
Nymphalidae	
Small Pearl-bordered Fritillary	Dog violet
(Large) Pearl-bordered Fritillary	Violet; Pansy
Dark Green Fritillary	Dog violet; Sweet violet
High Brown Fritillary	Dog violet; Sweet violet
Silver-washed Fritillary	Sweet violet
Marsh Fritillary	Devil's-bit scabious
Glanville Fritillary	Ribwort plantain
Heath Fritillary	Cow-wheat
Red Admiral	Stinging nettle
Painted Lady	Spear thistle
Small Tortoise-shell	Stinging nettle
Large Tortoise-shell	Common Elm; Whitebeam
Peacock	Stinging nettle
Camberwell Beauty	Willow (*Salix fragilis*)
Comma	Stinging nettle; Hop vine
Purple Emperor	Willow (*Salix caprea*)
White Admiral	Honeysuckle
Riodimidae	
Duke of Burgundy Fritillary	Cowslip
Lycaenidae	
Short-tailed Blue	Bird's-foot trefoil; Gorse
Long-tailed Blue	Tree lupin; Perennial pea; Common vetch; Gorse
Small Blue	Kidney vetch
Silver-studded Blue	Gorse; Heather

Species	Plant
Lycaenidae—cont.	
Brown Argus	Common rock rose
Common Blue	Bird's-foot trefoil; Rest harrow
Chalk-hill Blue	Horseshoe vetch
Adonis Blue	Horseshoe vetch
Holly Blue	Holly; Ivy
Large Blue	Wild thyme
Small Copper	Common sorrel; Dock
Large Copper	Great water dock
Green Hairstreak	Broom; Gorse; Rock rose
Brown Hairstreak	Blackthorn
Purple Hairstreak	Oak shoots
White-letter Hairstreak	Common and Wych elm
Black Hairstreak	Blackthorn
Papilionidae	
Swallow-tail	Hog's fennel (milk parsley)
Pieridae	
Black-veined White	Hawthorn; Blackthorn
Large White	Brassicas
Small White	Water cress and other *Cruciferae*
Green-veined White	Horseradish; Cuckoo flower
Bath White	Wild mignonette; Hedge mustard
Orange Tip	Lady's Smock; Dame's Violet
Pale Clouded Yellow	Lucerne
Berger's Clouded Yellow	Horseshoe vetch
Clouded Yellow	Red clover
Brimstone	Buckthorn species
Wood White	Tufted vetch; Yellow pea
Hesperidae	
Dingy Skipper	Bird's-foot trefoil
Grizzled Skipper	Wild strawberry
Chequered Skipper	Slender false-brome grass; Ground ivy
Small Skipper	Slender false-brome grass
Large Skipper	Yorkshire fog grass
Essex Skipper	Yorkshire fog grass
Lulworth Skipper	Slender false-brome grass
Silver-spotted Skipper	Bird's-foot trefoil

A separate small butterfly garden, in addition to or in place of a wild garden, will attract many species, and there their beauty and habits can be observed near to. Those species which will be drawn to the garden will depend upon its site and its location. A warm, sheltered garden will attract many more butterflies than a garden that is exposed to cold winds. The main areas for butterflies are East Anglia (which is still relatively untouched by industrial pollution and petrol fumes), and that part of the east Midlands covering the counties of Cambridgeshire and Northamptonshire and extending south to Oxfordshire and Berkshire. The chalk and limestone areas of southern England from Kent to Dorset are also a part of our islands where the butterfly count is still high; here will be found many of the migrating species discussed earlier in this chapter, amongst them the Queen of Spain Fritillary, Red Admiral, Painted Lady, Long-tailed Blue, Bath White and Clouded Yellow. Apart from the Red Admiral, which is common everywhere, it is only rarely that these species move further north than the south Midlands, for example, Northamptonshire Cambridgeshire, and Bedfordshire.

The Red Admiral's favourite flower is the buddleia, to be found in parks and private gardens everywhere, whilst it has become naturalized on railway embankments and elsewhere about our towns. The buddleia will also be visited by the Small Tortoise-shell (widespread throughout Britain), and the Comma in the west Midlands. The Brimstone and Peacock are also attracted to this plant. The less common species, *Buddleia alternifolia*, is a graceful shrub growing 5–6 ft. (1·5–1·8 m.) tall with silvery-grey willow-like foliage and bearing, in June, lavender-pink, honey-scented flowers in small groups. It is valuable in that it comes into bloom well before varieties of *B. davidii*, the familiar plant of old walls and seaside gardens, which blooms from mid-July until late September and bears its long elegant spikes of lavender-pink at the end of cane-like stems which grow up to 8 ft. (2·4 m.) high. Also loved by butterflies is the variety 'Empire Blue' which forms a large spike of soft powder blue, but 'Black Knight' should be planted as a companion too, for the Red Admiral is most striking when seen against the dark purple flowers in the late summer sunlight. 'White Profusion', though forming a more slender spike, is attractive to butterflies.

The buddleias will grow anywhere in full sun, being amongst the easiest of all shrubs, happy in poor soil and in the salt-laden breezes of a coastal garden. To prune, cut them well back early in spring when they will quickly come into new growth. Hard pruning will prevent the plants becoming a mass of woody stems with little foliage and few flowers.

Lilacs are frequently visited by butterflies, which are particularly attracted to the single pink variety 'Esther Staley'. The single-flowered Canadian hybrids, obtained by crossing the common lilac with *Syringa* × *prestoniae*, which bloom in June and July will also be visited by butterflies. The blooms have long thin tubes and the flowers are borne in small groups rather than in large trusses, being very different in appearance from the ordinary lilacs. Hermann Müller reported having seen the Swallow-tail (*Papilio machaon*) on lilacs on numerous occasions but I have never seen this. The Red Admiral, however, is a regular visitor to lilacs which are in bloom shortly after its arrival in England, and all the 'Whites' are to be seen on the flowers which secrete quite large amounts of honey.

The purple loosestrife, *Lythrum salicaria*, is visited by the 'Whites' and in the wild I have seen the long pink flower-spikes visited by the Swallow-tail. It makes a bushy plant 2–3 ft. (61–91 cm.) high, bears numerous upright flower-spikes during August, and has willow-like leaves. For the garden, 'Brightness' bears flowers of deeper pink whilst those of 'Robert' are a soft rose-pink. They like ordinary soil and are hardy. Plant any time between early November and early March, 3 ft. (91 cm.) apart.

Hyssop and marjoram are other plants which butterflies take

a delight in visiting. Hyssop is a native of Central and Southern Europe and has been growing in English gardens since Tudor times. It has become naturalized on the ancient walls of monastic buildings, as at Beaulieu Abbey, and was so often mentioned in the Bible that it was known as the Holy Herb. Michael Drayton, a contemporary of Shakespeare, wrote 'Hyssop is a herb most prime'. Plant hyssop in a well-drained soil 3 ft. (91 cm.) apart, for it grows 2 ft. (61 cm.) tall and bushy. In late summer its pink or blue flowers will be continually visited by many species of butterfly which will usually prefer the pink. Marjoram is a native plant growing only 12 in. (30 cm.) tall and is for the front of a border. The flowers appear in July and August, in a crowded terminal cyme, and are rosy-pink with reddish bracts. The sweet marjoram, a tender perennial of Southern Europe, is more sweet and aromatic and was used, as John Parkinson tells us in the *Paradisus* (1629) 'to put in ladies' nosegays'. It is also the 'knotted' marjoram, used to edge the flower-beds of Tudor knot gardens, together with hyssop and the upright thymes. It should always be included when a herb garden is planted.

As an alternative, pink, white or blue flowering lavender may be used for it will stand gentle clipping which is done in spring. In any case, the pink and white lavenders will not exceed 15 in. (38 cm.) in height. The flower-spikes which appear in June and persist until October (if not cut and dried) are a favourite source of nectar for butterflies. To make a low edge for a small border or herb garden, plant in April, 15 in. (38 cm.) apart.

Pinks of all types associate admirably with other butterfly flowers, especially with hyssop, marjoram and lavender. They may be planted in pockets of soil containing some lime rubble, and between paving stones or to the front of a border. The pink and cerise varieties seem to attract the most butterflies and it is the single varieties which produce nectar. Amongst these is the old Irish pink (deep cerise with white lacing);

'Inchmery' (shell-pink); 'Houston House' (salmon-pink) and 'Solomon'. All bear single blooms.

Pinks require a position of full sun and a well-drained soil containing some lime. Plant preferably from pots so that there will be the minimum of root disturbance. April is the best planting time and for continuity of bloom through summer, remove the dead flowers as they form.

Dianthus deltoides is a pink visited by butterflies. It makes a spreading plant and is for planting between paving stones. The honey is formed at the base of the stamens and ovary and is blocked from the short-tongued insects by the five inner anthers, so that it is accessible only to the long proboscis of lepidoptera. The flowers are rose-pink and the stamens and their anthers, coated with pollen, protrude beyond the narrow tube so that when inserting its proboscis, the butterfly must dust its head with pollen which it transfers to other flowers.

The leguminous plants should be in every shrub border, not only for the brilliance of their golden blooms, particularly welcome in spring and early summer, but to provide food for several of our loveliest small butterflies.

There must be many corners about the garden where seed of the common forget-me-not, *Myosotis arvensis*, can be sown in early summer to bloom the following year. The Small Copper and others early on the wing will visit the bright blue flowers which have a brilliant yellow eye at the centre, the nectar being available, somewhat surprisingly, only to those insects having a long proboscis. The Small Copper will also visit the fleabane with its bright yellow flowers in late summer. The forget-me-not blooms in spring, at the same time as the coltsfoot whose bright golden flowers are much visited by the Small Tortoise-shell after coming out of its winter hibernation. This plant can become an obnoxious weed in the garden and should be confined to an out-of-the-way corner, but one in full sun where it can be left to take care of itself.

The red clover of the meadows is a favourite butterfly flower but is not often sown in the garden; neither is bird's-foot trefoil, another plant of the meadows which bears yellow flowers rich in honey that are visited by the Common Blue butterfly.

The annual of field scabious too, a flower visited by a greater variety of insects for its readily accessible nectar than perhaps any other, will also be visited by butterflies. The Pale Clouded Yellow, the Brimstone, the Red Admiral and Painted Lady, will be frequent visitors. *Scabiosa atropurpurea* is the best form for the garden, seed being sown in April where it is to bloom. It will grow 3 ft. (91 cm.) tall.

The hemp agrimony is another wild flower for the border. It is perennial, growing 3–4 ft. (91 cm.–1·2 m.) high with pungently scented palmate leaves, bearing its flowers in trusses, like the valerian. It has pinkish disc florets and reddish bracts and it grows well in damp places such as by the side of damp woodlands, blooming from July until September. Müller reported having seen many butterfly species 'Sucking the flowers . . . taking no heed of neighbouring flowers'. Amongst ten species he saw on the flowers were the Purple Hairstreak, Small Copper, Silver-washed Fritillary and Silver-spotted Skipper.

The ragged robin, *Lychnis flos-cuculi*, preferably the semi-double form which bears pinkish-red flowers, will be visited by butterflies. The calyx tube is ⅓ in. (0·9 cm.) long and the honey is only available to those butterflies which are strong enough to push open the 'claws' of the petals. Müller reported having seen the stamens dusted with butterflies' scales.

Lychnis flos-jovis, also perennial, is another attractive plant for any wild garden visited by butterflies. It grows 2 ft. (61 cm.) tall and has woolly grey-green foliage, whilst early in summer it bears bright pink flowers. These two forms of the lychnis require a moist soil and are admirable plants both for a wild garden and for the border. Seed is obtainable from Thompson

& Morgan Ltd. of Ipswich who stock seed of many butterfly plants to grow in the wild garden.

Probably the best source of nectar for butterflies is *Centranthus ruber*, the garden valerian, a perennial which grows on cliffs and old walls. Chaucer called it Setwall and it is to this day to be found growing on the walls of the ancient home of the Greyfriars at Canterbury, which Chaucer would have known. The plant grows 2 ft. (61 cm.) tall and is extremely hardy. In bloom from May until September, the pinkish-crimson flowers, borne in large corymbs, have a long narrow corolla which makes their nectar accessible only to butterflies. The flower tubes are twice as long as those of *Valeriana officinalis*, with its pinkish-red flowers, present in woods and on grassy banks everywhere which are much visited by honey-bees.

Both plants are readily raised from seed sown in spring when they will come into bloom the following year. When established, the plants with their long woody roots are almost indestructible.

The annual cornflower may be grown in the border from seed sown in April and in the southern counties the flowers will be visited by the Pale Clouded Yellow when it has crossed over from France early in July.

The sweet rocket, *Hesperis matronalis*, also known as Dame's Violet, is a plant visited by butterflies. Here again, its flowers are usually pale pinkish-mauve, though there are white- and violet-coloured forms. Large amounts of nectar, which is obtained by bees and lepidoptera, are secreted from two fleshy glands at the base of the shorter stamens.

Perhaps at the back and sides of the butterfly garden will be trellis to enclose it, providing shelter from wind. It may be covered with the various species of honeysuckle, some to attract night moths, and with *Lonicera periclymenum* for the butterflies.

The plants mentioned here may be used with those shrubs

recommended for birds to nest in, planted in a border or garden within a garden, to attract as many butterflies and birds as possible.

Nor should the bramble be omitted from the garden. Grow it against a trellis or to the back of a border of butterfly flowers, for it is the chief source of nectar for the late summer butter-flies such as the Hedge Brown and Ringlet, and many others will spend hours on the open blossoms from early July until the autumn.

Other late-flowering plants are the golden rod and Michael-mas daisy, those bearing single (or semi-double) flowers pro-ducing nectar in large quantities. Many of these butterfly plants, which will bloom throughout the summer and autumn, will also be much visited by bees.

GARDEN FLOWERS MUCH VISITED BY BUTTERFLIES FOR NECTAR

Plant	Common Name	In Bloom
Aster novi-belgii	Michaelmas daisy	Aug.–Nov.
Buddleia alternifolia	Butterfly bush	June
Buddleia davidii and varieties	Butterfly bush	July–Sept.
Centaurea cyanus	Cornflower	July–Aug.
Dianthus deltoides	Cushion pink	June–Aug.
Dianthus (in variety)	Pink	June–Aug.
Eupatorium cannabinum	Hemp agrimony	July–Sept.
Hesperis matronalis	Sweet rocket	July–Aug.
Hyssopus officinalis	Hyssop	July–Aug.
Lavandula spica	Lavender	June–Oct.
Syringa hybrids	Canadian hybrid lilacs	June–July
Lotus corniculatus	Bird's-foot trefoil	June–Aug.
Lychnis flos-cuculi	Ragged robin	May–July
Lychnis flos-jovis	Jove's flower	June–July
Lythrum salicaria	Purple loosestrife	August
Myosotis alpestris	Alpine forget-me-not	July–Aug.
Myosotis arvensis	Common forget-me-not	April–June
Organum vulgare	Marjoram	July–Sept.

Plant	Common Name	In Bloom
Rubus fruticosus	Bramble	July–Sept.
Sedum spectabile	Ice plant	Aug.–Oct.
Silene acaulis	Moss campion	June–Aug.
Solidago officinalis	Golden rod	July–Sept.
Tussilago farfara	Coltsfoot	March–May
Viola odorata	Sweet violet	April–June

CHIEF SOURCES OF FOOD FOR BUTTERFLIES IN THE WILD

Adonis Blue	Horseshoe vetch
Bath White	Wild mignonette
Black Hairstreak	Blackthorn blossom
Brimstone	Buckthorn
Brown Hairstreak	Blackthorn blossom
Camberwell Beauty	Decayed fruit and birch tree sap
Chequered Skipper	Ground ivy
Clouded Yellow	Pink clover; Bird's-foot trefoil
Green Hairstreak	Gorse blossom
Green-veined White	Cruciferous flowers
Hedge Brown	Bramble blossom
Holly Blue	Flowers of holly and ivy
Large White	Cruciferous flowers
Long-tailed Blue	Tree lupin (naturalized)
Orange Tip	Lady's Smock; Dame's Violet (single forms)
Pale Clouded Yellow	Lucerne
Purple Hairstreak	Hemp agrimony
Red Admiral	Fruit juices
Ringlet	Bramble blossom
Small Blue	Kidney vetch
Small Copper	Hemp agrimony; Fleabane
Small Tortoise-shell	Coltsfoot
Small White	Cruciferous flowers
Speckled Wood	Bramble blossom
White Admiral	Bramble blossom; Honeysuckle
White-letter Hairstreak	Privet blossom
Wood White	Tufted vetch; Yellow pea

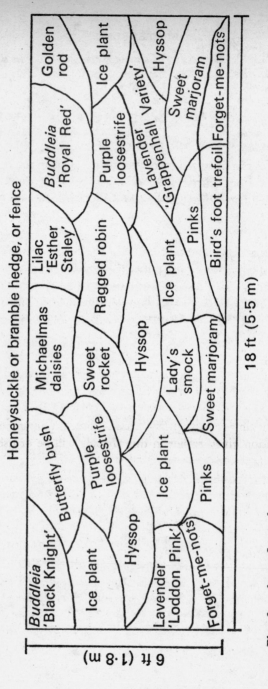

Honeysuckle or bramble hedge, or fence

Buddleia 'Black Knight'	*Buddleia* 'Royal Red'
Butterfly bush	Lilac 'Esther Staley'	Golden rod
Ice plant	Michaelmas daisies	Ice plant
Purple loosestrife	Sweet rocket	Ragged robin	Purple loosestrife
Hyssop	Hyssop	Lavender 'Grappenhall Variety'	Hyssop
Ice plant	Lady's smock	Ice plant	Sweet marjoram
Lavender 'Loddon Pink'		Pinks	
Pinks	Sweet marjoram	Bird's foot trefoil	Forget-me-nots
Forget-me-nots			

6 ft (1·8 m)

18 ft (5·5 m)

20. Plan for a butterfly garden

III. BREEDING BUTTERFLIES

Butterflies can be raised by collecting the eggs in the open and rearing the butterflies indoors, in a frost-proof shed or attic room. All that is needed is a rearing-box with muslin fixed to the sides instead of wood. The box should have a wooden base and lid and suitably strong upright pieces of $\frac{1}{2}$ in. (1·3 cm.) square timber at the four corners. To these, muslin is fastened all round by means of drawing pins. Children use a cardboard box with pieces of the sides cut away and with muslin pasted over them, and this serves admirably, though a wooden box is more durable.

Searching for eggs is not difficult if one understands where and when the butterflies can be found in their natural habitat. It is no use, for example, expecting to find the Clouded Yellow in Yorkshire for it rarely moves away from the south of England and the Home Counties. And whilst the Orange Tip is present almost throughout Britain it breeds only in May. The information given earlier in this chapter will be of use in the search for butterflies and their eggs. Some butterflies make only a fleeting appearance each year, being with us for a few weeks, and if the weather is cold, as it so often is in May, we can expect to catch but a quick glimpse of them.

One must take careful note of the plants on which the eggs are seen, for this will be the diet of the caterpillars and must be provided in the garden. Some species lay in large numbers, the Small Tortoise-shell being one, the Red Admiral another, so many will be reared together. Those which lay singly, often widely spaced apart, will be more difficult to collect and will be reared separately. Nature always has a purpose and the eggs will have been laid far apart to prevent the young caterpillars from eating each other. Caterpillars of the Orange Tip are cannibalistic, possibly because they have enormous appetites and need food in large amounts.

If one is familiar with Latin, the name of the species will often help one to decide where to find the eggs and the food to provide for the caterpillars. Butterflies and plants both follow the binominal classification introduced by the Swedish botanist Carl Linnaeus in 1735. The first name indicates the genus, the second the species. Thus *Aglaia urticae* is the Small Tortoise-shell; *urticae* is from Latin *urtica*, the stinging nettle, thus showing where the female lays her eggs. The Orange Tip is *Anthocharis cardamines* and one who knows about plants would expect her to lay her eggs on the Lady's Smock, *Cardamine pratensis*, so called because in olden times the plant's juice was thought to be able to strengthen the heart, and deriving from the Latin *cardiacus*.

If a butterfly lays on one member of a plant family, it will usually do so on another and in the case of the Orange Tip it will also lay on charlock (*Sinapis arvensis*), Dame's Violet or sweet rocket (*Hesperis matronalis*) and honesty (*Lunaria annua*), the latter taking its generic name from Latin *luna*, the moon, because of its large round transparent seed-capsules. The idea behind Linnaeus' nomenclature was not only to give each species an appropriate and definite name but was also so that this name, in Latin, would assist in the plant's recognition and be known throughout the world, whatever the spoken language of a country.

The eggs of butterflies are an interesting study in themselves for they are all different in shape and colour though this is not clear to see unless observed through a microscope. Those laid by the Black-veined White (also the Large White) are shaped like a cob of sweet corn, being long and cylindrical with grooves running from top to bottom, and are yellow. The Orange Tip, of the same family, lays an egg of similar shape. Those of the skippers are shaped like a sea-urchin, are also grooved, and are pale green. The eggs of the Red Admiral are longer, with more prominent ribs, and are also pale green. The egg of the Marbled White is shaped like a Grecian jar, and is free from grooves or other markings. Those of the Small Copper are flattened and marbled with white, the markings resembling a python's skin.

First find out where the species are likely to be found, for example, the Small Copper on dry heaths and sandy wastelands, throughout most of Britain; when they begin to lay, in this case early May; and on which plants—the Small Copper, for instance, lays on sorrel and dock leaves.

At the top of each egg is a tiny opening and it is here that the egg is fertilized by the male, and through this opening that oxygen reaches the unborn caterpillar. Usually, the eggs of the larger species are larger than those of the smaller species and in artificial warmth or during the height of summer will take only 7–10 days to hatch. Some hibernating species will, however, continue to lay until September when the eggs will remain dormant through winter, the caterpillars hatching in the first warm days of spring. Others may hatch in autumn when the larvae will hibernate during winter.

After hatching, the caterpillars will require large quantities of food which will be the same as that on which the eggs were found. When they have reached full size, they stop eating and will attach themselves to a twig (which must be provided) around which they will spin a girdle of silk so that it is held in an upright or horizontal position. Then, after another day or so, the skin begins to split behind the head and the chrysalis emerges. The chrysalis cannot move and may remain in position for some weeks, even months, until the butterfly has formed from the organs of the caterpillar, during what is known as pupation.

Emergence from the chrysalis may take an hour or more, the larger species taking longer, the very small ones rather less. At all stages, from the gathering of the eggs onwards, slightly moist conditions must prevail, otherwise the chrysalis will tend to shrivel, the butterfly will have difficulty in emerging and may be damaged in doing so. Line the box with moss which is kept slightly damp.

The colour of the wings and their markings are the last to form and can be seen through the shell of the chrysalis, just before the butterfly is ready to emerge. At this moment, the chrysalis splits from the head and the butterfly emerges. At first the wings hang limp until they dry and the insect pumps liquid into them, like inflating a balloon. The butterfly is then ready to fly, to feed and drink on nectar or decaying fruit. Those raised artificially can be released to the butterfly garden on a calm, sunny day and there they may remain long enough to suck nectar from the open flowers which they find to their liking.

One of the easiest species to manage is the Red Admiral and if a clutch of eggs is removed on a nettle leaf in May (when the first eggs are laid), the butterflies will be ready to release before the end of July when the much-visited buddleia and, later, *Sedum spectabile* will be in bloom.

There are firms who provide a valuable service for butterfly lovers in that at the appropriate time, May, June or early July, they will send the pupae shortly before they are due to emerge as butterflies. Prices of pupae range, at the time of writing this, from £2 for the Tortoise-shell to £5 for the Comma, and for these sums they will send you ten pupae. It is, of course, necessary to have the correct food in the garden for the butterflies to feed upon, so first make sure that one or more of the appropriate plants already mentioned are available.

As they emerge, the butterflies may be placed in the portable sun-cage as supplied by the Habitat Company. The cage is placed over a clump of valerian or *Sedum spectabile* and the butterflies can be studied near to as they feed upon nectar. Every two days or so the cage is moved to a fresh clump of flowers and it will be noticed that the butterflies will tend to stay about the garden when they are released from the cage. Like birds, they remain where they know there is a good supply of food.

They may be bred in the cages if a few pots of nettles are placed inside, for the Comma, Peacock, Tortoise-shell and Red Admiral lay their eggs on nettles and this is the food the caterpillars will feed upon. Each of these butterflies will produce two batches of eggs, the second in August when those from this batch will hibernate during winter in old buildings, to emerge again in the spring.

❋ 5. Moths and the night-scented flowers ❋

In the British Isles there are at least 2,000 species of moth. Of the order *Lepidoptera*, 97 per cent are moths, the remainder being butterflies.

With moths it is usually the female that is scented, attracting the male from considerable distances, though with the Ghost Swift moth (*Hepialus humili*) it is the male that releases a scent when in flight. After mating, the female will lay up to 300 eggs, dropping them as she flies. They hatch in about fourteen days, the caterpillars burrowing into the ground where they remain over winter to pupate in spring. This moth is a favourite food of the swift and the swallow which take it on the wing in the twilight of a summer evening. Moths range from the tiny micro-moths like the Green Oak moth and the Clothes moth which has a wing span of less than ½ in. (1·3 cm.) and will damage carpets and clothes considerably if allowed to remain for long in contact with them, to the giant hawk-moths of which the Elephant and Convolvulus moths are larger than any other of our lepidoptera. Another large species is the Puss moth (*Phalera bucephela*), one of the so-called 'prominents', night-flying moths which have a tuft of scales that prominently project from the inside edge of their fore wings. Closely related is the interesting Tussock moth, which is covered in hairs in all stages of its life-cycle, also the Tiger moth. The caterpillars too are covered in bristle-like hairs which can cause skin irritation when handled: this is part of the defensive system and birds shun them after the first bite. Their eggs are protected in the same way. Of the Vapourer moth (*Orgyia antiqua*) it is said that the males can detect with their antennae the presence of a female at more than a mile away by her scent. They then fly to her for mating, as the females are unable to fly.

The Noctuids are also night-flying and are the moths most attracted to lamps and lighted windows. They are, however, equally attracted to white or pale yellow flowers from which they obtain their nectar. Perhaps the Large Yellow Underwing is the most handsome of the Noctuids, its deep golden-brown hind wings having wide black bands around the outer edges.

Also night-flying is the Leopard moth (*Leuzera pyrina*) with long white wings speckled with black. It mostly confines its activities to south-east England. The Mother-of-Pearl moth, which is night-flying, deposits its eggs on nettles on which it hides by day.

Some moths are active by day. The Burnet moths, of which there are seven species, are day-flying and deposit their eggs on vetch and bird's-foot trefoil. The caterpillars take up prussic acid from these plants and this is passed on to the moth itself, making it poisonous to all its predators. These brightly coloured moths feed and live in colonies and are attracted to the garden by their host plants. Day-flying moths may be noticed when they are resting for, unlike butterflies, they have their wings spread open. Those which are nocturnal are of dull colouring, being white or pale yellow, green or brown, and with bodies much larger in proportion to the wings than the butterflies. There are, however, exceptions, one of which is the beautiful Emerald moth which closely resembles a butterfly with its long thin body and broad hind wings. It is nocturnal and common in England but not in Scotland.

Moths follow the same life-cycle as butterflies. Some are migrating species, as, for instance, the Humming-bird hawk-moths which come from Southern Europe in June and may have covered a hundred miles in a single day. They mostly confine themselves to the south of England and the south Midlands, like most of our migrating butterflies, but in a warm summer they will be seen in the north Midlands. They feed and mate during daylight hours, as does the Bee hawk-moth which so much resembles the bumble-bee that it is difficult to tell them apart. The Humming-bird may be encouraged into parks and gardens by planting petunias, dwarf convolvulus, and other plants whose flowers secrete nectar at the end of a very long tube, for the tongue of the hawk-moth is longer than that of any other. The tongue of the Convolvulus hawk-moth is more than 3⅛ in. (8 cm.) long, whilst its body is more than 5 in. (13 cm.) long.

Many of the hawk-moths are, however, nocturnal. They hatch during June, July and August when most of the night-scented plants are at their best. Each confines its egg laying to a separate plant, the Poplar hawk-moth depositing its eggs on poplar leaves, the Privet hawk-moth, which is mostly confined to southern England, on the privet and lilac, and the Elephant on the willow herb. The caterpillars feed upon the plants on which the eggs are laid during summer and at the approach of winter they burrow into the soil beneath the plants, pupating there early the following summer.

Flowers which attract moths

Moths resemble butterflies in that they lay their eggs on plants other than those they visit in search of nectar. Apart from midges and certain insects which move into flowers for warmth and protection at night, moths are the only insects which visit flowers during darkness, when they have no competition from other insects. They will visit the flowers in swift movements, visiting as many as possible in the shortest time. Certain flowers have adapted themselves to this activity by their conspicuousness in twilight and darkness, also by their time of opening and by their scent. Several of those which open only at night do so when released by a special mechanism which works in the coolness of evening and which prevents the flower from opening by day. The scent is retained in concentrated form in the closed bud by day and is thus more powerful when released at night. The evening primrose, *Oenothera biennis*, is prevented from opening its clear yellow flowers during the day by the hooks of the tapering sepals which clasp each other so that the bloom cannot open. As twilight descends and the air becomes cooler, the flower is seen to discard its protective hood and to open in all its fragrant loveliness. When the air is still, the scent is noticeable from a distance.

> *You, Evening primroses, when day has fled,*
> *Open your pallid flowers, by dews and moonlight fed.*

As with most other flowers which have adapted themselves to visiting lepidoptera, the nectar is secreted in long tubes which, in most cases, put it out of reach from all other insects. The evening primrose is a biennial and seed is sown in June for the plants to bloom during the summer of the following year. If the soil around the plants is left undisturbed, they will seed themselves to provide plants for future years.

There are other rewarding *Oenothera* such as *O. drummondii*, the Texas primrose, a biennial which grows less than 2 ft. (61 cm.) tall; it has attractive grey leaves and from June until September bears pale yellow flowers which open and are fragrant only at night. *O. caespitosa* is a perennial growing 12–15 in. (30–38 cm.) tall, its large single chalices of purest white having long slender calyx tubes, and at night diffusing the scent of tuberose. Two annual species are *O. triloba* and *O. tetraptera*, the latter being a native of Mexico and in Britain only half-hardy. It grows 9–10 in. (23–25 cm.) tall and bears large white flowers tinted with pink. At dusk they open and diffuse a more powerful scent than any other species, only to die as the sun begins to rise, others taking their place. *O. triloba* grows only 6 in. (15 cm.) tall and seed should be sown at the front of the border in April where the plants are to bloom, as it does not like transplanting. Its cups of pale yellow open in the evening and emit a rich penetrating scent.

Between these two lovely annuals, scatter in the soil in

groups or in small circles, seed of *Matthiola bicornis*, the night-scented stock; if sown early in spring, it will be in bloom by early June. Its tiny, dingy-looking flowers emit a surprising amount of perfume as darkness descends. It is a hardy annual growing 10 in. (25 cm.) tall and if there is no room in the garden to plant a border of scented flowers, sow seed in small beds beneath a bedroom window, especially if you live in a bungalow, and sleep with the window open: on a warm night the perfume will fill a large room. There is no need to stoop to inhale the perfume for this is noticeable from several yards' distance.

The night-scented honeysuckle, *Lonicera caprifolium*, has a tube so long that its honey is available only to those lepidoptera with a proboscis more than $1\frac{1}{4}$ in. (3 cm.) long—the Night hawk-moths come into this category. Such flowers usually have a mechanism that ensures their self-pollination should cold wet weather prevent moths from visiting them and they are of white or pale yellow colouring which makes them conspicuous in the dark. They are usually sweetly scented and the moths are drawn to them as much by their scent as by their colour. The honey-scented flowers which open by day are usually pink or pale mauve and attract butterflies.

Lonicera caprifolium and *L. periclymenum* are the most vigorous and free-flowering of the night-scented honeysuckles and the latter will also be visited by butterflies by day. *L. caprifolium* will be in bloom until the beginning of November when the earlier bloom will have given way to pale amber-coloured berries which the birds will enjoy: *L. periclymenum* has scarlet fruits.

Another lovely honeysuckle with deep yellow flowers, deliciously scented in the evening, is *L. etrusca* 'Superba', one of the most vigorous, which will climb to a height of 15 ft. (4·6 m.) or more in two to three years. Nor should the smaller flowering semi-evergreen species be omitted: these are forms of *L. japonica*, of which *halliana* bears creamy-white flowers, turning to yellow, during late summer and early autumn, which are much visited by hawk-moths in the warm evenings when the scent is most pronounced. In my garden it grows as vigorously as the Russian vine.

The new everlasting or perennial pea, *Lathyrus* 'White Pearl', raised from a crossing of *L. latifolius* with a white sweet pea, is delightfully scented in the evening. Easily raised from seed, which should be chipped before sowing, it is extremely hardy and will quickly cover a trellis 6–7 ft. (1·8–2·1 m.) tall.

Jasminum officinale, the white summer-flowering species, is equally vigorous, its tubular flowers most striking against the small dark green leaves, diffusing a sweet perfume at night and attracting numerous moths. It is, however, suitable only for a sheltered garden, for it may be cut back by cold winds. Birds will nest in spring in its dense twiggy growth, unseen by those who pass close by. The perfume the flowers emit after dusk is almost overpowering when the air is calm.

Grow a few tobacco plants, for their fragrance at night is pronounced. *Nicotiana affinis* is a half-hardy annual which will grow up to 4 ft. (1·2 m.) tall and is planted to the back of a border or bed. Its white trumpet-like blooms open star-shaped when twilight descends and as their fragrance is rich and spicy moths come to them in a continuous stream. The plants are given the usual half-hardy treatment, raised in gentle heat in March and planted out in May, after hardening. Plant them 15 in. (38 cm.) apart: the leaves are large and handsome in the border as a foil for brighter-coloured flowers. *N. sylvestris*, a woodland species, has even larger leaves and may be planted in a wild garden where it will often reach a height of 6 ft. (1·8 m.). The large creamy-white tubular flowers are borne in candelabra fashion and give out a lovely perfume. A new cultivar is 'Daylight', so called because its blooms, larger than those of *N. affinis*, remain open both by day and by night though, as is to be expected, the scent is not so pronounced after dark. A half-hardy annual, it grows 3–4 ft. (91 cm.–1·2 m.) tall, but for the front of the border there is a dwarf counterpart which grows to only 15 in. (38 cm.): it is an excellent bedding plant as it blooms from June until September.

Today few seed catalogues list that lovely old cottage garden perennial, *Hesperis matronalis*, the sweet rocket, which William Robinson, the Victorian gardener and writer, thought to be 'amongst the most desirable of garden flowers'. It is raised from seed sown in April or propagated by cuttings, removed in July and rooted in a sandy compost. Like most of the night-scented plants, it does well in partial shade and likes a moist, humus-laden soil. The plants grow 2–3 ft. (61–91 cm.) tall and the flowers which at night diffuse their delicious scent about the garden, are either mauve or white. Perhaps it has tended to become less well known by reason of its being difficult to keep unless divided each year or cuttings taken to maintain its vigour.

Hesperis tristis, the sand rocket, is also fragrant at night. It grows 18 in. (46 cm.) tall, being branched at the top with the leaves covered in hairs. The flowers are of dirty cream or purple-brown colouring and are as heavily scented as violets. By the close proximity of the sepals and claws of the petals, all insects, except night-flowering lepidoptera, are excluded from the honey.

With *Lychnis vespertina*, the night-scented campion, so deep is the nectar secreted that it requires an insect with a proboscis of $\frac{3}{4}$ in. (2 cm.) to reach it. The pure white flowers, free from any guiding lines, though open on dull days, emit no perfume until nightfall when the flowers, with their heavy and clove-like scent, are visited by moths of the same family as visit the dianthus.

The sand verbenas, the abronias, are not common plants. Being native of California they are, except in those warm gardens of the south-west, best treated as half-hardy annuals, though they really are perennial. They are readily raised from seed (first soaked in warm water) and should be sown in gentle heat in February, to be planted out after hardening. They will come into bloom in July. Or they may be propagated from cuttings, taken in spring and rooted in a sandy compost. *Abronia fragrans* is an erect plant of branching habit which will grow 2 ft. (61 cm.) in height and in July and August bears its pure white flowers in terminal clusters. They open only in the cool of evening, diffusing a vanilla-like perfume which attracts the moths. The true sand verbena is *A. latifolia*, a plant of trailing habit which should be allowed to ramble over paving stones. It has attractive kidney-shaped leaves and bears yellow flowers in dense clusters, which at nightfall diffuse the perfume of honeysuckle. They, too, are visited by moths.

It is not generally realized that *Myosotis alpestris*, the alpine forget-me-not, is scented after dark. Hermann Müller has told that on one occasion he counted thirty-three lepidoptera visiting the flowers in the space of a short time, but he does not record whether by day or by night. It must be one of the few blue flowers to be visited by lepidoptera, by night moths especially, for only after dusk do the brilliant blue flowers become fragrant. It is a native plant, to be found about rocky ground in the north of England, at quite high altitudes where it forms a tiny tuft 3 in. (7·5 cm.) high. It is perennial in a gritty, well-drained soil and is readily raised from seed.

Myosotis macrantha, native of New Zealand, is another distinctive species which may be raised from seed sown in spring. It grows 18 in. (46 cm.) tall and bears large funnel-shaped flowers of palest yellow which, with their evening fragrance, draw the night moths.

In a small garden, where their rich perfume can be enjoyed to the full, the old-fashioned summer-flowering heliotrope is a charming plant. It used to be called Cherry Pie, for its perfume is remarkably like the smell of cherries when baked in a pie. In Victorian days there were numerous varieties and it was grown in every garden, just for its perfume which is most noticeable at night when the moths will visit the rather insignificant flowers. These are of a pinky-mauve colour and attract butterflies by day. The plants may be treated like half-hardy annuals, seed being sown in gentle heat early in March, the plants set out in June after hardening; or they may be propagated from cuttings and wintered in gentle heat. The pure white 'White Lady' is especially richly scented at night.

The catchflies are also of the dianthus family and are noted for their evening scent, and whilst the moss campion, *Silene acaulis*, a perennial with rose-pink flowers, present in hilly parts of Scotland and the Lake District, is visited by so many butterflies that it has lost the power of self-fertilization, *S. vulgaris*, the bladder campion, with its white flowers, is scented only at night and is visited by moths. It is a plant of more bushy habit than the white campion and gets its name because the calyx is inflated to resemble a bladder.

The Nottingham Catchfly, *Silene nutans*, also has white flowers which with their sticky calyx trap any small flies that may be searching for honey by daytime. It is found on cliffs, usually by the sea, but at one time was present on the rocky outcrop on which stands Nottingham Castle. *S. noctiflora*, a plant of cornfields and hedgerows, with pale pink or white flowers, is also night-scented. By day, the flowers remain closed. *S. alpestris* also bears white flowers which are slightly scented at night and which appear in May. It makes a compact plant and is admirable for the alpine garden. All the silenes are readily raised from seed or may be propagated from cuttings taken in July.

Saponaria officinalis, the soapwort, a native plant (so called because in former days the sap from its stems was mixed with water, when it would make a foamy lather in which the body or clothes could be washed), is visited only by night moths. The flowers are white or palest pink and are made conspicuous after dark by being held on 2 ft. (61 cm.) stems. Only slightly scented by day, the flowers emit a pronounced fragrance by night. The honey is hidden at the end of a long narrow tube and is available only to long-tongued lepidoptera which will often visit it after dark. *S. caespitosa*, also perennial, blooms in July and August, its heads of rose-pink flowers appearing on short, sturdy stems.

Also scented at night is *Viola cornuta*, the Alpine Violet or Horned Pansy of the Pyrenees, with its dainty tufted habit, being one of the few pansies to reproduce itself by division of the roots which are fibrous so that each piece readily becomes established. The flower has a longer spur than any of the family so its nectar is available only to night-flying lepidoptera. It is a plant that was widely used in raising the bedding viola and also the lovely violettas, so much used for bedding by Victorian gardeners, which emit the same vanilla-like perfume at night.

The night-scented flowers can be included in a border of those plants which are attractive not only to moths but also to butterflies, so that during the summer there will be interest by day and by night. One may visit the garden during twilight hours and after dark when the moths will be fluttering about the open scented blossoms. The moths may be seen by the diffused light of a lantern or torch and on any warm evening one may sit quite close to the plants with the light dimly shining so that the flowers and their visitors are just visible. When the moon is shining, one may watch without artificial light.

In my garden I have made a small walled enclosure and in one corner have built a simple shelter over a floor of paving stones which have been cemented in. The corner where two walls join provides two sides and the third, of wood, has an opening for entry: on each side are two lattice 'windows'. A roof of bitumen-treated felt keeps out the evening dew. There is ample room to take in a chair which provides some degree of comfort whilst one watches the after-dark activities of the moths and other creatures by the light of the moon or a lamp. Night-scented flowers are grouped together, as near to the shelter as possible, with the honeysuckles climbing over the trellis on each side of the entrance.

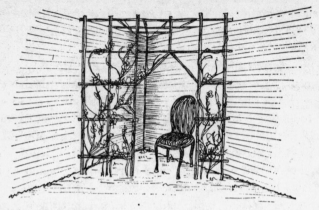

21. A small garden enclosure

NIGHT-SCENTED FLOWERS THAT WILL BE VISITED
BY MOTHS

Plant	Common Name	In Bloom
Abronia fragrans	Verbena	July–Aug.
Abronia latifolia	Sand verbena	July–Aug.
Heliotropium peruvianum	Cherry Pie	July–Sept.
Hesperis matronalis	Sweet rocket	July–Aug.
Hesperis tristis	Sand rocket	July–Aug.
Jasminum officinale	White jasmine	June–Sept.
Lathyrus 'White Pearl'	Everlasting pea	July–Sept.
Lonicera caprifolium	European honeysuckle	July–Nov.
Lonicera etrusca superba	Italian honeysuckle	July–Aug.
Lonicera japonica halliana	Japanese honeysuckle	Aug.–Oct.
Lonicera periclymenum	Honeysuckle	July–Aug.
Lychnis vespertina	Night-scented campion	June–Aug.
Matthiola bicornis	Night-scented stock	June–Sept.
Myosotis alpestris	Alpine forget-me-not	May–June
Nicotiana affinis	Tobacco plant	July–Sept.
Nicotiana sylvestris	Woodland tobacco	June–Aug.
Oenothera biennis	Evening primrose	July–Sept.
Oenothera drummondii	Texas primrose	June–Sept.
Oenothera tetraptera	Mexican primrose	July–Sept.
Oenothera triloba	Californian primrose	July–Sept.

Plant	Common Name	In Bloom
Saponaria officinalis	Soapwort	July–Sept.
Silene noctiflora	Night-scented catchfly	July–Sept.
Silene nutans	Nottingham catchfly	May–July
Silene vulgaris	Bladder campion	June–Aug.
Viola cornuta	Alpine violet	June–Aug.

⚜ 6. Bees ⚜

The *Hymenoptera*, the bees, are amongst the most interesting of nature's children. They rival butterflies in their pollinating abilities though are more important in that they are able to tolerate cold, wet weather. Of vital importance to the setting of fruit, bees are welcome in every orchard and where there are only a few fruit trees in the garden, possibly two or three growing against a wall, as many bees as possible must be encouraged to visit the garden at blossom-time, for only a few varieties of fruit are able to fertilize themselves without the aid of pollinators. In addition, bees will suck up nectar from flowers and also collect the pollen which they convert into honey, this being the best of all forms of sweetening and a reliable substitute for sugar.

Wherever possible, those who are interested in bees should first learn the art and mystery of bee-keeping from those who already keep bees, and then obtain a colony of their own. A new hive and equipment for the extraction of honey will cost about £50 but have an almost indefinite life, whilst second-hand equipment (or some of it) may very often be obtained from a keeper who is giving up or reducing his stocks, though it is unusual for anyone who has learnt to understand bees and to have a colony or two, ever to give them up unless because of ill-health or for some other compelling reason.

Women make excellent bee-keepers for they have a gentleness that bees appreciate and bee-keeping seems to be an ideal occupation, not only to provide an interest but as a means of earning a useful additional income. There is always a demand for well-produced honey from local shops and Women's Institutes which are so valuable in promoting country crafts. As with all country crafts, experience counts for a great deal in achieving success in this occupation and it is obtained only through studying bees and their requirements.

At the time of writing (1976), it is estimated that there are about a quarter of a million colonies of honey bees in the British Isles and there are now over 13,000 members of the British Bee-keepers' Association.

Honey

In 1974, a survey was carried out with the help of the Bee Research Association of Chalfont St. Peter to determine the 'honey potential' of a unit of land: in other words the amount of honey to be obtained, including the sugar value, and also the floral density and duration of flowering time of the plants growing in that unit of land. Dr. Eva Crane, Director of the Research Association, reported that after exhaustive trials, it was determined that a colony of honey bees foraged over an area of about 1 sq. mile in their search for pollen and nectar, and that the highest yields, amounting to about 500 lb. (227 kg.) of honey an acre, were obtained from garden sage, deadnettle, clary, borage, common thyme, sweet clover, black locust and lime tree blossom, all of which can be planted in the garden. It is estimated that up to a million flowers in each unit (depending on species and a wet or dry summer) are needed to produce a pound of honey.

Bees collect nectar in a special stomach or pouch which is entirely separate from the digestive system, though the two are connected. This enables the bee to utilize some of the nectar when in need of it as it goes about its work. In the pouch, the nectar is converted into honey which it disgorges upon its return to the hive, some being stored for winter use whilst the rest is put in the honeycomb and is available for the larvae to eat. During a good honey-flow, as from a clover field in warm weather in June, 100 lb. (45 kg.) of nectar may reach a hive, collected from more than 50 million flower-heads. The occupants of a hive may consume more than 500 lb. (227 kg.) in a year, so the bee-keeper must always leave sufficient for the bees to feed upon in winter. In a poor summer (as in 1974), this may leave the keeper a surplus of only a few pounds, whereas in a good year there may be 100 lb. (45 kg.) or more surplus from each hive. A single mature lime tree may yield a year's supply of nectar for a hive.

The walls of the comb are made of wax which is secreted by the bees from under their abdomens and which they make malleable by chewing. The nectar from different flowers varies in taste, colour, scent and medicinal qualities. The ancients so greatly prized it that they named it *ghoneg*, a Hebrew word meaning 'delight', and it is one of the most valuable foods known to man. It is said that Pythagoras, originator of several geometrical theories learned at school, lived to be over ninety and existed only on wholemeal bread and honey.

Pure honey contains 70 per cent glucose, so it is an important source of energy. This is the part which crystallizes and usually sinks to the bottom of the jar. The rest is fruit sugar, which is similar to the brown syrup of cane sugar. When honey is eaten, it is absorbed at once into the blood-stream, whereas cane sugar has first to be masticated with saliva to convert it into honey sugar.

Bees also collect pollen from flowers and when examined under a microscope pollen grains may be recognized as being from a particular plant in the garden. The pollen sticks to strong hairs, which are sticky with nectar, on the bee's abdomen and hind legs where there are pollen baskets into which the pollen is transferred as the bee flies back to the hive. By the action of the bee's legs, the pollen is made into tiny balls which are then readily transferred to the collecting sacks. Once back at the hive, the bees remove the pollen for other workers to place in the cells. At the end of summer the bee-keeper removes the honey from the combs and replaces it with sugar for the bees to live on during winter.

Widely used today in beauty preparations, honey is also a valuable medicine. Dissolved in hot water and then cooled, it is a capital gargle for a sore throat, whilst honey mixed with the juice of rose petals is a valuable 'pick-me-up' during serious illness. Honey water, mixed with that of rosemary and rubbed on to the scalp, will often promote the growth of new hair where all other remedies have failed. In olden times, a health-giving wine called mead was made from honey and it is still made today in some places, for example on the island of Lindisfarne.

Bees and pollination

There are about 250 species of bee in the British Isles; the most important are the honey- and bumble-bees, the former, *Apis mellifera*, being domesticated and inhabiting specially made hives. These are placed by the bee-keeper in selected places about the countryside such as on moorlands, for heather honey is much to be desired, together with that from clover, and in orchards. In larger gardens where bees are kept, flowers are planted especially for the amount of nectar they produce but all gardens should grow these same flowers, for not only are bees a source of great interest when taking nectar and pollen, but now that so many of our wild flowers have become lost to us through the indiscriminate use of herbicides (chiefly to counteract the ever-rising cost of labour needed to keep the verges of our roads under control) bees must rely on gardens for a greater part of their food.

A colony may be composed of between 30,000–50,000 workers, together with a queen and drones. The workers, so named because they are bees which hunt for nectar and pollen, are sterile females, the queen being the only one to lay eggs. She mates only once and always outside the hive, but from then onwards spends her entire life inside, living as long as five years, though at some time she may swarm with half the workers to a new place. The workers protect her with their barbed stings, and feed her.

Not only do the workers seek out nectar but they also look after the larvae which they feed with secretions from their glandular system, no easy task when it is remembered that the queen, when she begins laying in spring, will lay up to 2,000 eggs a day. Eggs laid in worker cells produce worker bees; eggs laid in drone cells produce drones. An egg laid in a queen's cell produces a queen. The workers born in autumn live through winter and will continue to be active throughout summer, dying at the approach of winter, otherwise the hive would be too crowded. Those born in spring and early summer also die at this time.

The drones are the males which evolve from unfertilized eggs; their only function is to fertilize the queen and towards the end of summer they are driven out of the hive by the workers, to die when the weather becomes cold.

The eggs are placed in the wax-walled cells and the larvae fed on nectar, pollen and a juice which is secreted by the mouth glands of the workers. This substance is also produced by the queen, in more concentrated form, and it covers her body. It is known to beauticians as royal jelly.

Sometimes the queen will leave her hive, accompanied by a large number of workers and drones, to begin a new colony. The air will be filled with the swarm of excited bees which will settle on a tall tree or may enter an old building. When this happens, a bee-keeper should be informed at once so that he can remove the swarm and place it in an empty hive, for a young queen will already have taken the old queen's place. I have seen honey-bees swarming almost in the centre of Birmingham and by the time the bee-keeper could reach them they were in a very hostile mood, though when first they swarm they are most docile.

Fruit-growers depend upon bees for the setting of their

orchard crops and invite bee-keepers with their portable hives during blossom time. This extends from early April until about mid-June, beginning with Early Rivers cherry, the first of all fruit trees to bloom, which needs, to set heavy crops, Bradbourne Black or Merton Heart as a pollinator. Then come the plums and gages, followed by the pears with their greyishwhite blossom, lastly the apples which, being late, usually escape the spring frosts. It is important not to spray any fruit trees from the time when the blossom begins to show colour, or the bees will be seriously harmed.

The importance of planting fruit trees with the right pollinating varieties, and the way in which they rely on bees to carry the fertile pollen from one variety to another, may be noted from the results of experiments carried out by Sir Daniel Hall and M. B. Crane at the John Innes Institute. Of 12,000 flowers on a tree of Cox's Orange Pippin which was covered to exclude insects bringing pollen, less than 100 flowers set fruit. Yet on a nearby tree, pollinated by bees with fertile pollen from Egremont Russet, 13·4 per cent of blossom set fruit. From all tests carried out with apple blossom at the John Innes Institute it was found that cross-pollination gave a fruit set of 11 per cent, whilst from self-pollination the set was only 2·5 per cent.

Bees should never be killed, as they so often are, being mistaken for wasps, for they play a prominent part in the fertilization of flowers. Workers are small and of dull brown colourings, their bodies tapering almost to a point.

Next in the order of *Hymenoptera* are the bumble-bees, *Bombus*, amongst the most handsome of all bees; in Britain there are more than twenty species. The nest, which is about the size of a grapefruit, is made in a tuft of long grass or in a crevice of a quarry by a queen who has been in hibernation through winter. Here, with her own wax and by collecting pollen, she makes a small comb in which six or more eggs are laid in spring. The larvae become the first workers (sterile females) and gradually throughout the summer the nest be-

comes filled with wax cells and with a colony of between 100–
150. Late in summer a number of eggs hatch out to queens and
drones which fly away to mate; then these new queens go into
hibernation and the rest of the colony perishes in the cold.

Bumble-bees will frequently make their nests in the dense
tufty grass of a spinney and will often use a mouse's old nest
or that of a bird which may have been built on the ground. The
grass should be left uncut, for the presence of the bees may not
be noticed for some time until larger numbers have hatched out
and have begun to fill the nest. If one is considering the
fascinating hobby of bee-keeping, such a spinney would be a
suitable place to have hives.

Included amongst the species of bumble-bee is our largest
bee, *Bombus terrestris*, the Digger bumble-bee, the queen
measuring about 1 in. (2·5 cm.) long and the workers only
slightly less. All parts of the body are covered in black bristles
or hairs, apart from the outer surface of the tibia of the hind
legs which is smooth. Across the back are three wide orange-
red bands. It is distinguished from the slightly smaller 'Cuckoo'
bee (*Psithyrus vestalis*), of which there are six species, in that the
body of the latter, the most common of the 'Cuckoos', ter-
minates in a large red area or zone with the two horizontal
upper bands nothing like as prominent as with *B. terrestris*.

As imagined from its name, the 'Cuckoo' bee is unable to
feed its own young, having no pollen sacks on its legs. A queen,
therefore, occupies the nest of a queen bumble-bee, killing it
and then becoming accepted by the workers, but her eggs
become only queens and drones which mate, the queens
hibernating as is usual and the drones dying during winter.

Another species of bee is the Leaf-cutter bee (*Megachile
centuncularis*), confined to the south of England, similar to the
honey-bee but with larger jaws. These it uses to cut out circular
pieces from leaves which it rolls up and holds under its
abdomen with its legs as it flies to its nest which is usually built
in a rotten tree stump and is long and cylindrical. It is lined

with cells in which honey and pollen are stored. From the one main tunnel, several others are made and in each cell the eggs are deposited when the bee flies away and dies. The larvae remain in the pupal state until the following spring when the bees leave the tunnels. The value of these bees lies in their pollinating of fruit trees, for they are as important in this respect as the honey- and bumble-bees.

The honey-bee stands on a higher level than the bumble-bee in the arrangement of its collecting apparatus and its torsal brushes. In *Bombus*, the pollen-collecting sack is enclosed by many stiff hairs showing traces of the feathery branching of more primitive species. In *Apis*, these have become smooth bristles with no trace of feathering and are arranged in regular rows. The more primitive bees collect pollen entirely by their abdominal brushes, *Apis* and *Bombus* by their hind legs. At the same time, the tongue for collecting nectar is of far more intricate design in the honey- and bumble-bee than in the sand wasp and other more primitive species. At the end of the tongue of the honey- and bumble-bee is a capillary tube which enables these bees to reach the nectar at the end of quite long tubular flowers, though not those having as long a tube as flowers visited by certain lepidoptera. The bee's capillary tube which is at the end of the tongue and sheaths it, acts as a suction device by which the tongue conveys the nectar to the back of the mouth. After removing the nectar from a flower, which may require the act of suction to be performed six or seven times or even more, the tip is drawn back into the sheath which is then brought up to the mouth. The bee flies from flower to flower with its sucking apparatus extended as it alights, but the tongue remains concealed within the sheath until the moment of suction arrives.

Dr. Müller has told that when watching a honey-bee on a greater plantain he observed that after collecting nectar it ejected a small amount on to the anthers so as to make the pollen adhere as it was collected into a ball. Never does the bee

suck nectar and collect pollen at the same time, and the search
for nectar always precedes the gathering of pollen. When
collecting pollen, the bee does so with its tongue withdrawn.
As large quantities of pollen remain adhered to the hairs of the
abdomen and (or) the legs, the honey- and bumble-bees are
able to transfer it from one flower to another, thus ensuring
that pollination is most effective. Some bees are entirely without
hairs and so play only a limited part in the pollination of
flowers.

It is of interest that by its very long spur *Viola cornuta*, most
heavily scented at night, is pollinated by night-flying lepidoptera whereas *V. odorata*, the violet, scented by day, has a spur
of sufficient length to enable the nectar to be taken by honey-
and bumble-bees. Here, the pistil that bears the stigma is bent
downwards at a short distance from the lower petal. When the
bee thrusts its proboscis beneath the stigma it pushes up the
pistil and opens the ring of anthers which shed their pollen on
the inserted organ. By experiment, it has been proved that
when bees are excluded from *V. odorata*, the flowers bear no
seed and so cannot reproduce themselves. Flowers, therefore,
depend as much on bees and lepidoptera for their survival as
bees do on flowers.

Flowers which attract bees

Whereas butterflies and moths are drawn to flowers chiefly by
their perfume, bees make use of their sight rather than their
sense of smell when seeking nectar and pollen. In the main
those flowers visited by bees are purple or blue and have distinguishing marks to direct the bees to their organs of repro-
duction so that the bees lose no time as they move from one
flower to another. Not only is this important to the bees in their
collection of honey and pollen, but it also ensures that the
pollen is transferred from one flower to another without undue

deterioration. It was Sprengel who first maintained that the distinguishing marks served as guides to the nectary.

Bees can readily distinguish colours, except for red to which they are colour-blind; they are unable to distinguish red from green and are rarely, if ever, seen visiting red or orange flowers. They concentrate their energies on purple or blue flowers, such as borage, lavender, balm and lobelia and early flowering forget-me-nots, and, to a lesser extent, on yellow which is the predominant colour of the spring and early summer flowers. Wallflowers will be constantly visited; the latter in reddish-brown and yellow being one of the few flowers of these colourings to have an attraction for bees, possibly because there are few other flowers in bloom around this time, from March to May. (For the same reason, bees make frequent visits to the pink and white blossom of fruit trees.) Yellow and white flowers, however, are those most visited by moths and most of those visited by bees possess little or no perfume which in this case is not necessary for the survival of either plant or insect. Of the large number of blue flowering plants which have no scent, most are representative of the *Violaceae*, *Campanulaceae*, *Boraginaceae* and *Labiatae* families, bearing tubular or bell-shaped flowers or having a pronounced lip upon which the bees (in this case bumble-bees) alight, pressing down the lip to enable them to probe deep into the flower. It may be thought that the Labiates, such as lavender and sage, are the exceptions to the rule that flowers with scented attractions are not usually visited by bees, but this is not so, for lavender, the most highly scented of the Labiates, derives its perfume not from the flower petals but from tiny green bracts immediately beneath them. It is only these parts which are scented.

It will be noticed that many of those flowers visited by bees droop downwards, to preserve the pollen from rain and dew, as in the case of borage.

Herman Müller has told of the acute powers of vision

possessed by bees, confirmed also by Darwin and described in the latter's *Cross- and Self-Fertilisation of Plants* in which he has shown how a bee will single out flowers of the same species (especially those coloured blue) for visiting in search of pollen, flying from one to another and entirely neglecting all other flowers on their way. 'On one occasion', Darwin relates, 'I observed bumble-bees flying in a straight line from a blue-flowered larkspur (*Delphinium consolida*) which was in full bloom, to another plant of the same species 15 yd. away and which had not a single flower fully open, the buds showing only a slight tinge of blue.' That larkspur flowers are scentless must confirm that the bees were able to distinguish them by their powers of discrimination, being able to tell the blue colouring of the larkspur from the blue of other flowers.

That bees work entirely by sight was determined by Darwin on another occasion on a warm day when large numbers were observed visiting the blue flowers of *Lobelia erinus*. Darwin removed the petals of a number of flowers and noted that no bees visited them again, though they continued to search for nectar and pollen from flowers nearby. But he noticed, too, that if the sun ceased to shine for only half an hour, the visits of the bees slackened and if the sun stayed covered by cloud, the bees stopped altogether, from which it would seem that a certain degree of warmth is necessary to promote a generous secretion of nectar.

More than 2,000 years ago, Aristotle had observed that bees and certain insects usually visit flowers of the same species for as long as possible before going on to another species, the reason for this possibly being that, learning the exact arrangements of the parts of a flower of a certain species by repeated visits, they are able to work faster than if they moved from one species to another. This is important when considering all that the bees have to do with the nectar and pollen they save.

For the same reason, it is observed that where large numbers of flowers of a certain species are growing in close proximity, bees will bore through the side of the flowers at the point where the nectar is secreted in order to save time.

That all flowers and this includes the, to us, virtually scentless blue flowers, do possess some degree of perfume, perhaps a leafy smell, was confirmed by von Frisch who found that when a worker returns to the hive with nectar the other workers probe her with their antennae, at the end of which is the olfactory organ, and then will fly off to the plants which have provided the nectar, in the same way that the housewife will pass the word round to her friends that some scarce commodity is to be obtained from a certain supermarket! In this way the bees will lose no time in obtaining the necessities of their life, for to delay whilst searching for nectar from other plants could mean that other insects might be first on the scene.

The needs of insect and plant are inter-related and those flowers which rely on insects for perpetuating the species are often proterandrous, releasing their pollen before the stigma is ready to receive it. But for insects, they would be unfertilized. Bees and other insects will carry the pollen from one flower to another when the stigma is most ready to receive it. In the same way, birds of the tropics fertilize plants by the pollen which adheres to the front of their heads as they search for nectar with their long beaks.

Not all flowers of the same family have the same pollinators. In *Oxalidaceae*, the oxalis family, those species where the flower is funnel-shaped are scentless and pollination is by bees, but where they are of narrow tubular formation, pollination is by butterflies and moths with their longer tongues, and the flowers are highly scented as, for example, in *Oxalis enneaphylla*.

Blue flowers are the most highly developed of flower colours whilst the honey-bees are amongst the most highly intelligent of insects. In New Zealand, where there are few bees, there are few blue flowers. There is no blue-flowered clematis, violets are white, and the gentian, the bluest of flowers in Europe, is white in New Zealand. Most blue flowers are European and have been developed by nature to satisfy bees which abound there, especially in the Mediterranean regions.

The following blue-flowering species are frequently visited by honey-bees and may be used to make a bee garden or border. They are most attractive when grown with silver leaf plants, the silver and blue enhancing the colouring of each other. Those marked * are annual or biennial, all others are perennial.

Species	Height	
Aconitum napellus (monk's hood)	4 ft.	(1·22 m.)
Agastache oenothiodora	2 ft.	(61·0 cm.)
Allium schoenoprasum (chives)	6 in.	(15·2 cm.)
Anchusa officinalis	3 ft.	(91·4 cm.)
Anchusa sempervirens	18 in.	(45·7 cm.)
Arabis purpurea	2 in.	(5·1 cm.)
Aster novi-belgii	3 ft.	(91·4 cm.)
Borago officinalis	2 ft.	(61·0 cm.)
Borago orientalis	3 ft.	(91·4 cm.)
Camassia quamash	18 in.	(45·7 cm.)
Campanula latifolia	3 ft.	(91·4 cm.)
Cardamine pratensis	18 in.	(45·7 cm.)
* *Carduus nutans* (purple)	2 ft.	(61·0 cm.)
Carduus vulgare (purple)	3–4 ft.	(91·4 cm.–1·22 m.)
Centaurea cyanus	18 in.	(46·0 cm.)
Chionodoxa luciliae	4 in.	(10·2 cm.)
Cichorium intybus	15 in.	(38·1 cm.)
Codonopsis ovata	2 ft.	(61·0 cm.)
Colchicum autumnale	6 in.	(15·2 cm.)
Cyananthus lobatus	4 in.	(10·2 cm.)
Cynoglossum nervosum	18 in.	(46·0 cm.)
Delphinium consolida	2–6 ft.	(61·0–1·83 m.)
Downingia pulchella	6 in.	(15·2 cm.)
Echinops ritro	3 ft.	(91·4 cm.)
Echium vulgare	1 ft.	(30·5 cm.)
Endymion non-scriptus (bluebell)	15 in.	(38·1 cm.)
Erigeron speciosus	15 in.	(38·1 cm.)
Eryngium maritinum (sea holly)	18 in.	(46·0 cm.)
Euphrasia officinalis	6 in.	(15·2 cm.)
Hyssopus officinalis	2 ft.	(61·0 cm.)

Species	Height	
Jasione perennis	1 ft.	(30·5 cm.)
Knautia arvensis	2–3 ft.	(61·0–91·4 cm.)
Lavandula spica	10–30 in.	(25·4–76·2 cm.)
Limonium vulgare (sea lavender)	1 ft.	(30·5 cm.)
Lithospermum gastonii	3 in.	(7·6 cm.)
*Lobelia erinus	6 in.	(15·2 cm.)
Lythrum salicaria	3 ft.	(91·4 cm.)
Melissa officinalis (bluish-white)	15 in.	(38·1 cm.)
Melittis melissophyllum	2 ft.	(61·0 cm.)
Mentha spicata (mint)	10 in.	(25·4 cm.)
Mertensia dahurica	10 in.	(25·4 cm.)
Mertensia virginica	18 in.	(46·0 cm.)
Muscari spp.	4 in.	(10·2 cm.)
Myosotis sylvestris	6 in.	(15·2 cm.)
**Nemophila menziesii insignis*	8 in.	(20·3 cm.)
Nepeta cataria (catmint)	1 ft.	(30·5 cm.)
Nepeta mussinii (catmint)	15 in.	(38·1 cm.)
**Nigella damascena*	18 in.	(46·0 cm.)
Origanum vulgare (pot marjoram)	18 in.	(46·0 cm.)
Ostrowskia magnifica	2 ft.	(61·0 cm.)
**Phacelia tanacetifolia*	30 in.	(76·2 cm.)
Platycodon grandiflorum	18 in.	(46·0 cm.)
Polemonium coeruleum	18 in.	(46·0 cm.)
Pulmonaria angustifolia	1 ft.	(30·5 cm.)
Scabiosa caucasica	15 in.	(38·1 cm.)
Scilla sibirica	6 in.	(15·2 cm.)
Stokesia laevis	20 in.	(51·0 cm.)
Thymus drucei (purple)	4 in.	(10·2) cm.
Trachelium caeruleum	20 in.	(51·0 cm.)
Trachystemon orientalis	2 ft.	(61·0 cm.)
Vernonia noveboracensis	4 ft.	(1·22 m.)
Veronica beccabunga	3 in.	(7·6 cm.)
Veronica longifolia	3 ft.	(91·4 cm.)
Wahlenbergia gracilis	6 in.	(15·2 cm.)

When planting a bee flower border, use the taller plants at the back and the dwarf to the front unless planting an island bed when the tall plants should be at the centre, planting those

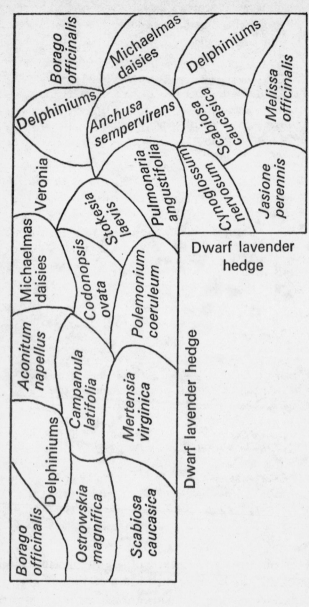

Dwarf lavender hedge

Dwarf lavender hedge

22. Plan for a bee garden with blue plants

of more dwarf habit around them. Early spring is the best time
to plant those with blue flowers which for some reason never
do well from autumn planting, especially if the winter is unduly
wet.

❦ 7. Other wildlife in the garden ❦

In addition to birds, butterflies, moths and bees, there are many other visitors to watch, and this chapter discusses some of the small mammals which will often be found where the garden is situated close to open countryside or woodland. Most of them will come during the hours of darkness and can be observed from a small garden shelter.

HEDGEHOGS

One friend which comes after dark is the hedgehog, for, except just before hibernation, it is only at night that it comes in search of slugs which make up its main diet. With the front of my garden close to the main road, I am sad to see so many of these interesting animals run over by passing cars as they make their way across the road to get to the fields on the other side, so I do all I can to keep them in the garden during summer when they are most active and when the roads are busy with holiday traffic. In winter they hibernate and so are not slaughtered in such distressing numbers. I often sit quite still for hours in my garden shelter where each evening I put down a saucer of milk which is, apart from insects and slugs, their favourite food. They will become quite tame if milk is put down for them and will come into the garden each evening looking for it. As this animal is a great friend of the gardener, it should be widely encouraged and there is nothing which will do this better than a saucer of milk. Hedgehogs lap up milk as quickly as do cats, and with the same enthusiasm, and will then sit in the half-light of dawn, cleaning their snouts. Of the same natural order as moles and shrews, when curled up in the hand a hedgehog will just about fill it, but as an adult it will measure 8–9 in. (20–

23 cm.) long when it is feeding. The inch-long spines are not very sharp and it is quite easy to pick up an adult without the spines penetrating the flesh of one's hand. The spines lie flat when the animal is feeding but become erect when it shows fear and it will then roll into a ball to protect itself. This it will do when a car is approaching, thus presenting a sitting target, for its dull brown colouring is difficult to see at night against the surface of a road and the driver rarely has time to avoid it.

To prevent the hedgehogs from reaching the highway, I have put wire netting inside the hedge, let into the ground to a depth of 6 in. (15 cm.), and reaching 3 ft. (91 cm.) above ground. Though they can climb, they will not often do so to a greater height than this: though young hedgehogs may climb up stone walls in their search for birds' eggs, it is rare for adults to do so.

The eyes and ears of the hedgehog are small in relation to its body size and its legs are scarcely strong enough to support it, so it has a comical appearance when running. During the day it remains hidden in a tuft of long grass, or amongst the roots of trees, covered by dead leaves. Out it comes looking for food just as soon as dusk descends. Slugs, worms and the larvae of insects are its main diet, though it will suck the juice from pears or plums lying on the ground. Its snout, like that of a pig, is strong yet highly sensitive and it will recoil from anything which may irritate it. Occasionally it will attack small birds whose nest is on the ground and it will take lizards and frogs which it may find hiding under stones. It has been known to tackle adders where they are prevalent and usually comes off best in any contest, for it is immune to their poison.

Hedgehogs hibernate between mid-October and early April. They will select a place like that chosen for their daytime sleep in summer, where they can curl up comfortably, and will line it with moss and leaves which they also use to cover themselves to keep out the frost and heavy rain of winter. At this time their body temperature will fall from 95° F. (35° C.) to between 36°–40° F. (2°–4½° C.) which is maintained through-out their hibernation period, during which time they are in a state of complete torpor.

During the few weeks of autumn before its hibernation, the hedgehog may often be seen during daytime, searching for as much food as it can possibly consume, for this has to last it through the winter. Late in March or early in April, depending on the spring temperature, it will emerge in an emaciated state and have difficulty in remaining long on its feet. But little by little its strength returns as it begins to feed and at this time I break an egg into the saucer of milk, for this is also a food which it enjoys and one which will be nourishing after hiber-nation. It will also consume scraps from the kitchen, bacon rind cut up small and other little bits of meat.

When the hedgehogs have fed again and have become plump and active, they will mate during May and June and will leave the garden at this time to have their young. The mother feeds her young for about a month after their birth and will return to the garden as soon as she has finished doing this. By then the young will have formed spines and will be able to fend for themselves.

To persuade them to have their young in the garden and to stay there, provide them with a wooden box about 15 in. (38 cm.) square and of similar depth, let into the ground almost to the rim; put in some moss and dead leaves or bracken and partly cover the top with bracken and leaves. The hedgehogs will usually find it and have their young in it. Or a hole in the ground, close to the bottom of a hedge, will suffice and should be prepared in the same way. If it is used, you will notice that the covering has been disturbed. If so, peep in to see if it is a hedgehog that is using it and not some other animal, then leave it alone until you see the young come out during one evening several weeks later. It may be possible to see foot-marks on the ground nearby; they resemble those of the badger but are larger and not as broad and will be almost in a straight line. The hedgehogs' presence in the garden may be confirmed by their droppings.

BADGERS

The badger is also nocturnal and though nothing like as frequently seen in gardens as the hedgehog, it is an occasional visitor, even to gardens of Greater London, for it still breeds in Richmond Park. 'Brock' as he is affectionately called (the name is derived from an Anglo-Saxon word), is a native of Africa. The badger must, however, have been a visitor to Britain some thousands of years ago for it has long been naturalized here, certainly since the Stone Age. It is one of the largest mammals of our islands, measuring about 3 ft. (91 cm.) from nose to tail, and its diet consists of rats and mice and possibly a few rabbits. Its habitat is mostly woodlands, but during darkness it will range far and wide in search of food, often coming into gardens and farmyards where it will obtain much of its diet about a haystack. Like the hedgehog, it will also eat slugs and snails and if there are hives about it has been known to upturn them in search of the honey it needs to satisfy its sweet tooth. Its presence in the garden may be detected by its broad footmarks and its five-toe imprint, as against the fox's four-toe markings. It will always come into the garden by the same path; this it makes from its sett where it lives deep underground. The sett is composed of a series of tunnels along which, at regular intervals, are chambers where the badger sleeps on moss or leaves and makes a nest to rear a family which may consist of two to five cubs, rarely one. The badger is a protected animal though it is believed that a certain strain is able to pass on tuberculosis to cattle and where this is known, badgers can be exterminated under official supervision. Mating takes place during the summer but it is February before the cubs are born. They remain with their parents for a year or more.

Badgers are most fastidious in their habits and will never foul their sett with droppings or with the remains of food as foxes do. Their claws are sharp and they keep them so by sharpening and cleaning them daily on a nearby smooth-barked tree, as do cats. Their bite is powerful and their jaws have a locking device which, should it get a hold, can be released only by the badger's death, so never go too close to one when it is out looking for food. You may, however, encourage it to come into a garden situated near woodlands, by placing ripe fruit in its season on the ground, near where the badger is believed to enter. Badgers can be seen by the light of the moon but be careful not to let them get your scent or they will keep away. If you find a sett in a wood, it may be watched from a tree on any moonlit night, but you should be in position by sunset, for the badgers will emerge soon after. On a dark night use a large torch fitted with a red glass; this will help to diffuse the light, for artificial light scares them away.

Badger cubs will play for hours outside their sett whilst their parents go in search of food. Young badgers are almost like black bear cubs, being ash-grey in colour with jet-black legs. A badger's head is broad and is white with wide black stripes running from behind the ears to just in front of the eyes. The tail is short, the nose long and tapering. The coarse bristles which cover the body are used to make shaving brushes, a good brush being quite expensive but lasting for anything up to fifty years, even when in almost daily use.

DORMICE AND SHREWS

One of the most delightful of garden visitors is the common dormouse (*Muscardinus avellanarius*) which is a hibernating mammal, possibly taking its name from the French *dormir*, to sleep. It is of hazel colouring with a body 4 in. (10 cm.) long and a tail 2 in. (5 cm.) in length. It mostly inhabits woodlands from which it makes its way into the garden. During the day it will hide in a nest of grass and dead leaves made in a hollow tree or in a hole in the trunk of an old apple tree; or perhaps it will make its nest in a drain-pipe, or low down in the branches of a hedge. In appearance it resembles a small red squirrel but, unlike the squirrel, it hibernates when its body temperature is reduced to 38°–40° F. ($3\frac{1}{4}$°–$4\frac{1}{2}$° C.). It may make its winter nest below ground or at the bottom of a hedge or, like the hedge-hog, between tree roots where it curls up into a ball. It is a nut-eater and is to be found in hazel copses or in any garden where there are hazels or beech trees. Though storing food for its hibernation, it will eat berries. Early in autumn it feeds voraciously, opening the hard shells of the nuts with its incisor teeth, sitting upright as it does so and, like a squirrel which it rivals in agility, for ever climbing up and down the branches of nut-producing trees. Just before hibernating, it becomes fat and then lives on its fat through the winter. It is nocturnal in its habits and is seen mostly when one comes upon its nest by day; it will rarely awaken if it is disturbed whilst sleeping. The nest is beautifully made of grasses, moss and dead leaves, being quite distinct from the winter nest.

The female will often have two litters a year, each of three to five young, the first brood being usually born in early summer and perhaps a second brood early in autumn. The young will remain with the mother during winter hibernation.

Dormice live for four years or more, though when they are out feeding during summer nights they are often taken by owls. Nut-bearing and berried trees will encourage them into the garden, especially where there is a spinney or some rough ground to provide them with material for their nests. Now becoming scarce, the common dormouse is covered by the Conservation of Wild Creatures and Wild Plants Act. The fat or edible dormouse (*Glis glis*), introduced by Lord Rothschild early this century, is seen in gardens around Aylesbury.

Interesting when they come into the garden are the shrews which do not hibernate and are active both by night and by

day. They are insect-eaters and consume much unwanted
larvae, though they also find earthworms greatly to their liking.
Like moles, they tunnel deep into the ground, the tunnels being
so narrow that the animals clean their fur against the sides
when coming in and out. The shrew's bite is venomous and can
kill a mouse or small bird, but if one's finger is bitten, one will
feel no more than a stinging sensation.

Shrews have a long pointed snout through which they make
grunting and squeaking sounds as they fight amongst themselves for the right to claim a worm or slug. The common
shrew (*Sorex araneus*) is 3 in. (7·6 cm.) in its body length whereas
the pigmy shrew (*S. minutus*) is no more than 2 in. (5 cm.) long,
with a tail almost as long again. Their fur is mousy-brown with
white on the underside. Both species are to be found throughout the British Isles but only the pigmy in Ireland. They are
usually present where there is a spinney or orchard and will hide
beneath dead leaves and rough grass which they use to line
their tiny nests.

Shrews have glands which release a scent by which they
keep in contact with each other and which also makes them
unpleasant to cats and other animals, which will take mice and
rats but leave the shrews alone. Shrews are, however, taken at
night by owls who find them a great delicacy. Their life-span
is short, being little more than a year even if owls do not find
them, and so to compensate they have three or four litters a
year, each with up to eight young. They remain with their
mother for about a month. They are quite aggressive for such
small creatures and will guard their tunnels from all intruders,
making terrifying squeaks which soon frighten other animals
away. Where they are known to be nesting, one may sit up in
the branches of a tree to watch them come out to feed or, if
one prefers to be more comfortable, erect a roughly constructed shelter beneath mature trees; if one keeps quite still
the shrews will come close to it in their continuous search for
food. They are quite comical as they push through the dead

leaves and grass with their snouts, occasionally stopping to sit up and sniff around, possibly to reassure themselves that they are alone.

The water shrew (*Neomys fodiens*) is found near ponds and streams where it makes its nest below ground and feeds on snails, fish and small frogs. It is slightly larger than the common shrew and has black fur which is accentuated by the snow-white underside. A handsome mammal, it is more nervous than other mammals and will only come into gardens where there is a large pond or lake with rough herbage around the sides.

MOLES

The mole (*Talpa europaea*) is not to be encouraged into the garden, for it pushes up the soil into mounds of up to 12 in. (30 cm.) high as it digs below ground in its search for worms and larvae. It will severely damage a large lawn in a few hours and will be a serious pest in those gardens adjoining unculti-vated land. Often the tunnels are made only 2–3 in. (5–7·6 cm.) below the surface, when the outline can clearly be seen like a maze. For all that, they are most interesting, their black glossy fur, sleek to touch and always clean, making their skins valuable for coat trimmings.

Present throughout the British Isles but not in Ireland, moles grow to about 6 in. (15 cm.) long and are almost sausage-shaped, with amazingly powerful front limbs which they use to push away the soil. A mole will move as much as 28 lb. (12·7 kg.) in an hour and when busy will cover a con-siderable area, provided the soil is in a loose condition. Like the shrew, it keeps its fur clean by rubbing against the sides of the tunnels. There is one main gallery which it makes directly from the hole where it goes below ground and where a nest is made, usually beneath a large mound. From the nest it makes a series of underground tunnels along which it travels in its search for food.

As with shrews, the mating season is April and May, and in June, two to five young are born. Like rats, they are born blind and without fur but after a month, when they leave the nest, they have thick shiny coats. Closely related to the hedgehog and shrew, moles live for three years or more. They do have eyes, contrary to popular belief, but these are no larger than pin-heads and are completely hidden by the fur. In any case, they are of little use to them, though moles will often be seen during daytime tunnelling along the surface if the soil is hard after a long period of drought, and their movements may then be closely studied. When they are above ground during darkness, they will often fall prey to owls and to cats which will wait for them to emerge from their holes.

VOLES

There are three common types of vole in the British Isles. The field vole (*Microtus agrestis*), when seen from a distance, resembles the rat, but differs from it in that it has a short tail and blunt snout. When fully grown it measures about 4 in. (10 cm.), excluding the tail, and is yellowish-brown in summer, becoming more chocolate-brown in winter, and is grey on the underside. It frequents hedgerows and spinneys where it builds in tufts of dense grass on which it also feeds, though it also nibbles at young trees and does considerable damage to new forest plantations. It rears two or three litters a year, always during the summer months, and there are usually four young in each litter.

The bank vole (*Clethrionomys glariolus*) is more chestnut-coloured and makes its nest in banks, usually beneath the roots of an old tree. It will raise three or four litters a year, with generally three or four in each.

Both species feed on hedgerow fruits and may be encouraged to visit gardens situated on the outskirts of towns, where there are thick hedges or areas of rough grass.

The water vole (*Arvicola amphibius*) is twice the length of the other two species and is greyer in colour. It makes its nest in a burrow in a bank near water, the entrance to the nest being just below water level to keep out predators such as owls and foxes, and especially weasels. The burrow itself runs in an upwards direction, away from the water. The water vole will often be seen near a natural pond and it will eat the vegetation growing around, leaving large areas quite bare. It will, however, do no damage to trees and shrubs. A characteristic which distinguishes it from the water rat is that it swims beneath the surface of the water. After a swim, it will sit on the bank for hours, drying and cleaning itself, and it will then feed on waterside plants before disappearing into its burrow.

MICE

The two that are most interesting are our smallest rodents, the harvest mouse (*Micromys minutus*), and the field or wood mouse (*Apodemus sylvaticus*), both possessed of the most endearing qualities. Neither is nocturnal. The harvest mouse is the smallest, measuring about 2 in. (5 cm.) in the body and with a tail about the same length. Its fur is pale yellowish-brown and it has a blunt rounded nose. It is a regular summer visitor to gardens that are close to open country and situated roughly south-east of a line from the Severn to the Humber. It makes its round untidy nest above ground using corn stalks (hence its name), reeds or rough grass, around which it cleverly intertwines lengths of dead grass. In a few hours the nest is made and, safe inside it, the tiny creature will peep out on all who pass by. Though now much less common than it used to be, it makes an interesting pet and until recent times harvest mice were kept by children in small boxes lined with moss and dead grass, and were fed on bran, but they are now covered by the Wild Creatures Protection Act. In the wild they will move from stalk to stalk in cornfield or reed bed, supporting themselves by their long tails. As a rule they will stay above ground. During winter hibernation they will make their nests in clumps of grass or in hay, or even amongst old clothing.

Three or four litters are born every year in summer and each may consist of eight or nine young.

As the harvest mouse will occupy its summer nest until early in November and may have built it in a spinney or beneath a hedge, it is not advisable to cut down the long grass for the autumn cleaning until this time: these mice are often present on roadsides, especially in remoter areas, and the Highway Authorities in the various counties are co-operating with the County Trusts for Nature Conservation in this respect.

The field or wood mouse is an inch longer than the harvest mouse, but with a rather shorter tail. It has larger ears and is chestnut-brown, with white on its throat and belly. It will make its nest in a hole in the ground where there is rough grass, or beneath tall trees where the roots are exposed and it can form a hollow between them, lining its nest with dead leaves and grass. It is a common visitor to the garden for it loves berries of all sorts, especially hips and haws, and beech nuts. The field mouse is a timid fellow and one needs to be as quiet as the proverbial mouse to see him feeding or carrying off to his nest a supply of food for the bleaker days of winter. Several litters are produced, usually in summer, and each with up to eight or nine young.

Another of our more interesting mice is the yellow-necked (*Apodemus flavicollis*), the longest of all with a body measuring 4 in. (10 cm.) and a tail even longer. Its fur is bright chestnut and it has more white on its underparts than the field mouse. It also has a yellow mark on its throat. Common throughout southern England and breeding in colonies, it is found in woodlands and gardens where it feeds on beech nuts, acorns and fallen berries.

SQUIRRELS

Whilst the red squirrel (*Sciurus vulgaris*), a native rodent, is a most desirable garden visitor, the comparatively recently introduced grey species (*S. carolinensis*) has already become a serious woodland and garden pest, stripping bark off trees and causing many thousands of pounds of damage each year. The red species has no such bad habits and is a delightful creature, usually found in the conifer woodlands of northern England and East Anglia, from whence it can be attracted to nearby gardens where there are mature pines, for cones are its staple diet. It is said that the red squirrel needs 5 acres (2·02 ha.) of pine woods for a year's food. For winter feeding it collects cones and hazel nuts and stores them in a hole in a tree.

The red squirrel builds its nest (a drey) of twigs and moss high in the fork of a tree and rears two litters a year, mostly of two or three kittens, as young squirrels are called. If disturbed the mother will, like a cat, remove the kittens in her mouth and may build another nest for them.

When the red squirrel is sitting up on its hind legs, with a cone in its front paws, it measures about 9 in. (23 cm.) long; it has a bushy tail which rises almost perpendicular and is nearly as long as its body. The fur is a rich chestnut-red colour. Whilst the grey squirrel is quite tame and may even feed from the hand, and certainly from a bird-table, the red is extremely shy and will hop from branch to branch, watching all the time for anything coming too close, when it will bound away at amazing speed.

WEASELS

The weasel (*Mustela nivalis*) is a vicious killer of small birds, so is not wanted in the garden, but it will often intrude in those gardens situated close to open country. Some 9 in. (23 cm.) in length, it is only about half the size of the stoat which it resembles in its summer coat, being fawn with a broad white area extending from the mouth and neck to the belly and beneath the back legs. The stoat, however, changes to an all-white coat in winter. The tail of the weasel is also considerably shorter than that of the stoat and is without the black tip that the stoat's has.

The weasel is present throughout Britain, except in Ireland where a smaller type of stoat is found and where it is known, incorrectly, as a weasel. The stoat hunts mainly by day but the weasel hunts by night and will take chickens if they are not securely fastened up; it is, however, useful in keeping down rats and mice about farm and estate buildings. Weasels usually have two litters of six kittens, as their young are called, each year, one in spring and the other in early autumn, a nest being made with dead leaves at the bottom of a hedge or between the exposed roots of a tree. Stoats have only one litter, in spring.

Like all nocturnal hunters, and like cats, weasels have large and extremely sensitive whiskers to enable them to judge the width of holes they enter. They also have a highly developed sense of smell, but poor eyesight. They kill with a bite at the back of their victim's neck and are fierce when approached, rising upon their hind legs and hissing. They will bite one's hand if it is near enough and no attempt must be made to handle them. They may be seen in a country garden by the light of the moon or of a lamp, if one keeps quite still and there is little air movement to carry a human's scent.

If rodents should become a nuisance in the garden and home, they should be exterminated with Warfarin which kills painlessly and does not act along food-chains, as do so many poisons.

BATS

These are amongst the most primitive of creatures, resembling

the pterodactyl of long ago in wing construction and mostly inhabiting tropical regions. Included amongst nearly 1,000 species
is the dreaded Vampire bat, a carrier of rabies. In Britain there
are fourteen species of bat, only seven or eight being at all
common, and they are thought by many to have unpleasant
characteristics, though there is no truth in the popular belief
that they will fly into one's hair and be difficult to disentangle.
They are to be found about churches, castles, and other old
buildings, roosting amongst the rafters where they also hibernate as they do in caves and in old hollow trees in dense woodlands.

The bat is the only flying mammal and it has a life of up to
five years. Only one is born to the female each year, in mid-
summer. Though bats usually hang head down when sleeping,
after giving birth the mother hangs with her head upwards and
for about a month keeps her young one in a pouch beneath her
breast, all the while feeding it with her milk. Then for about
another month she will show it how to hang correctly and it
remains in this position whilst she collects insects on the wing
at night to feed to it.

The two largest species are the Greater Horseshoe (*Rhino-
lophus ferum-equinum*) found mostly in Wales, and the Long-
eared (*Pletocus auritus*), the former having a wing-span of about
14 in. (35·5 cm.) and always flying close to the ground in search
of insects. The Long-eared has a 10 in. (25 cm.) wing-span and,
with its large upright ears, is quite fearsome in appearance.
Among the smallest of the species are the Whiskered bat
(*Myotis mystacinus*), with a body 3 in. (7·6 cm.) long and a
wing-span of 8–9 in. (20–23 cm.), and the Pipistrelle (*Pipistrellus pipistrellus*) which is only 2 in. (5 cm.) long and weighs less
than half an ounce; it is a regular visitor to many of London's
parks and squares during summer nights. It flies higher than
most bats and is that mostly seen about old buildings. The
equally small Natterer's bat (*Myotis nattereri*) rarely moves far
from the woodlands where it is born, whilst the closely related

Daubenton's bat (*M. daubentoni*) keeps close to still water, flying over the surface. Surprisingly, it flies by daytime and is the only bat to do so.

A bat's wings are really its skin, stretched over four of the five long fingers. Possessed of weak eyesight, it hunts by means of a powerful radar mechanism which is one of the wonders of nature. When flying, it utters almost continuously a high-pitched sound which echoes back to it as it strikes a moving insect; from this the bat knows exactly where to find the insect. The tiny screech to be heard when bats are flying nearby is quite a separate sound. The presence of bats can be detected by the Holgate Ultrasonic Receiver which is able to pick up sounds which are made by bats in flight but which cannot be detected by the human ear. Each species has its own particular sound which is received at about 50,000 cycles a second, compared with only about 3,000 cycles a second for the highest note of a piano. The sounds of certain species are received on the detector by way of short metallic clicks, but each species comes through in a different way, making recognition simple to those trained in the receiver's use. Some sounds are so loud that an experienced person using the equipment can pick them up at a distance of 50–60 yd. (45·7–54·8 m.), whilst others at such a distance will be scarcely audible.

LIZARDS

Our two native lizards are the common lizard (*Lacerta vivipara*) and the rare sand lizard (*L. agilis*), though the slow-worm (*Anguis fragilis*), which resembles a snake and is occasionally present in damp woodland, is really a lizard. The common lizard is often a visitor to those gardens situated close to moorlands or mountainous country. It will bask in the sunshine on a stone, darting beneath it if disturbed. When fully grown it will measure up to 6 in. (15 cm.) in length, its tail being almost half of the body length. It moves rapidly, like the iguana, and

like it is able to shed its long tail and grow a new one, should it
be trapped by the tail. It has a hard, scaly skin and is usually
grey-brown, yellow on the underside. It is unusual amongst
reptiles in that it bears live young which are enclosed only in a
thin transparent membrane from which they emerge almost at
once: between six and ten are born during July.

The sand lizard, which is greyish-green, confines itself
mainly to sand dunes. It may be seen around the coasts of
Devon and Dorset and, occasionally, Kent, but it is not at all
common and it rarely comes into the garden, even near the
coast. It is now protected by the Conservation of Wild Creatures and Wild Plants Act.

❧ 8. The garden pond ❧

In the landscaping of gardens in the eighteenth and nineteenth centuries, use was always made of water in lakes, pools and streams, for the designers were fully aware of the additional interest it provided. Water, whether it be moving or still, never fails to fascinate us with its many moods and reflections and it may be the means of attracting all manner of wildlife. It is therefore well worthwhile to plan a garden pond with wildlife in mind, banking the sides up with additional soil and surrounding it with rough grass and with trees and shrubs to give suitable cover to the visitors. Few will be fortunate enough to have a large pond, let alone a lake, in their gardens, but a small pool may be made in any garden and it will be a source of beauty and interest for much of the year. Birds will visit it to drink, whilst some will use it to catch those insects which are attracted to water. Sand-martins may build in the banks, possibly a kingfisher too, whilst the water vole may make its nest of rushes and reeds just below the water-line and feed on nearby herbage, and produce three or four litters a year. In the bank the water shrew can tunnel to a suitable nesting place. The reed warbler prefers running water but the sedge- and willow-warblers will often be present, whilst swallows and martins will use the water and any mud round the edges of the pond for their nest building. Dragonflies, amongst the oldest of the earth's insects, will be an attraction as they dive over the surface of the water to catch small flies and midges on the wing, as will the smaller damselflies. These differ from dragonflies in that they rest, like butterflies, with their wings closed, whilst dragonflies, like moths, rest with wings outstretched. Both fly about at the most amazing speed and, with their brilliantly coloured bodies, some red, some green or blue, and their bright markings, are amongst the most attractive form of wild-life in the garden.

If in one corner of a pool you build up stones, using cement with waterproofing added, and keeping the top stone just above the water-level, many more birds will use it for drinking, rather than just coming to the side of the pool. They feel safer out in the water and will often use the stone as a perch from which to catch flies or take beetles which skim the surface. The birds will come back time and time again to the stone, but remember to keep, if you can, the water-level almost to the top of the stone during hot days in summer when there is some evaporation.

Another idea is to place an old tree branch across one end of the pool; the birds will perch upon it before diving to take flies and beetles from the water. Alternatively, use a rough builder's lath which will soon be covered in moss and become partly hidden by marginal plants as they become established.

The pool can be made at one end of the garden, surrounded by an evergreen hedge in which birds will build. An arbour where one can sit to watch the wildlife, or simply a wooden seat sheltered by the hedge, will increase one's enjoyment of the pool. One side of this separate little garden can be paved with flagstones which will dry quickly after heavy rain. If the hedge is allowed to grow to about 6 ft. (1·8 m.) it will form a sun-trap which will encourage wild visitors and it will become something of a tiny nature reserve, especially welcome in a city garden. Buddleias and other plants to attract butterflies may be planted at one end, together with berried shrubs for the birds; a corner should be kept for night-scented plants to attract the moths. Planted in this way, the little garden will provide continuous interest for almost twenty-four hours a day through-out the spring and summer.

So long as there is dense vegetation by the waterside, coots and moorhens may, in a garden of suitable size, be introduced. The coot is slightly larger than the moorhen, measuring about

15 in. (38 cm.) from head to tail, and is black, readily distinguished by the white mark on its forehead. It will build by the side of water and lays six to eight eggs in May. The moorhen has a red patch on its forehead and, when diving below the water, displays a white mark under its tail. Moorhen is a corruption of its true name, mere-hen, which indicates its liking for water. When it swims it moves its head backwards and forwards. It, too, will build in waterside vegetation and during April, May or June it lays from five to ten eggs. Both birds provide hours of interest as one watches them swimming and diving down for food, feeding on almost anything that can be found in or about the water.

Several of the wild ducks may be attracted to a large garden pond or lake, especially the mallards and tufted ducks which are present almost throughout the British Isles and are frequently seen in our municipal parks. Mallards build by the lakeside in the grounds of Buckingham Palace, and bring up their families there. The mallard usually nests away from water, in long grass or nettles, but usually only a short distance away. Or it may nest beneath gorse bushes and hedgerow plants, as does the pheasant. It lays from eight to twelve greenish-grey eggs which hatch in twenty-eight days. The young take to the water after about eight weeks and, when swimming with their parents, are a most attractive sight.

The tufted duck prefers to build close to water and will do so in the overhanging branches of trees and shrubs, or amongst reeds, its large solid nest resembling that of the coot and moorhen. It lays from six to twelve greenish-grey eggs and the young take to the water only six weeks after hatching. These ducks and others may be obtained from those who specialize in their rearing, and provided there is a good area of water and some rough vegetation near it, they will be quite at home in an urban garden.

The larger the pool and the more abundant the waterside plants, the greater will be the attraction for birds and other wildlife. One is often asked whether it is essential for there to be a natural supply of water before a garden pool is made. It is certainly not essential, so long as the pool has the correct proportion of the correct oxygenating plants (see p. 230) for they will keep the water clear and birds and insects will drink from it. These plants prevent algae from choking up the water. The oxygenators obtain their sustenance from minerals in the water and absorb the sunlight which, by the process of photosynthesis, they convert into oxygen. It is not necessary to drain and clean the pool more often than once every five years, when the plants in it can be divided.

Making a pool

A pool can be of any shape and any size, so long as it is in scale with the rest of the garden. The smallest pool, which may be sited on a terrace or veranda if there is no garden space, may be made from an old oak cask cut in half crossways, each part being about 18 in. (46 cm.) deep. Make sure that the iron bands which hold the staves in position are sound, and treat them with a rust-proof paint, both on the outside and inside, before they are filled with water. When the tub is filled the staves will swell and close up any slight gaps, provided of course that the wood is sound.

A pleasing effect will be obtained if the tub is inserted into the ground to about half its height, or to within 1 in. (2·5 cm.) of the top with paving stones set into cement around the rim. The latter method will allow the pool to be maintained without treading the soil or grass around it. Lay the stones on a 2 in. (5 cm.) bed of cement which the weeds will not grow through, but leave small pockets between the stones, filling them with soil for carpeting plants.

Inside the tub several large stones are placed and soil pressed into the pockets between them. Arrange the stones so that when the tub is filled there will be no more than 9 in. (23 cm.) of water covering them, for the marginal plants which are to be set in the pockets must not be planted deeper than this. Three or four marginals will add to the pond's natural beauty and two or three oxygenating plants will maintain the purity of the water. The plants should be set into a 4 in. (10 cm.) layer of soil and should be in position before the tub is filled with water.

23. A miniature garden pool in a tub

To make a tub or cask into a miniature water garden is a comparatively simple operation but the construction of a larger pool, lined with concrete or cement, requires considerable expertise. It can well be done by those with the necessary skills but careful rules must be followed and the majority of people will find it best to seek professional help or to study a manual which gives detailed advice. Such advice is outside the scope of this book but is readily available elsewhere (see Bibliography).

A pool may be lined with PVC, polythene, or Butylite, a

synthetic rubber membrane made of Butyl rubber; these materials have a long life and do not harden or crack when under water. A pool lined in this way is easier to construct than one lined with concrete or cement, but here again, expert advice should be followed. Pool liners may also be prefabricated from fibre-glass.

If a pool is to contain both plants and fish, its size must be determined by the necessity of achieving the right balance to maintain the clarity of the water, as well as by the size of the garden. The minimum size required to maintain water clarity is about 48 sq. ft. (4 m².).

Whatever the size and type of pool, it must have a shelf for marginal plants, and this should be about 9–10 in. (23–25 cm.) wide and the same in depth.

The stone edging to a pool should be in proportion to its size. If the pool is made in a lawn, the turves are removed to the depth of the stone so that a lawn-mower can be taken over the side. At one end an area of rough grass can be left, with trees and bushes to encourage wildlife, but these should be planted some little distance away so that the leaves will not foul up the water. Always site a pool well away from existing trees. If a

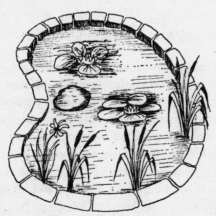

24. A small formal pool

small formal pool is made the centre-piece of a little courtyard or constructed on a terrace, its surround may be of the same kind of flagstones as are already *in situ*. Room should be left to plant small trees or shrubs, some of which may be wall-plants.

Stocking the pool

As with pool construction, expert advice should be taken on the initial stocking of a pool and what I give here are simply general guide-lines.

Where a new pool is lined with cement or concrete, one must allow a little time for it to become weathered, but a pool with a liner can be put into use right away. In any event, a pool should be filled with water about a week before planting, to allow the water to warm up a little, for water straight from the mains will be too cold for most plants. Any soil required should be put into position before the water goes in. Good turf loam which has previously been well manured is recommended but it should be covered with loam without manure or fertilizer for these, when they come into contact with water, will encourage algae.

Planting should, ideally, be in spring and summer when the plants are making new growth, rather than resting.

First to go in are the oxygenators which are planted in polythene containers or crates measuring 8 in. × 8 in. × 4 in. deep (20 cm. × 20 cm. × 10 cm.) for a small pool, larger sizes being available for bigger pools. These crates will last as long as the pool lining. Not only do they make planting easier, they also prevent the oxygenators from filling up the whole pond to the exclusion of other plants. As the crates are made with openings around the sides, it is advisable to place a piece of hessian in each before adding the soil. The hessian will, of course, decay, but not before the plants' roots have bound the soil together. Plant the oxygenators in the crates which are then placed at the

bottom of the pool. As a rough guide, four or five containers
should be used for a pond measuring about 6 ft. × 5 ft.
(1·8 m. × 1·5 m.) and each container may contain two or three
plants. If by the end of the summer the plants have made too
much growth and are choking up the pond, remove as much
as seems necessary to allow other plants room to develop.
Simply put in your hand and pull out large wads of growth.

Water-lilies suitable for a small pool must have at least 12 in.
(30 cm.) of water over them to protect the rhizomes (roots)
from extreme cold. They may be planted straight into the soil
or in containers; in either case use bricks or stone blocks to
bring the plants to the required level. Be sure to make the
plants firm in the soil, leaving the growing point uncovered.
They may be covered with an inch of shingle after they are in
position, which will give them a clean appearance. Allow one
water-lily for each 20 sq. ft. (1·9 m².) of water surface. Water-
lilies may be planted at any time from the end of April to the
end of July, when they come into new growth as the water
becomes warmer. They and other surface-flowering plants are
planted chiefly for their beauty but they and floating aquatic
plants are valuable in that they reduce the amount of sunlight
which can penetrate to the bottom of a pool, thus regulating
the growth of algae and also providing shade for fish. The
same is true of marginal plants. Whereas surface-flowering
plants go in in crates or into pockets of soil, floating plants, as
their name implies, float on the surface and they need no soil—
they are simply dropped gently into the water. Use only three
in a pool measuring 6 ft. × 5 ft. (1·8 m. × 1·5 m.).

Marginal plants go either by the side of the water or on the
shelf provided for them. If planted on the shelf they may go
straight into soil or into crates which, as with those containing
water-lilies, can be raised on bricks or blocks to bring them to
the required depth. They should have not more than 3–4 in.
(7·6–10 cm.) of soil over the roots and be covered by not more
than 6–8 in. (15–20 cm.) of water. If planted on the bank, they

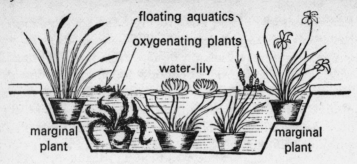

floating aquatics

oxygenating plants

water-lily

marginal plant

marginal plant

25. A larger garden pool stocked with four types of plants

should be in rich damp soil and should be raised in irregular dense groups to attract birds and other wildlife.

Earthenware pots are excellent containers for pool plants but these have now become very expensive and difficult to obtain.

With all these plants, follow the planting instructions given by their supplier with great care, especially with regard to the recommended depth. In the case of plants in crates, gradually remove the supporting bricks so that the crates are at the required level as the plants become established and make new growth.

The larger the pool, the better balanced it will be, and this is particularly important where fish are to be introduced. Algae, which cause clouding of the water, are difficult to clear where the pond is small. The water is liable to become green and cloudy until the oxygenating plants are established. If it is slow to clear, treat the water with Acurel E, using a 2 oz. (57 g.) bottle for every 500–1,200 gal. (2,273–4,546 l.) of water in the pond. This preparation is harmless to fish and plants but the amount recommended must not be exceeded. (To calculate the cubic contents of a pool, multiply the length × breadth × depth. A pool measuring 6 ft. × 5 ft. × 18 in. deep (1·8 m. × 1·5 m. × 46 cm.) will have a capacity of 45 cu. ft. (1·3 m³.). Deduct 5 cu. ft. (142 dm³.) for the shelf and sides, leaving a capacity of 40 cu. ft. ($1 \cdot 1$ m³.). As 1 cu. ft. (28 dm³.) contains $6\frac{1}{4}$ gal. ($28 \cdot 4$ l.), the pond will contain 250 gal. (1,136 l.).

Blanket weed may also cause trouble. It is a green slimy mass which adheres to the sides of a pool and also floats on top. Though not really dangerous, it is unsightly and will choke up plant life if not controlled. Treat the water, following the manufacturer's instructions, with Algizin, a non-toxic algicide which will also kill the White Spot parasite on fish.

Notes on some plants for garden ponds

OXYGENATING PLANTS

Callitriche autumnalis

The water starwort, one of the most useful of the oxygenators, for it is active all the year, its leaves floating on the water like green stars.

Ceratophyllum demersum

The hornwort has thin freely branching stems and whorls of dark green narrow leaves. It grows without soil and is just fastened to a stone and dropped into the water.

Elodea crispa

The Canadian pondweed is another very useful plant, though not entirely hardy. Its stems are clothed in leaves with reflexed edges.

Hottonia palustris

The water violet is inclined to be difficult to establish but is a good oxygenator. The roots attach themselves to stones at the bottom of a pond, the leaves being always under water with the flower stem arising 12 in. (30 cm.) or more, bearing whorls of pale lilac flowers in May and June.

Potamogeton crispus

The pondweed, with crinkled foliage of bronzy green, is the most common of the oxygenators.

Ranunculus aquatilis

The water crowfoot. Its deeply cut foliage, from which it gets its name, is like a crow's foot and its handsome flowers look like white buttercups. An excellent plant for still and flowing water.

FLOATING AQUATICS

Hydrocharis morsus-ranae

One of the most charming, its flat dark green leaves floating on the surface, like those of water-lilies. In July and August it bears small white flowers. Water-snails, however, enjoy the leaves as food and it is often a difficult plant to establish.

Lemna trisulca

The ivy-leaf duckweed has pale green fronds which seem to clarify any ponds they float in. This is the only duckweed suitable for a garden pool.

Stratiotes aloides

Known as the Water Soldier on account of its upright spiny leaves. A valuable plant which bears snow-white flowers in summer. In the wild it is found only in limestone districts.

SURFACE-FLOWERING AQUATICS

These are planted chiefly for their beauty.

Aponogeton distachyus

This is the water hawthorn which requires at least 18 in.

(46 cm.) of water to be successful. Its oval dark green leaves float on the surface and during summer and autumn it bears white flowers with black anthers, which smell powerfully of hawthorn.

Nymphoides peltata (syn. *Villarsia nymphaeoides*)

Known as the Floating Heart, for its heart-shaped leaves float on the surface. In July and August it bears bright yellow flowers.

SOME NYMPHAEA SPECIES AND HYBRIDS

The *Nymphaea*, the water-lilies, are the most beautiful of flowering aquatics. Varieties of medium vigour (M) should grow at a depth of 2 ft. (61 cm.), those of less vigour (L) at 15–18 in. (38–46 cm.), whilst the miniatures for tubs (T) need only 12 in. (30 cm.) of water. Those listed here are all hardy.

Nymphaea 'Albatross' (L)

The finest white for small pools. The flowers have golden anthers and are enhanced by bright glossy foliage.

N. 'Aurora' (T)

A free flowering variety for tubs or small pools, the large flowers opening yellow, turning to orange-red with age.

N. 'Ellisiana' (L)

A beautiful variety, the flowers being of deepest crimson-red with orange-red stamens.

N. 'Froebeli' (L)

The scented flowers are blood-red, the leaves dark green. The outstanding red variety for a small pool.

N. 'James Brydon' (M)

The fully double blooms are of deep carmine-red and are held above bronze-green leaves.

N. 'Laydekeri lilacea' (T)

The best pink for tubs or shallow ponds, being free flowering with small lilac-pink flowers.

N. 'Marliacea flammea' (L-M)

Interesting in that the wine-red flowers, freely produced, are speckled with white.

N. odorata 'Turicensis' (L)

The rose-pink flowers are freely produced and emit a soft sweet perfume, as does *N. o.* 'William B. Shaw' which has sweetly scented star-like flowers of soft pink.

N. 'Paul Hariot' (L)

Its flowers are the largest of the small pool varieties and open pale yellow, turning orange with age.

N. pygmaea alba (T)

A charming pygmy for tubs and small pools, the star-like flowers of purest white measuring 2 in. (5 cm.) across. *N. p.* 'Helvola' is equally dainty with star-shaped blooms of prim-rose yellow. *N. p.* 'Rubra', with crimson blooms, is also suit-able for tubs.

N. 'Rose Arey' (L-M)

One of the loveliest, the scented flowers of cerise-pink having incurved petals and orange stamens.

N. 'William Falconer' (M)

For a large pool. The flowers are deep red with a velvet-like texture, and golden anthers. The dark red foliage matures to a deep green.

MARGINAL PLANTS

Acorus calamus

The sweet flag, its sword-like leaves orange-scented when crushed, grows up to 3 ft. (91 cm.) in height. There is also an attractive variegated form, with cream and pink stripes. Its spikes of yellowish flowers appear in June.

Alisma plantago-aquatica

The water plantain, with large ribbed leaves. In July and August it bears spikes of small pink flowers on leafless 2–3 ft. (16–91 cm.) stems, opening in the afternoon.

Butomus umbellatus

The flowering rush (though it is not a true rush), it grows 3 ft. (91 cm.) tall. In August and September it bears dense clusters of rose-pink flowers at the end of the stems.

Caltha palustris

The marsh marigold, valuable in that it blooms in March and April, bearing large globular buttercup-like flowers on 18 in. (46 cm.) stems. *Flore-pleno* is double.

Cyperus longus

The sweet galingale which bears pretty feathery plumes on slender 3 ft. (91 cm.) stems.

Glyceria maxima variegata

The variegated manna grass, growing 3 ft. (91 cm.) tall, the strap-like leaves being striped with cream and white, turning pink in autumn.

Hippuris vulgaris

The mare's-tail has roots creeping in the mud. It bears tiny whorls of leaves on 2 ft. (61 cm.) stems and its green flowers are only a single stamen.

Hypericum elodes

It grows only 6 in. (15 cm.) tall and spreads over the edge of a pool, its handsome grey foliage enhanced by its yellow star-like flowers.

Iris laevigata

Forming a clump of grass-like leaves and from June to September bearing deep blue flowers on 2 ft. (61 cm.) stems.

Iris pseudacorus

The bog or yellow iris which grows 3 ft. (91 cm.) tall. It has razor-edged leaves and in May and June bears yellow flowers. The form variegatus has foliage striped cream and green.

Mentha aquatica

Planted at the side of a pool, it will spread to form a grey-green mat of aromatic foliage above which it bears whorls of lavender flowers on 9 in. (23 cm.) stems.

Menyanthes trifoliata

The bogbean, it is a handsome plant with large clover-like leaves, measuring 4 in. (10 cm.) across, which float on the water. In May and June the flower-spikes appear as large pink buds, opening to white flowers shaded with pink.

Pontederia cordata

The pickerel weed which has glossy heart-shaped leaves and bears pale blue flowers on 2 ft. (61 cm.) stems.

Sagittaria sagittifolia

The common arrowhead, it will flourish in water 16–18 in. (41–46 cm.) deep. Its arrow-shaped leaves rise 3 ft. (91 cm.) above water. In July and August it bears spikes of pure white flowers on leafless stems.

Sagittaria sagittifolia flore-pleno

This is the double Japanese arrowhead which bears flowers similar to those of stocks, borne on 2 ft. (61 cm.) stems.

Scirpus albescens

The ornamental bullrush which has pale green leaves striped with creamy white and grows 4 ft. (1·2 m.) tall.

Scirpus tabernaemontanii 'Zebrinus'

A most handsome plant, its thin stems being marked with alternate bands of cream and green.

Typha angustifolia

The reed mace, with slender leaves and thick brown spikes borne on 3 ft. (91 cm.) stems, like bullrushes. Its leaves are only ½ in. (1·3 cm.) wide but it may reach a height of 6 ft. (1·8 m.).

Typha minima

The lesser bullrush, with neat leaves and bearing small brown poker-like inflorescences on 20 in. (51 cm.) stems. The 'pokers' have a wide gap in the middle.

Fish for natural garden ponds

Whilst there is a number of ornamental fish that may be purchased for artificial ponds, these are really outside the scope of a book on wildlife, so this section is concerned with some freshwater fish that may be introduced to natural ponds. Such fish may attract kingfishers to build in a bank at the side of the pond.

It is important that the water be kept as clear as possible: pollution can be caused by decaying leaves from nearby trees, by the use of chemicals such as weedkillers too close to the water and by over-stocking the pool. Keep a watch on the habits of the fish in order to learn about their health and requirements. If they come up frequently for air it will signify that there are insufficient natural oxygenating plants and a container or two should be provided.

Fish in a large pond where plant life is established should not require feeding, or only very occasionally in winter. A high-protein food in pellet form can be provided, but only sufficient should be given for the fish to consume within a few minutes. Fish will remain healthier if they are underfed, rather than overfed.

During a prolonged frost, you may prevent ice from forming by floating logs on the surface, but if there is a covering of ice more than several inches thick, carefully make holes of 6 in. (15 cm.) diameter to allow gases to escape.

SOME NATIVE FISH FOR NATURAL PONDS

Carp

Its original home is the Black Sea but it is believed to have been introduced into England by monks returning from visits to the Holy Land and Asia Minor. It will also flourish in man-made ponds and in medieval times it was a valuable source of food. It is a lover of warmth and is often seen lying on the surface of a pond, enjoying the sunlight. It will only breed in warm water and is best confined to southern England, south of the Thames. The carp is slate-green, yellow on the underside, and it will grow to 2–3 ft. (61–91 cm.) in captivity and to 30–40 years of age. In a large pool an old carp will become quite a pet.

Roach

A handsome fish with a blue back and orange underfins. It has a silvered appearance and a mature specimen may weigh more than 3 lb. (1·4 kg.). It is present in lakes and rivers throughout England and Wales but is less common in Scotland and was only recently introduced into Ireland. It is more tolerant of polluted water than any other fish and is present in rivers and canals around industrial towns. It spawns in April and May and the eggs are laid about the marginal vegetation. The fish feed on insect larvae and small water-snails.

Rudd

Distinguished from the roach by the brighter red colour of its fins. It is present in ponds and lakes in England and Ireland, feeding on insects which fly just above the surface. They spawn during May and June and the young feed on algae. Rudd are left alone by other fish, so a pond where the conditions suit it will soon be heavily stocked. There should be a plentiful number of marginal plants.

Stickleback

The most common of our freshwater fish, present in ponds and rivers everywhere. Fishermen know it as the 'tiddler', for it measures only 2–3 in. (5–7·6 cm.) long when adult. It has three dorsal spines in front of the dorsal fin and is partly coloured blue-black or green. During the breeding season, which extends from April to July, the male's throat becomes brilliant orange. With this he attracts the female to a nest he has built amongst the vegetation, the materials being held together by sticky matter secreted from his kidneys. He will act as guard to the fry, as the young are called, for a week or so after hatching. The stickleback does not reach the adult state for at least a year and will live for about another year, unless taken by birds or larger fish.

Tench

It is dark brown and lives for the most part in ponds and shallow lakes where it lies for weeks during periods of cold weather, almost as if in hibernation, maturing at about three years when it will have grown 12 in. (30 cm.) long. Spawning is in early summer, the green eggs hatching in a week. The young feed on algae, the adults on larvae and snails. The adults are covered in a coat of slime which is said to benefit the health of other fish.

Notes on the insect life of ponds

Alderflies (Megaloptera)

One of the water-flies which closely resemble moths in appearance. They live in alders, close to water, but are found on many waterside plants. The wings are pale brown with darker veins. Alderflies live for only three to four weeks and in June or July lay as many as 500 long eggs on plants or moss-covered stones. After hatching the larvae hide beneath the stones or in mud by the water's edge and they are a favourite food of fish. Those which survive will remain in the larval state for two years before coming out of the water to pupate.

Caddis Flies (Trichoptera)

Resembling but differing from moths in that their wings are covered with minute hairs and not scales, but, like moths, they drink nectar and do not eat. The caddis is nocturnal and is found about vegetation by the side of ponds or rivers. The larger species have a wing-span of more than 2 in. (5 cm.) and are used for bait by anglers. The eggs are laid by the water's

edge, the larvae making pencil-like tubes of pieces of vegetation in which they hide during the day so that fish cannot take
them, but at night they come out to feed on decayed matter.
But for all their careful camouflage, large numbers of larvae are
taken by pond fish which find them a great delicacy.

Dragon and Damselflies (Odonata and Lygoptera)

These beautiful insects will spend hours about a pond, alighting on reeds and rushes, and from their perch will make continuous forays over the water to take any flies up to the size of
a small butterfly. Amongst the fastest of insects on the wing,
they are known, from fossilized remains, to have been here for
more than 300 million years.

In the British Isles are twenty-seven species of dragonfly,
one of the largest being the Emperor with a greenish-purple
body and a wing-span of nearly 4 in. (10 cm.). Their eyes
almost cover the head and this enables them to see in all
directions at the same time. Damselflies are smaller and have
smaller eyes. They both catch gnats and midges and are on the
wing throughout summer when mating takes place, the eggs
being in most cases laid on the stems and leaves of marginal
plants, also in mud around the edge of a natural pond. Though
adults live for only a month or so, the nymphs, as the young
are called, will take up to a year to grow, some species taking
longer. Whilst damselflies inhabit low-growing marginals or
surface aquatics, dragonflies live in mud at the bottom and edge
of a pond, feeding on larvae and tadpoles. When almost
mature, the nymphs climb a plant's stem and once clear of the
water shed their skins and fly away.

Ladybirds

Though the tiny marsh ladybird (Coccidula rufa) is to be found
on plants by the waterside, it is not merely a water-insect but a
beetle of great value to the gardener, living on aphis, thrips
and mites which do great damage in orchards. An adult lady-

bird will eat up to fifty small insects in a day, but they themselves are evil-tasting to birds so are not taken by them. If
attacked, they exude a fluid which their predators find unpleasant. Ladybirds hibernate beneath the bark of apple and
other trees and in spring lay their eggs on plants, especially
where there are nettles and long grasses. The eggs hatch in
about eight days and after about a month the grubs pupate,
like those of a butterfly, turning in another eight days into
ladybirds. They are familiar to all with their hard orange wing-
coverings and black spots, perhaps the most common species
being the Seven-Spot Coccinella and the Two-Spot Adalia. The
warm, dry summer of 1975 saw a big increase in their numbers.

Mayflies (*Ephemeroptera*)

Mostly seen about natural ponds, for the nymphs bury themselves in the mud and it may be as long as three years before
some species reach the surface, to cast off their skins and
emerge as adult mayflies. They are an important part of a fish's
diet and, even as adults, will be taken from the surface of the
water by fish and birds. Some find their way to marginal plants
where they throw off another skin to reveal their brilliantly
coloured bodies. They live for only a day or two during which
time they mate over water, the female dropping her eggs on the
surface. Some are eaten by fish, but others will float to the
bottom to hatch as nymphs and begin the life-cycle again.

Most of the forty-six species of mayfly are green and measure
between $\frac{1}{2}$-1 in. (1·3-2·5 cm.) long. They have transparent
wings and are distinguished from the dragonfly in that most
have three tails, though several species have only two. These
tails are present in the nymph state, so one can distinguish
them from other aquatic larvae, but at that stage they are
shorter and broader. Nymphs will store up enough food to
carry them through their adult life.

Stoneflies (*Plecoptera*)

With their long antennae, they measure almost 1 in. (2·5 cm.) long overall, with widely separated pairs of wings. The eggs are laid amongst moss on stones, the nymphs moving to the muddy banks of a pool or beneath stones to emerge as adults after a year or more. As adults they live for only 2–3 weeks and spend most of the time hiding beneath stones at the water's edge. They have twin tails. The closely related Needlefly is so called because when resting it rolls its wings tightly around its body, looking like a needle on a stone; otherwise its habits are similar.

Water-Boatman (*Netonecta glauca*)

When its wings are folded it is shaped like a boat. It is pale brown with three pairs of legs, its back ones shaped like oars, yet it is always seen swimming upside down. Though less than 1 in. (2·5 cm.) long, it can take a small fish with its harpoon-like tongue and inject into it a poison to cause its death before it eats it. In turn, it is consumed by larger fish and birds. The eggs are laid in spring in the stems of water-plants and hatch in about two months. At first the young are wingless and it will take another two months for them to grow.

Water-Measurer (*Hydrometra stagnorum*)

So named from the slow manner of its walk as it strides on the surface of pond or pool looking for water-fleas. A long-lived creature, it winters beneath stones around the pond side, mating in spring. An adult is about ½ in. long.

Water-Scorpion (*Nepa cinerea*)

Not related to the scorpion, though at the end of its brown beetle-like body is a sharp spine which it uses for breathing when submerged. It has no sting but it catches its prey, usually small fish, with its front pincer-shaped legs, and then kills it with its powerful bite. It spends its life by the side of a pond, amongst plants, and will pounce on the fish as it swims nearby. The eggs are laid in the stems of marginal plants, the young taking two to three months to reach the adult state when they will measure about 1 in. (2·5 cm.) long and be quite ferocious in appearance.

Water-Skater (*Gerris lacustris*)

Like a daddy-long-legs with its long thin legs and lightweight body, it can walk on water, the ends of the legs being fitted with minute 'shoes', to prevent them from breaking the surface. It feeds on surface flies and will catch anything from a midge to a bluebottle with its small but strong, front legs. Like most pond insects, the adults winter beneath marginal stones to emerge and mate in spring. As soon as they emerge, the young begin to 'skate' over the water and catch small flies.

Water-Stick (*Ranatra linearis*)

It has a long thin body, measuring about 2 in. (5 cm.) including its snorkel, and resembles a piece of brown stick. It spends its life in reeds by the side of a pond, feeding on small flies. When under water, it breathes by a long tube fitted to the end of its body, in the manner of the water-scorpion, which enables it to stay just beneath the surface for some time. The eggs are laid in spring in reed stems, but usually just below the surface, for each egg has a tiny tube which enables it to breathe. It likes warmth and is rarely seen north of the Thames.

Whirligig Beetle

It takes its name from the erratic manner in which it swims. Spending its entire life on water, it frequents ponds and lakes. It has a shiny black back and legs with hairs which enable it to swim extremely fast for its size. It has two sets of eyes, one set on the lower part of its head, enabling it to see under water, and the other on the upper part, to enable it to see on the surface. Its food consists of insects which have become water-bound.

The eggs are laid in spring, on water-plants, the larvae spending their entire life at the bottom of the pond. Later in summer they climb up the stems of waterside plants and pupate towards the end of summer.

Water-Snails

Interesting to watch as it climbs the stems of marginal plants, the red-blooded Ram's Horn snail (*Planorbis corneus*) will eat up any left-over fish food, whilst the fish will feed on its eggs. One snail should be introduced for each 3 sq. ft. (28 dm².) of water surface. The Whirlpool Ram's Horn has a large circular shell like a Catherine-wheel, or like the ripples of a whirlpool. The shell is transparent, so the snail may be seen inside. The White Ram's Horn is also interesting, with a shell like a small white coil.

The Ram's Horns have eyes at the base of the tentacles, not at the ends as have most snails. They attach themselves to marginal plants or to stones to which strings of eggs are also fastened as they are laid. The adults die after spawning and the eggs hatch to young snails in four weeks.

Amphibians

There are a number of creatures which spend part of their life on land, part in water. They may visit a garden pool and are valuable in the garden in that their diet consists of slugs and larvae harmful to plants. They breed in water and it is usual for them to do so only in natural ponds, often going several miles until they find the one which is most suitable to them. It could be that they return to the pond in which they were born.

Newts

They may be distinguished from lizards in that they have smooth skins. They also spend most of their time in or near water, whilst lizards stay on the land. Like lizards, newts have long tails.

The most common is the smooth newt, *Triturus vulgaris*, pale brown in colour with a spotted throat shaded with red. The males have a spinal crest, not so pronounced as in the great crested (*Triturus cristatus*), and they grow to 4 in. (10 cm.) long, the females not quite so large. Males of the great crested will grow to twice the size and are charcoal coloured with white and orange on the underside, and are covered in hard warts. These are glands which release a sticky fluid, bitter to taste, when attacked by predators. The third British species is the palmate newt (*Triturus helveticus*), smallest of the three, with a central stripe of orange down the tail. It is less common than the others and mostly frequents moorland ponds.

In spring, the females lay as many as 300 eggs, enclosed and held together by a sticky fluid. They hatch to a tadpole-like state and will have grown into efts (the name for young newts) with fully grown limbs in about ten to eleven weeks. They then leave the water and spend their life in damp places but may not return to the pond for several years, until ready to breed.

Frogs

As with newts and lizards, there are three species in Britain: the common (*Rana temporaria*), edible (*Rana esculenta*) and marsh (*Rana ribunda*) frogs. The common which, is olive-brown, is present in most parts of Britain but the edible, a quite recent introduction, is found mostly in Essex, Middlesex and Surrey. The brown marsh frog is of even more recent introduction and has become established only in Kent, about the Romney Marsh area. It is the largest of the three. Frogs

hibernate; early in spring they emerge and make their way to
ponds where they mate and spawn, the female laying several
thousand eggs which the male fertilizes. Covered in a protective fluid, they hatch into tadpoles in the warmth of the early
summer sunshine and swim around for almost two months, by
which time they have grown into small frogs. They then leave
the water. Many will have been taken by ducks or large fish
before reaching this state and many more will be taken for food
by the larger birds when they leave the water. Making use of
their long back legs, frogs can jump several feet.

Toads

The charcoal-coloured common toad (*Bufo bufo*), broader and
with shorter legs than the frog, has a dry wart-covered skin
and walks along the ground rather than jumps. A nocturnal
creature, it hides in holes (toad-in-the-hole!) by day and is
active at night, feeding on grubs, aphis and woodlice.

The natterjack toad (*Bufo calamita*) gets its name from its loud
croak. It is found mostly in Wales and the west and is now
protected. At one time it was prevalent about the sand dunes
at Southport but with the encroachment of house building it
has almost died out there. It is smaller than the common toad
and is olive-brown, with a bright yellow line down its back. It
spawns in shallow water, the common toad in deep water,
neither of them frequenting pools except during mating time.
They hibernate from early November then lay between 5,000
and 7,000 eggs which are mostly eaten by fish. Toads follow a
similar life-cycle to that of frogs.

❀ Appendix I. Birds and the law ❀

Under the Protection of Birds Acts 1954–67, all wild birds are protected by law, though there are certain exceptions such as those classed as pests to farmers, and sporting birds. The latter are, however, protected in their close season and they are:

Partridge	1 February–31 August
Pheasant	1 February–30 September
Ptarmigan (in Scotland)	11 December–11 August
(In England and Wales it is protected at all times)	
Red Grouse	11 December–11 August
Wild Duck and Geese	21 February–31 August

Those birds which may sometimes be classed as pests and which may be killed by authorized persons are:

Bullfinch	Magpie
Crow, Carrion	Merganser (Scotland)
Dove, Collared (Scotland)	Rock Dove (Scotland)
Gooseander (Scotland)	Rook
Gull, Great and Lesser	Shag
Black-headed	Sparrow, House
Gull, Herring	Starling
Jackdaw	Wood Pigeon
Jay	

All other birds and their eggs are protected at all times. By provision of the Acts, it is an offence, punishable by heavy fines, wilfully to

(i) kill or attempt to kill or injure a wild bird;

   (ii) take, damage or destroy the nest of any wild bird whilst in use;

  (iii) take or destroy the eggs of any wild bird;

  (iv) ring or mark any wild bird (except by an authorized person for scientific purposes);

   (v) disturb any wild bird whilst on or near a nest or with young;

  (vi) have in one's possession or control, any wild bird recently killed;

 (vii) sell any live bird which is protected;

(viii) sell, barter or exchange the eggs of any wild bird;

  (ix) sell any dead wild bird or skin or plumage;

   (x) sell a dead wild goose or wild duck between February and 31 August;

  (xi) import live or dead common quail;

 (xii) import any dead wild duck or geese (except those listed in their season;

(xiii) import dead lapwings or their eggs;

(xiv) import any live bird of prey or owl.

※ Appendix II. Pesticides and fungicides ※

Only those which are known to be non-toxic to animals and birds should be used. These include:

(i) Derris powder or liquid (though it must not be used near fish) which will control:

Asparagus: beetle
Broad bean: black fly
Cabbage: caterpillar (and of other brassicas)
Dwarf bean: black fly
Gooseberry: sawfly
Pot plants: greenfly
Raspberry: beetle and moth
Strawberry: aphis
Turnip: fly (and of swedes)
(Derris will also exterminate wasps in their nests.)

(ii) Orthocide (containing 65 per cent Captan) which will control:

Blackcurrant: leaf spot
Cauliflower: damping off (seedlings)
Lettuce: botrytis
Pear tree: scab
Peas: pre-emergence damping off
Rose: grey mould and black spot
Strawberry: botrytis
Strawberry: mildew compounds
Sweet corn: damping off

(iii) Malathion and Menazon compounds which are organo-phosphorus compounds with low toxicity. They should not be used on sweet peas and antirrhinums but will control:

Cabbage: caterpillar (and of other brassicas)
Fruit trees: aphides, capsids, winter moth and woolly aphis

(iv) Bordeaux Mixture (made by dissolving 1 lb. (454 g.) quick lime and 1 lb. (454 g.) copper sulphate in 12 gal. (54·6 l.) water) which will control:

Antirrhinum: rust
Asparagus: rust
Beetroot: downy mildew
Begonia: grey mould
Blackberry: cane spot
Blackcurrant: rust and leaf spot
Broad bean: chocolate spot
Brussels sprout: downy mildew
Cabbage: dark leaf spot
Celery: heart rot
Celery: leaf spot
Chrysanthemum: blotch
Dahlia: leaf spot
Delphinium: black blotch
Dwarf bean: anthracnose
Dwarf bean: halo blight
Gladiolus: botrytis
Gooseberry: leaf spot
Lily: botrytis
Peas: leaf spot
Peppers: fruit spot
Potatoes: blight
Radish: white blister
Rose: powdery mildew

Tomato: blight
Turnip: mildew

Insecticides based on Gamma-BHC (Lindane, Lindex), an organo-chlorine compound, should be used with care. It is persistent but nothing like so much as DDT which was banned for use in home gardens in 1971.

Compounds of mercury must be used with the greatest care. Calomel is one and it will control:

Cabbage: club root and root fly
Onion: fly and white rot
Radish: club root and root fly
Turnip: club root and root fly

It is highly effective and is used by dusting seeds when sown in drills with it or by dipping the roots of brassicas in a solution before planting. In this way, the preparation is out of reach of animals and birds.

Metaldehyde, used for slug control, is harmful to wildlife and should be partially covered by an upturned pot or box.

※ Appendix III. Some useful societies and their addresses ※

Bee Research Association,
  Hill House, Chalfont St. Peter, Bucks.
British Bee-keepers' Association,
  55 Chipstead Lane, Riverhead, Sevenoaks, Kent.
British Ecological Society,
  Monks Wood Experimental Station, Abbots Ripton, Hunts.
British Naturalists' Association,
  Willowfield, Boyneswood Road, Four Marks, Alton, Hants.
British Ornithologists' Union,
  Zoological Society of London, Regents Park, London NW1.
Fauna Preservation Society,
  c/o Zoological Gardens, Regents Park, London NW1.
Mammal Society of Great Britain,
  62 London Road, Reading, Berks.
Nature Conservancy,
  19 Belgrave Square, London SW1.
Royal Society for the Protection of Birds,
  The Lodge, Sandy, Beds.

❋ Bibliography ❋

These books I have found indispensable additions to my library in searching after knowledge of the wildlife of the British Isles. Several may now be out of print but may be obtained from secondhand book dealers.

All about Photographing Animals and Birds, David Hodgson. Michael Joseph (1974)
Animals of the Dark, Clive Roots. David & Charles (1974)
Beetles of the British Isles (2 vols.), E. F. Linssen. Warne (1959)
A Beginner's Guide to Bird Watching, Reg. Harrison. Pelham Books (1970)
A Bird Book for the Pocket, Edmund Sanders. Oxford University Press (1927)
Birds of our Country (2 vols.), F. Finn and E. K. Robinson. Hutchinson (1924)
Birds of the British Isles and their Eggs (2 vols.), T. A. Coward. Warne (1969)
Birds of Town and Suburb, Eric Simms. Collins (1975)
Birds of Town and Village, W. D. Campbell. Hamlyn (1968)
Birdwatcher's Year, L. A. Batten and J. Flegg. Poyser (1972)
Birdwatching (Discovering Books), J. Flegg. Shire Publications (1973)
Book of British Birds, Reader's Digest. Collins (1969)
The Book of the British Countryside. Drive Publications (1973)
The Book of the Garden Pond, George Hervey and Jack Hems. Faber (1970)
Breeding Birds of Britain and Ireland: Historical Survey, John Parslow. Poyser (1973)
Butterflies, E. B. Ford. Collins (1948)
Climbing and Screening Plants, Noël Prockter. Faber (1973)
The Complete British Butterflies in Colour, L. Hugh Newman and E. Mansell. Ebury Press (1968)
Covering a Wall, Roy Genders. Robert Hale (1957 and 1973)
The Dictionary of Butterflies and Moths, A. Watson and P. E. S. Whalley
Exploring Woods, Peter Schofield. Independent TV Books (1970)

An Eye for a Bird: The Autobiography of a Bird Photographer, Eric Hosking. Hutchinson (1970)

Fertilisation of Flowers, Hermann Müller. Macmillan (1883)

Field Guide to Birds' Nests, Bruce Campbell and Jas. Ferguson-Lees. Constable (1972)

A Field Guide to the Birds of Britain and Europe, R. Paterson, G. Mountford and P. A. D. Hollom. Collins (1974)

A Field Guide to the Insects of Britain, Michael Chinery. Collins (1971)

The Flower Garden, Roy Genders. Ward Lock (1975)

Hedges, E. Pollard, H. D. Hooper and N. W. Moore. Collins (1975)

The Honey Bee, T. W. Cowan. Longmans (1890)

A Lifetime of Badgers, Peter Hardy. David & Charles (1974)

The Lives of Bats, D. W. Yalden and P. A. Morris. David & Charles (1975)

The Living World of Animals, *Reader's Digest*. (1971)

Modern Water Gardening, Reginald Kaye. Faber (1973)

The Moths of the British Isles (2 vols.), R. South. Warne (1963)

New Bird Table Book: A Guide to Food and Shelter for Wild Birds, Tony Soper. David & Charles (1973)

A New Dictionary of British Birds, A. Lansborough Thomson. Nelson (1964)

Owls, John Sparks and Tony Soper. David & Charles (1972)

Pictorial Encyclopaedia of Insects, V. J. Stanek. Hamlyn (1969)

Plants and Bee Keeping, F. N. Howes. Faber (1946)

Popular Handbook of British Birds, P. A. D. Hollom. H. F. & G. Witherby (1968)

The Roadside Wildlife Book, T. Mabery. David & Charles (1973)

Rodents, Peter Hanney. David & Charles (1975)

The Titmice of the British Isles, J. A. G. Barnes. David & Charles (1974)

Trees for Smaller Gardens, Roger Grounds. Dent (1974)

Watching Birds, James Fisher and J. Flegg. Poyser (1970)

Waterfowl's World, Oscar Merne. Poyser (1970)

❧ Index ❧

Acurel 'E', for pond cleansing, 232
Alderflies, 242
Algae, clearing of, 227, 232
Algizin, for pond cleansing, 233
Amphibians, 247
Aquatic plants: floating, 231, 234, species of: *Hydrocharis morsus-ranae*, 234; *Lemna trisulca* (ivy-leaf duckweed), 234; *Stratiotes aloides*, 234; surface-flowering, 231, 234–7, species of: *Aponogeton distachyus* (water hawthorn), 234; *Nymphoides peltata* (syn. *Villarsia nymphaeoides*), 235; see also *Nymphaea* (Water lilies)
Aristotle, 202

Badgers, 211–12, Pl. 14
Bats, species of: Daubenton's, 222; Horseshoe, 22, 221; Long-eared, 221; Mouse-eared, 22; Natterer's, 221; Pipistrelle, 221
Bee Research Association, 193
Bees: bumble, 197–9, 202; 'Cuckoo', 198; Digger bumble, 198; hives, 192, 196; honey, 191–5, 199, 203; keeping, 192; Leaf-cutter, 198; life cycle of, 195; plants for, 15, 193, 200, 204, 206; and pollination, 197
Bird bath, 83
Bird songs, 84
Bird watching, 83
Birds: building in walls, 20, 128, in nest boxes, 70; feeding habits of, 79, 84; migrating, 89; nesting habits of, 29, 68
Birds, species of: Barn owl, 91; Blackbird, 20, 29, 37, 45, 87, 126; Blackcap, 16, 29, 49, 88, 89, 92, 126; Blue tit, 20, 92, 126, Pl. 1; Brambling, 17, 49, 88, 93; Brown owl, 94; Bullfinch, 87, 94, 126, 251; Chaffinch, 29, 35, 40, 44, 88, 94, 126; Chiffchaff, 20, 29, 40, 45, 88, 89, 95, 127; Coal tit, 96; Coot, 225; Corn bunting, 96, 126; Dunnock (Hedge sparrow), 15, 29, 35, 45, 88, 97, 126; Fieldfare, 17, 49, 97, 129; Firecrest, 98, 129; Garden warbler, 15, 16, 29, 40, 88, 98, 127; Goldcrest, 44, 88, 98, 126; Goldfinch, 88, 99, 127; Great-spotted woodpecker, 74, 88, 99, 126; Great tit, 87, 100, Pl. 2; Green woodpecker, 88, 101, 126; Greenfinch, 29, 35, 50, 101; Hawfinch, 49, 102, 126; House martin, 102, 127; House sparrow, 103, 126; Jackdaw, 74, 76, 88, 104, 126, 251; Kingfisher, 105, 240; Lesser redpoll, 45, 88, 105, 126; Lesser spotted woodpecker, 106; Linnet, 16, 49, 89, 106, 126; Little owl, 86; Long-tailed tit, 51, 86, 107; Magpie, 108, 251; Mallard, 226; Marsh tit, 53, 96, 108, Pl. 3; Mistle thrush, 44, 88, 109, 126; Moorhen, 226; Nuthatch, 16, 110, 126; Pheasant, 16, 49, 111, 126, 251; Pied flycatcher, 112; Pied wagtail, 20, 45, 88, 89, 112; Red-backed shrike, 113; Redbreast (robin), 15, 17, 49, 53, 69, 88, 114, 126, Pl. 5; Redstart, 29, 44, 114, 127, Pl. 4; Redwing, 17, 115, 129; Reed bunting, 115; Sedge warbler, 116; Song thrush, 20, 29, 88, 116, 126; Spotted flycatcher, 18, 29, 40, 69, 88, 117, 127; Starling, 118, 126, 251; Stonechat, 49, 88, 118; Swallow, 18, 88, 89, 119, 127, Pl. 6; Swift, 20, 77, 88, 120, 127; Tawny owl, 76; Tree creeper, 15, 29, 68, 75, 88, 121, 126; Tree pipit, 69, 121, 127; Tree sparrow, 122, 126; Waxwing, 17, 49, 122, 129; Whitethroat, 29, 88, 122, 127; Willow warbler, 44, 53, 73, 123; Wren, 17, 20, 87, 88, 124,

Birds—cont.
126; Wryneck, 74, 88, 124, 127; Yellow hammer, 16, 44, 50, 125, 126; Yellow wagtail, 53, 126, 127

Blanket weed, 233

British Bee-keepers' Association, 256

British Ecological Society, 256

British Naturalists' Association, 256

British Ornithologists' Union, 256

Bumble bee, *see* Bees

Butterflies: breeding habits of, 133, 175; characteristics of, 131; eggs of, 177; life-cycle of, 132; migrant, 133; protection of, 131

Butterflies, plants for: bird's-foot trefoil, 153, 164, 170, 181; blackthorn, 149, 165; brambles, 134, 136, 144, 163, 172; buckthorn, 153, 160, 161, 173; buddleia, 132, 162, 166, 172, 178, 225; clover, 153, 162, 169, 173; cocksfoot, 137, 160, 163, 164; coltsfoot, 173; common rock rose, 155, 160, 163; couch grass, 155, 160, 163; Dame's Violet, 152, 161, 165, 171, 173, 176; dog violet, 139, 161; dogwood, 161; fennel, 150; field scabious, 170; fleabane, 148, 173; forget-me-not, 169, 172; golden rod, 172; gorse, 161, 164, 173; ground ivy, 155, 173; heather, 164; *Hebe* 'Midsummer Beauty', 52; hedge mustard, 165; honesty, 161; honeysuckle, 144, 160, 163, 164, 171, 173; hop vine, 143, 160, 164; hyssop, 168, 172; ice plant, 132, 162, 173; kidney-vetch, 146, 164, 173; Lady's Smock, 152, 161, 165, 173, 176; lavender, 163, 168; lilac, 167, 172; lucerne, 153, 165, 173; marjoram, 168, 172; meadow grass, 163; milk parsley, 150, 165; nettles, 143, 161, 164, 179; pinks, 169, 172; privet, 150; purple loosestrife, 167; ragged robin, 170; Scottish thistle, 162; *Sedum spectabile*, 132, 162, 173, 178; sheep's fescue, 136, 160, 164; sorrel, 148, 177; sweet violet, 164; tree lupin, 145, 161, 164, 173; tufted hair-grass, 160, 164; valerian, 171, 178; whitebeam, 164; willows, 144,

161, 164; Yorkshire fog grass, 155, 165

Butterflies, species of: Adonis Blue, 130, 147, 157, 159, 173; Bath White, 152, 158, 159, 165, 166, 173; Black Hairstreak, 149, 158, 159, 160, 165, 173; Brimstone, 153, 158, 161, 165, 166, 170, 173, Pl. 8; Brown Argus, 146, 157, 165; Brown Hairstreak, 149, 160, 165, 173; Camberwell Beauty, 133, 143, 157, 164, 173; Chalk-hill Blue, 147, 157, 165; Chequered Skipper, 154, 158, 159, 165; Clouded Yellow, 152, 158, 165, 166; Comma, 133, 143, 157, 158, 160, 164, 166, 178; Common Blue, 146, 157, 165, 170; Dark Green Fritillary, 139, 157, 162; Dingy Skipper, 154, 158, 159, 165; Duke of Burgundy, 144, 157, 164; Essex Skipper, 155, 158, 165; Grayling, 136, 156, 159, 160, 164; Green Hairstreak, 148, 158, 159, 161, 165; Green-veined White, 151, 158, 165, 173; Grizzled Skipper, 154, 158, 165; Heath Fritillary, 140, 157, 159, 164; Hedge Brown, 136, 156, 164, 172, 173; High Brown Fritillary, 139, 157, 162; Holly Blue, 147, 157, 165, 173; Large Blue, 22, 130, 131, 148, 157, 165; Large Heath, 137, 156, 159, 164; Large Skipper, 155, 158, 168; Large Tortoise-shell, 131, 142, 159, 164; Large White, 151, 158, 165, 173; Long-tailed Blue, 145, 157, 159, 161, 164, 166, 173; Lulworth Skipper, 131, 159; Marbled White, 135, 156, 160, 164, 177; Marsh Fritillary, 140, 157, 159, 164; Meadow Brown, 136, 156, 164; Mountain Ringlet, 135, 156, 159; Orange Tip, 152, 158, 161, 165, 173, 176; Painted Lady, 133, 141, 157, 162, 164, 166, 170, Pl. 7; Pale Clouded Yellow, 133, 152, 158, 165, 170, 173; Peacock, 133, 142, 157, 158, 161, 166, 179, Pl. 9; Pearl-bordered Fritillary, 138, 156, 164; Purple Emperor, 134, 144, 157, 159,

Butterflies—cont.

161; Purple Hairstreak, 149, 158, 165, 170, 173; Queen of Spain Fritillary, 133, 138, 157, 159, 166; Red Admiral, 133, 140–1, 157, 161, 164, 166, 170, 173, 175, 179; Ringlet, 137, 156, 164, 172, 173; Scotch Argus, 135, 156, 159, 163; Short-tailed Blue, 145, 157, 164; Silver-spotted Skipper, 155, 158, 165, 170; Silver-studded Blue, 146, 157, 161, 164; Silver-washed Fritillary, 139, 157; Small Blue, 145, 157, 159, 164, 173; Small Copper, 148, 158, 159, 169, 170, 173, 177; Small Heath, 136, 156, 164; Small Pearl-bordered Fritillary, 137, 156, 162, 164; Small Skipper, 155, 158, 165; Small Tortoise-shell, 133, 141–2, 161, 164, 166, 169, 173, 175; Small White, 151, 158, 165, 173; Speckled Wood, 134, 156, 159, 160, 163; Swallow-tail, 131, 150, 158, 159, 165, 167; Wall Brown, 135, 156, 163; White Admiral, 144, 157, 160, 164; White-letter Hairstreak, 150, 158, 165, 173; Wood White, 153, 158, 165, 173

Caddis flies, 242
Chrysalis, 177, 178
Conservation of Wild Creatures and Wild Plants Act, 22, 131, 213, 217, 223
Council for Nature, 23
'Cuckoo' bee, see Bees
Cuprinol, 73

Damselflies, 224, 243
Darwin, Charles, 202
Digger bumble bee, see Bees
Dormice: common, 21, 22, 212, 213; edible, 213
Doughty, K., 86
Dragonflies, 224, 243, Pl. 12
Drinking water, 22, 83, 224

Fauna Preservation Society, 256
Feeding tables, 77, 81, 82
Fish for ponds, 239–40; species of: carp, 240; roach, 241; rudd, 241; stickleback, 241; tench, 241

Flowers, night-scented: *Abronia fragrans*, 187, 190; *A. latifolia*, 187, 190; Alpine forget-me-not, 187; Alpine violet, 189, 191; campion, 186, 190; catchflies, 188, 191; evening primrose, 183, 190; heliotrope, 187, 190; *Heliotropium peruvianum*, 190; *Hesperis matronalis*, 186, 190; *H. tristis*, 186, 190; honeysuckle, 184, 190; *Jasminum officinale*, 185, 190; *Lathyrus* 'White Pearl', 185, 190; *Lonicera caprifolium*, 184, 190; *L. etrusca* 'Superba', 184, 190; *L. japonica halliana*, 184, 190; *L. periclymenum*, 184, 190; *Lychnis vespertina*, 186, 190; *Matthiola bicornis*, 184, 190; *Myosotis alpestris*, 187, 190; *M. macrantha*, 187, 190; *Nicotiana affinis*, 185, 190; *N. sylvestris*, 185, 190; *Oenothera biennis*, 183, 190; *O. drummondii*, 183, 190; *O. tetraptera*, 183, 190; *O. triloba*, 183, 190; perennial pea 'White Pearl', 185, 190; sand rocket, 186, 190; sand verbena, 186, 190; *Saponaria caespitosa*, 189, 191; *S. officinalis*, 188, 191; *Silene acaulis*, 188, 191; *S. nutans*, 188, 191; soapwort, 188, 191; summer jasmine, 185, 190; sweet rocket, 186, 190; tobacco plant, 185, 190; *Viola cornuta*, 189, 191, 200

Foxes, 17, 87, 212
Frogs: common, 248; edible, 248; marsh, 248
Fungicides, 253

Garden enclosure, 189–90
Glover, R., 86

Hall, Sir Daniel, 197
Hardy, Peter, 22
Hedgehogs, 21, 87, 208–10, Pl. 13
Hedges, 56–67; plants for: *Berberis stenophylla*, 58, 61, 66; *Buxus sempervirens*, 61, 66; *Chamaecyparis lawsoniana*, 60, 66; *Cupressocyparis leylandii*, 60, 66; *Escallonia*, 63;

Hedges—cont.
   Euonymus fortunei, 64; fuchsia, 64, 66;
   Hippophae rhamnoides, 63; holly, 57,
   66; *Ligustrum ovalifolium*, 58; *Lonicera nitida*, 58, 66, 79; privet, 58, 67,
   95; *Prunus* 'Cistena', 62; *P.* 'Pissardii', 62, 67; *P. spinosa*, 62; *Pyracantha
   rogersiana*, 62, 67; *Pyrus communis*,
   62, 67; *Rosa alba*, 66; *R. canina*, 66,
   67; *R. moyesii*, 65, 67; *R. rubiginosa*,
   66; roses, 64; *Taxus baccata*, 60, 67;
   Thuya occidentalis, 60, 67; *T. plicata*,
   58, 59, 67; whitethorn, 57, 67
Honey, *see* Bees
Honey bee, *see* Bees
Hymenoptera, 192, 197

Ladybirds, 243
Leaf-cutter bee, *see* Bees
Lepidoptera, 130, 132, 180, 199
Lizards: common, 222, Pl. 15; sand,
   23, 223

Mackenzie, J. D., 75
Mammal Society of Great Britain, 256
Marginal plants, 227–8, 229, 231;
   species of: *Acorus calamus* (sweet
   flag), 237; *Alisma plantago* (water
   plantain), 237; *Butomus umbellatus*
   (flowering rush), 237; *Caltha palu-
   stris* (marsh marigold), 237; *Cyperus
   longus* (sweet galingale), 237; *Gly-
   ceria maxima variegata* (manna grass),
   237; *Hippuris vulgaris* (mare's-tail),
   238; *Hypericum elodes*, 238; *Iris
   laevigata*, 238; *I. pseudacorus*, 238;
   Mentha aquatica, 238; *Menyanthes
   trifoliata* (bogbean), 238; *Pontederia
   cordata* (pickerel weed), 238; *Sagit-
   taria sagittifolia* (common arrowhead), 239; *S.s. flore-pleno* (double
   Japanese arrowhead), 239; *Scirpus
   albescens* (ornamental bullrush), 239;
   S. tabernaemontanii 'Zebrinus', 239;
   Typha angustifolia (reed mace), 239;
   T. minima (lesser bullrush), 239
Mayflies, 244
Mice: field, 217, 218; harvest, 217,
   218; yellow-necked, 218

Moles, 215–16
Moths: characteristics of, 131, 180,
   181; flowers to attract, *see* Flowers,
   night-scented; at night, 182
Moths, species of: Burnet moth, 181;
   Clothes moth, 180; Convolvulus
   hawk-moth, 180, 182; Elephant
   hawk-moth, 180, 182; Emerald
   moth, 181; Ghost Swift moth, 180;
   Green Oak moth, 180; Humming-
   bird hawk-moth, 36, 181, 182, Pl. 10;
   Large Yellow Underwing, 181;
   Leopard moth, 181; Mother-of-
   Pearl moth, 181; Poplar hawk-
   moth, 182; Privet hawk-moth, 182,
   Pl. 11; Puss moth, 180; Tiger moth,
   180; Tussock moth, 180; Vapourer
   moth, 180
Mulching, 33, 44
Müller, Dr. Hermann, 132, 167, 170,
   187, 199, 201

Natterjack toad, 22, 249, Pl. 16
Nectar, collection of, 162, 183, 193,
   200
Needleflies, 245
Nest boxes, 39, 68; construction of,
   73; fixing, 70, 75; siting, 68, 69, 75;
   in trees, 46, 75; types of, 75; on
   walls, 39, 78
Nesting: in boxes, 68; in hedges, 56;
   in shrubs, 49; in trees, 45; in wall
   plants, 28; *see also* Shrubs for nesting
   and Trees for nesting
Newts: common, 248; great crested,
   248; palmate, 248
Night hawk-moths, 184
Noctuids, 181

Oxygenating plants, 227–8, 230, 232,
   233; species of: *Callitriche autumnalis*
   (water starwort), 233; *Ceratophyllum
   demersum* (hornwort), 233; *Elodes
   crispa* (Canadian pondweed), 233;
   Hottonia pallustris (water violet),
   233; *Potamegeton crispus* (pondweed),
   234; *Ranunculus aquatilis* (water
   crowfoot), 234

Peat, use of, 27, 31, 37, 41

Pesticides, 253
Pollination, by bees, 192, 197
Pond: to attract birds, 112, 116, 224; cleansing of, 227, 232–3, 240; construction of, 227–30; for drinking water, 22, 224; fish for, 240; insects of, 242; planting of, 230–3; siting of, 225
Pool, *see* Pond
Protection of Birds Act, 251

Royal Society for the Protection of Birds, 23, 74, 84, 86

Shrews: common, 214; water, 215
Shrubbery, 44; planting of, 45
Shrubs for nesting: *Berberis darwinii*, 49, 54, 112; *B. julianae*, 49, 54; *Cornus alba*, 50; *C. mas*, 50, 55; *Cytisus kewensis*, 53; *Eleagnus fungens*, 50, 55, 73; *Griselinia littoralis*, 50, 55; *Laurus nobilis*, 51, 55; *Lonicera fragrantissima*, 51, 55; *L. purpusii*, 51; *L. tartarica*, 51, 55; *Mahonia aquifolium*, 49, 55; *M. japonica*, 49, 55; mistletoe, 53; *Olearia* × *haastii*, 50, 55; *O. macrodonta*, 50, 55; *Osmanthus delavayi*, 52; *O. hetrophyllus*, 52, 55; *Photinia serrulata*, 52; *P. villosa*, 52, 55; *Prunus lusitanica*, 51; *Spiraea arguta*, 53; *Ulex europaeus*, 49, 55; *Viburnum burkwoodii*, 52; *V. davidii*, 53; *V. lantana*, 53; *V. opulus*, 53; *V. tinus*, 52, 55
Smooth snake, 23
Society for Promotion of Nature Reserves, 23
Squirrels: grey, 219; red, 219
Stoats, 220
Stoneflies, 249

Times, The, 86
Toads: common, 249; natterjack, 22, 249
Trees for nesting, 44–55: apple, 44; *Carpinus betulus*, 48, 54, 57; *Chamaecyparis*, 45, 54, 95; *Crataegus crusgalli*, 48, 55; *C. oxycantha*, 47, 55; *C. submollis*, 48, 55; *Cupressus glabra*, 46, 55; *Ilex aquifolium*, 48;

Juniperus squamata, 46, 55; *Metasequoia glyptostroboides*, 47, 55; *Pinus sylvestris*, 46; *Populus alba*, 69; *Thuja occidentalis*, 46, 55
Trellis, 25, 26, 39
Tub, for a water garden, 228

Voles: bank, 217; field, 217; water, 217, 224
von Frisch, 203

Wall plants, 20, 25–43; species of: *Actinidia chinensis*, 32, 42; *Akebia quinata*, 32, 42; *Berberidopsis corallina*, 34, 42; *Camellia japonica*, 41, 42; *Campsis grandiflora*, 31, 42; *C. radicans*, 30, 42; *Ceanothus* 'Burkwoodii', 36, 42; *C.* 'Charles Detriche', 37; *C.* 'Gloire de Versailles', 37, 42; *C. veitchanus*, 36, 42; *Celastrus scandens*, 33, 42; *Choisya ternata*, 36, 42; *Cissus striata*, 28; *Clematis armandii*, 37, 42; *C. montana*, 20, 27, 38, 39, 42, 88; *C. tangutica*, 38, 43; *C. vitalba*, 38, 43; *Cotoneaster henryanus*, 41, 43; *C. simonsii*, 41, 43; *Cytisus battandieri*, 34; *Decumaria barbara*, 31, 43; *Freemontodendron californicum*, 33; *Garrya elliptica*, 33, 43; *Hedera canariensis*, 30; *H. colchica*, 30; *H. helix angularis aurea*, 30; *H. helix* 'Caenwoodiana', 30; *H. helix purpurea*, 30; honeysuckle, 20, 27, 189; *Hydrangea petiolaris*, 28, 47, 49; ivy, 29; jasmine, 27, 34, 43; *Jasminum nudiflorum*, 34, 43; *J. officinale*, 34, 43; *Lonicera japonica halliana*, 20; *L. tragophylla*, 36; *Parthenocissus quinquefolia*, 18, 28, 29, 43; *Passiflora coerulea*, 40, 43; *Polygonum baldschuanicum*, 31, 43; *Pyracantha angustifolia*, 35; *P. atalantioides*, 35, 43; *P. rogersiana*, 35, 43, 122; Russian vine, 20, 32; *Solanum crispum*, 34; *S. jasminoides*, 34; *Trachelospermum jasminoides*, 35; Virginia creeper, 18, 28; *Vitis* 'Brant', 32; *V. coignetiae*, 32; *V.* 'Miller's Burgundy', 32; *V.* 'Purpurea', 32; *Wistaria sinensis*, 33

Walls, preparation of, 25-7
Water-boatman, 245
Water lilies, 231; species and varieties of: *Nymphaea* 'Albatross', 235; *N.* 'Aurora', 245; *N.* 'Ellisiana', 235; *N.* 'Froebeli', 235; *N.* 'James Brydon', 236; *N. odorata* 'Turicensis', 236; *N.* 'Paul Hariot', 236; *N. pygmaea alba*, 236; *N.* 'Rose Arey', 236; *N.* 'W. Falconer', 236

Water-measurer, 245
Water-scorpion, 245
Water-skater, 246
Water snail, 246
Water-stick, 246
Weasel, 219-20
Whirligig beetle, 246
Windbreak, 56
Wire feeders, 80
Wire netting, 27, 31